Industry and Society in Europe

Industry and Society in Europe

Stability and Change in Britain, Germany and France

Christel Lane

Lecturer in Sociology, Faculty of Social and Political Sciences, University of Cambridge and Fellow of St John's College, Cambridge

Edward Elgar
Aldershot, UK • Brookfield, US

Published by
Edward Elgar Publishing Limited
Gower House
Croft Road
Aldershot
Hants GU11 3HR
UK

Edward Elgar Publishing Company
Old Post Road
Brookfield
Vermont 05036
US

British Library Cataloguing in Publication Data
Lane, Christel
  Industry and Society in Europe: Stability
  and Change in Britain, Germany and
  France
  I. Title
  338.094

Library of Congress Cataloguing in Publication Data
Lane, Christel.
    Industry and society in Europe: stability and change in Britain,
  Germany, and France / Christel Lane.
      p.   cm.
    Includes bibliographical references and index.
    1. Industries—Great Britain.   2. Industrial organization—Great
  Britain.   3. Industries—Germany.   4. Industrial organization—
  Germany.   5. Industries—France.   6. Industrial organization—
  France.   I. Title.
  HC255.L268   1995
  338.0941—dc20   94–43574
                                                                  CIP

ISBN 1 85278 394 X (hardback)
     1 85898 274 X (paperback)

Printed and bound in Great Britain by
Biddles Ltd, Guildford and King's Lynn

Contents

Figures and tables

FIGURES

TABLES

Introduction

This book explores changes in patterns of industrial organization in the three largest European societies – Germany,[1] Britain and France – during the period between 1973 and 1993 and draws on both economic sociology and political economy to offer an interpretation of this transformation process. Its aim is to conceptualize these changes, study their social foundations and explore some of their consequences. The focus will be mainly on the industrial sphere, where numerous analysts have detected what is variously referred to as a fundamental developmental break, a major disjuncture or a second industrial divide. Although major qualitative change is now widely acknowledged there is as yet no agreement on the extent and precise nature of that change. This book, it is hoped, will provide the material and interpretations to arrive at more informed discussion of this issue. It critically engages with some of the main theoretical approaches in this field – the flexible specialization thesis of Piore and Sabel, regulation theory and the New Institutionalism in sociology – and tries to assess their explanatory value in the systematic analysis of empirical material on three advanced societies.

The work has three main objectives. The first is to foster a sociological understanding of economic processes and structures by focusing on the way they are embedded in the social-institutional frameworks of the societies in which they are situated. Such frameworks are seen as the outcomes of historical developments going back to the start of industrialization and beyond. This Institutionalist sociological approach is supplemented by a perspective from political economy which tries to understand the production and consumption of social wealth in terms of power relations, involving capital, labour and the state. This understanding will entail an examination of how globally engendered processes of economic change become expressed in nationally distinctive ways, shaped by the different ways in which capital, labour and the state are structured and in their different modes of interaction. Such an analysis will therefore continually counterpose processes of structural convergence and divergence. Although integration in the European Union and wider processes of economic globalization have led many analysts to assume a process of convergence between European societies this work will give greater emphasis to the enduring distinctiveness in patterns of industrial organization.

The second objective is to study empirically aspects of industrial organization and change in the three largest European societies. This entails a juxtaposition of stable early post-1945 structures with recent processes of industrial change in a number of areas: first, the restructuring and growing internationalization of large European corporations; secondly, the resurgence of
smaller firms and the changing interconnections between corporate and small
capital; thirdly, the organizational and technological transformation and massive rationalization of whole production systems and the impact on labour
processes, trends in employment policy and forms of industrial relations;
finally, there will be consideration of the way all these developments have
impacted on the role of the nation state, that is, on the way in which states are
attempting to redefine their relation to the industrial economy and, through
changed modes of intervention, create new competitive regimes.

The focus of the book is thus mainly on manufacturing industry and its
mode of regulation by other societal institutions. This I consider justified
because, despite a substantial reduction in the size of this sector, its overall
importance remains undiminished (Greenhalgh and Gregory 1994). The whole
economy remains very much shaped by the manufacturing sector, and social
and material well-being dependent on it.

The third objective of this work is to pursue the study of current economic
transformations in a rigorously comparative manner. Each major topic is thus
examined first in terms of general issues and problems and then in its German, British and French appearance. This approach is designed to counteract
ethnocentric explanations and the constant temptation to present the particular as the general pattern. Thus the book will challenge readers to move
beyond the knowledge of their own society and to become familiar with
several European societies. In more substantive terms, such comparative and
historical analysis should also alert readers to the wide range of options open
to capital and to its enduring dynamism and creativity when faced with crisis.
Finally, the use of comparative method is also intended to foster the adoption
of more firmly grounded explanations of socio-economic change by keeping
constant some of the economic and social variables while varying others. But
such explanation, as the following exploration of theories of political economy
will make clear, can only be tentative, due to the overwhelming complexity
of the subject matter under examination.

A systematic and broad examination of change in all important aspects of
industrial organization over the last two decades concludes that European
societies have, indeed, been experiencing a fundamental developmental break
and that a new industrial paradigm is emerging. Reluctance to define the new
paradigm is partly due to the fact that some transformation processes are still
in flux. But this hesitation to apply labels is also conditioned by the circumstance that convergence in general processes remains always refracted in

nationally peculiar ways. Thus the book wishes to distinguish between different types of capitalism, based on distinctive national patterns of industrial organization, embedded in society. The latter I refer to as industrial order (Lane 1991 and 1994). There is an assumption that different degrees of social embeddedness or, conversely, social isolation of firms define divergent national competitive regimes. In other words, they make a difference to the capacity of firms and industries to adjust and respond to the current international environment and to the new competitive challenges it poses.

Britain and Germany can be presented as polar types on most aspects of industrial organization whereas France is much more difficult to typify in such terms. The British model remains that of financier-dominated capitalism, characterized by voluntarism, 'arm's-length' relationships and by a high degree of fragmentation and diversity. Firms are loose associations of lowly committed actors which, moreover, are exceptionally socially isolated. Unable to share risks, they undertake mainly short-term and low-risk investments in both fixed capital expenditure and human resources development. The absence of collectivistic orientations at the level of the firm is replicated at the level of industries, due to the absence of either self-regulation or significant state intervention. The low degree of embeddedness and of formal regulation, together with highly individualistic orientations among the main actors, permit flexible and often innovative responses to new challenges while, at the same time, impeding their effective implementation. Although the traditional adversarial approach to conflict resolution within and between firms is now becoming less marked, it has not yet been replaced with a stance of active involvement and co-operation.

The German model of production-orientated capitalism, implying both a greater concern with, and a closer integration of management and labour around, productive tasks, is the expression of an industrial order in which economic actors adhere to a limited communitarianism. Both the productivist bias and the greater collectivity orientation is dependent on a mode of finance provision which allows the development of long-term horizons in developing strategy for both individual firms and whole industries. It is further reinforced by a system of education and training which puts a strong emphasis on skill development at all levels and responsiveness to industrial needs. These orientations are supported by strong and dense associational networks and by both local and national state organizations. This high degree of embeddedness of firms and markets, together with a penchant towards consensual solutions, slows down responsiveness to outside challenges and limits options. But once restructuring is agreed upon by various interested parties, implementation is usually more effective than in the British model.

The high degree of stability of '*Modell Deutschland*' during the post-war period has been challenged by the reunification process begun in 1990. The two Germanies shared some common cultural orientations, such as the emphasis on skill development and an education system close to the needs of industry. However, most economic and political institutions have been radically different – those of liberal democracy and capitalism in the West as opposed to the structures of state socialism and the command economy in the East. Although the latter have either crumbled on impact or been pushed aside almost totally by West German economic and political institutions, one can neither expect a simple assimilation of West German industrial order in the East, nor should one envisage that industrial organization in the Western *Länder* will remain unaffected by the merging processes. The culture of state socialism has become part of the mind-set of East German citizens and will linger long after the demise of the institutions which originally shaped cultural orientations. This circumstance has led to serious problems in finding indigenous 'agents of change' and has led to the demoralizing occupation of most leading positions by citizens of the former West Germany and to the perception of imposed change. This circumstance has obvious consequences for the acceptance of the new institutions and cultural orientations. Although the resulting conflict is having a negative feed-back effect on the whole German industrial order the invigorating and thought-provoking effects of reunification on industrial policy-makers at various levels should not be ignored. While the final outcome of the reunification process cannot yet be predicted some effort will be made in the various chapters to indicate emerging trends.

The French model shares some features of the German industrial order in attenuated form, such as longer-term horizons and a strong concern with qualifications. But French industrial order lacks the integrative force, asserted by homogeneity in qualification terms between hierarchical levels of the firm, as well as Germany's more consensual industrial culture and dense network of support structures, facilitating self-administration by industrial communities. The French model depends instead on a more limited state-sponsored communitarianism which diminishes the effectiveness of the production orientation. It is perhaps more appropriate to speak of a strong concern with product design rather than with production organization as a whole, as in the German case. Moreover, while the model centred on the state as entrepreneur was reasonably successful in the establishment of a competitive regime during earlier post-war periods it appears less well suited to meet the challenges of the current more volatile and less predictable economic context.

The European Project has greatly increased the interest in understanding the economic and social structures of European nations, both among Europeans themselves and among members of competitor countries, and much writing on European economies and societies has emerged in recent years. But many publications in this area have been either 'individual country' studies, or, if comparative, have focused only on selected issues of industrial organization. Moreover, a sociological understanding of economic structures and processes is still comparatively rare. Since the publication of my previous book in 1989, *Management and Labour in Europe*, there has not emerged any work of comparable scope. Whereas the 1989 book focused mainly on business organization, the current work is concerned with the broader understanding of industrial organization and change. In other words, it tries to place the individual firm in a web of relationships with other industrial firms and with organizations, supplying the factors of production and/or safeguarding their timely and efficient co-ordination.

The text is addressed to academics and students in the following fields: economic sociology, political economy, management, business and European studies. As it does not presuppose extensive knowledge of social science concepts, it should also be of interest to practitioners in the fields of business or economic policy-making who are attempting to understand the wider social and economic contexts in which their own work is undertaken. Although the work does not presuppose prior knowledge, students in their final years of study or on post-graduate courses are probably more likely to appreciate the wide comparative sweep of the analysis. The book is the result of lecturing to both business and social science students in their second and final years.

The book has drawn on a widely dispersed literature and has often crossed national and disciplinary boundaries, as well as considering accounts aimed at practitioners. Thus I have made forays into economics, business studies and politics and have made extensive use of German sources and, to a much lesser extent, French ones. Given the very recent occurrence of some of the developments discussed, as well as the relative underdevelopment of the subdiscipline of economic sociology, empirical accounts are still rare in some of the areas covered. Inevitably, this makes for unevenness in both empirical documentation and in evaluation of theoretical claims. Thus, while we possess an extensive and well-informed literature in the field of comparative industrial relations – a mature British field of study – the topic of restructuring of large corporations and of multinational companies – an equally or even more vital aspect of understanding current processes of industrial transformation – has received very little systematic empirical study from a comparative social science perspective.

The first chapter introduces and evaluates four important theoretical approaches in the fields of political economy and economic sociology which, singly or in combination, inform the discussion of substantive issues in the chapters which follow. Chapter 2 explores the historical foundations of various aspects of industrial organization and focuses particularly on the fifty-odd years around the turn of the last century when the points were being set for many industrial developments of the post-Second World War period. One of the most important influences on the pattern of industrial organization – the industry–finance nexus – receives detailed consideration in Chapter 3. Chapters 4 and 5 deal with traditional structures and recent transformations in the corporate sector and explore the evidence, relating to the theses about corporate fragmentation and the emergence of transnational companies, respectively. Whereas Chapter 4 deals with general issues, relating to corporate structure and strategy and to newly emerging patterns of industrial organization, Chapter 5 seeks to make a contribution to the globalization debate. Chapter 6 is devoted to the sector of small and medium-sized enterprises and discusses the differing claims about the contributions this sector makes to both economic vitality and to the quality of the employment relation. By highlighting the divergent character of this sector in the three societies, it cautions against easy generalizations about the roles small and medium-sized firms can play in the current restructuring process. In Chapters 7 and 8 we move on to consider the impact of changes in industrial organization on labour. Chapter 7 concentrates on issues in the fields of industrial relations and employment, exploring interactions between the two, as well as considering the impact of wider economic and political changes on the structure and conduct of industrial relations. Here I highlight the differential loss of industrial and political clout of the three national union movements and attempt to explain these developments both from an Institutionalist and a political economy perspective. Chapter 8 studies the varying extent and degree of consistency in the transformation of production policy and organization in the three manufacturing sectors and draws out the differential consequences for skill development, patterns of management control and employment trends.

In the concluding chapter, the discussion of changing patterns of industrial organization considers the role played in this process by the nation state. It explores the extent to which the scope of this role has been diminished and the many ways in which governments have tried to develop a new balance between state and market during the last two decades. As in previous chapters, examination of processes of change takes care to consider ideological and political structural starting points in the three countries, as well as differing economic preconditions. Throughout the book, it is attempted to achieve a balance between highlighting the common economic and political challenges faced by the three European societies and between emphasizing the often highly distinctive routes taken to deal with these challenges.

NOTE

1. The discussion of German industrial organization focuses mainly on the former West Germany, due to the shortage of comparable data on a reunified Germany, as well as to the unsettled and transitional nature of many developments in the former GDR. However, the impact of reunification on German industrial organization is not ignored. Every chapter includes at least a few observations on how structural features and ideological orientations have been affected by reunification and to what extent such changes might modify German industrial order. It should also be noted that the two parts of Germany are of very different size, and that both the East German population share (20 per cent) and the share of industrial production (3–4 per cent) (Kern 1994: 33) are discrepantly low.

1. Theories of industrial organization and change

Comparison of industrial organization in several countries has to be guided by a theoretical framework which specifies both the purpose and focus of comparison. Such theories can be orientated towards an emphasis on structural similarities between societies and thus towards examination of a process of convergence. Alternatively, theories can dwell on divergencies between societies and underline enduring distinctiveness. Ideally, however, theories of industrial organization should sensitize us to both commonalities, flowing from common location in the capitalist global economic system, and towards remaining national specificities, stemming from historically grown social-institutional features. In addition to the comparative element, theories can be used to sensitize us to the issues to be investigated and the questions to be asked, besides helping to organize the empirical detail on industrial organization and change. This chapter will introduce four such theories and indicate their relevance to the empirical issues to be covered in subsequent chapters: the first – the Marxist analysis of capitalist society – will be outlined very briefly; then three more recent theories of industrial organization and transformation – institutionalism, the 'flexible specialization' thesis of Piore and Sabel and French regulation theory will be covered in more detail. In each case a general outline of the theory will be followed by an evaluation of strengths and weaknesses.

MARXIST THEORY OF CAPITALIST SOCIETY

This theory gives prime emphasis to transnational influences on industrial organization, emanating from a common location in the world capitalist system. Societies share a common mode of production, distinguished by private ownership of productive property, competition between capitals and production of commodities for profit. The compulsion to continually increase capital accumulation, due to the competition between capitals, entails the need for capital to reduce unit costs of labour and to develop and maintain forms of labour control to achieve this objective. An important weapon in the competitive struggle to raise labour productivity and increase profits is the constant revolutionizing of technology and the eventual domination of living labour by the machine. Consequently, the interests of capital stand in conflict to those of labour who try to maintain or raise levels of pay, as well as maintain skill and control over their labour process. This conflict, together with the intensifying economic crises resulting from overproduction, provide the dynamic of social development which will eventually lead to the supercession of capitalism.

A second focus of Marxist theory is on the relation between diverse fractions of capital, particularly that between monopoly capital and the capital of small owners. Here Marx outlines parallel processes of growing concentration of capital and control and the absorption of petty by monopoly capital. A last important tenet for our purposes is the claim that all social and political institutions, but particularly the state, are ideologically and materially committed to the perpetuation of capitalism.

The Marxist theory thus emphasizes relations at the level of production above those of distribution, and these relations are inherently conflictual and do not allow for co-operative solutions. Concerning comparisons between societies, Marxist theory dwells on common constraints and the convergence towards a common final stage of development. Divergences are regarded either as temporary phenomena or as being marginal to basic developmental trends.

In many ways the Marxist analysis seems eminently plausible in the current context of growing internationalization of economic processes, increasing interdependence, rapid technological change and intensifying global competition. The last decade or so has also made more obvious the pronounced pressures on management to improve competitiveness and to pass on some of these pressures to labour. It is also evident that the demands of capitalism have been articulated more stridently at the ideological and political level. At the same time, there have occurred new economic developments which are not readily understood from within a Marxist framework, such as a resurgence of smaller firms, a growing management concern with fixed capital rather than labour, as well as a new preoccupation with distribution and markets. Most importantly, the Marxist homogenizing perspective leaves no purchase for understanding the highly distinctive ways in which different national economies have responded to the new international challenges. A deeper consideration of the three largest European societies soon reveals that there has occurred no complete convergence and that historically evolved social and economic patterns have mediated the impact of global influences in nationally distinctive ways. Thus, to conclude, although many Marxist insights remain important for understanding current processes of industrial transformation, they are insufficient to encompass this diversity, as well as being too one-sided in their exclusive emphasis on production, on economic determinism and on the capital–labour conflict.

THE INSTITUTIONALIST PERSPECTIVE

In contrast to the Marxist approach, institutionalism accords overriding importance to national distinctiveness in industrial organization, attributing this to the influence of historically grown, enduring institutional frameworks which 'create the lenses through which organizational actors come to view the world' (DiMaggio and Powell 1991: 13). In the process, institutions both constrain and enable actors, and, in the words of Jepperson (1991: 146), 'are vehicles for activity within constraint'. The concern of institutionalists to understand how social choices are shaped, mediated and channelled by institutional arrangements has long informed scholars in all the social sciences, and a variety of different institutionalist approaches are on offer. The following discussion is mainly concerned with three more recent developments in this field: the elaboration and tighter specification of this approach from a sociological perspective by New Institutionalists in organizational analysis (Powell and Dimaggio 1991); the work of some political scientists in the tradition of political economy (for example, Hall 1984 and 1986; Thelen 1991); and lastly, the work of economic sociologists trying to apply the institutionalist analysis to the understanding of whole national industrial orders or national competitive regimes (Lane 1991 and 1994; Orru et al. 1991; Whitley 1992; Hollingsworth et al. 1994).

The New Institutionalists

In common with other institutionalists, theorists under this label attempt to clarify the processes through which institutions shape organizational structure and action. They adopt, however, a distinctive view of institutions which then shapes their analysis of how influence is exerted, as well as moulding their understanding of organizational actors and processes of change. Institutions, in their view, are not necessarily the outcomes of conscious human design by instrumentally orientated individuals. They have turned from the 'rational actor' model towards a phenomenological approach which emphasizes cognitive and cultural explanations. Institutions are viewed as supra-individual units, irreducible to the motives of individuals (DiMaggio and Powell 1991: 8). Social relationships and actions are seen to possess a 'taken for granted' and routine quality, resulting in shared cognitions which define 'what has meaning and what actions are possible' (quoted in DiMaggio and Powell 1991: 9).

This phenomenological perspective seems to be developed in opposition to one emphasizing the normative quality of social action (ibid.: 15). But it remains unclear why the cognitive and normative aspects cannot be combined, and it is suggested by this author that such a combination can even strengthen the institutionalist approach. While it is plausible that the 'taken for granted' quality is dominant and that unreflective conformity to institutionalized patterns of action is the rule it is also the case that breaches of such patterns call forth sanctions which imply some normative force, even if it remains dormant until such challenges arise. Although patterns of action are mostly reproduced in this unreflective, almost automatic manner there are occasions – brought about by external shocks or cross-cutting institutional pressures – when a more active agency is needed to reassert legitimacy in the face of challenges from those deriving less benefit from existing institutional arrangements. In other words, institutional reproduction occasionally depends on the reassertion and even enforcement of norms.

The phenomenological approach of New Institutionalists to the understanding of institutions also implies a rejection of the notion of institutions held by many economists who see their creation and persistence as due to their efficiency in regulating economic transactions. The sociological New Institutionalists, in contrast, reject functionalist explanations and attribute institutional persistence to the inability of individual actors to break out of, and transcend, established modes of cognition. Actors' preference for familiar patterns of decision-making and problem solution creates resistance to change. This is an important difference in as far as it helps us to understand why patterns of action or whole organizations persist even when they have long been associated with poor economic performance. Their persistence is due not only to sunk economic costs, but also to sunk psychological costs (Scott 1991: 194). According to the phenomenological approach, institutions maintain their legitimacy by explaining and justifying social order in such a way to make institutional arrangements subjectively plausible (ibid.: 169).

This 'taken for granted' quality of modes of thinking prevents individuals from perceiving alternatives and thus results in structures which are to some extent self-sustaining and, hence, resistant to change. New Institutionalists do not want to rule out change within organizations and attribute it mainly to the impact of external shocks. But their understanding of institutions as self-perpetuating and self-reinforcing structures, together with their notion of actors and interests as being constituted by institutions, makes their new emphasis on change problematic and unconvincing. The emphasis on common understandings and conformity downplays conflicts within organizations and hence eliminates one dynamic of organizational change. It does not probe the possibility that some actors benefit more than others from the perpetuation of institutionalized practices. Also the exclusive focus on external shocks as sources of institutional change neglects their impact on power relations within organizations and the creation of new manoeuvring space for various groups of actors. Opportunities for change may be created by external shocks but actual implementation of such change necessitates the mobilization of internal actors in support of such change. Both differential power and interests within organizations and 'the active political side of the story' need more attention, as DiMaggio and Powell freely admit (1991: 30–1).

Lastly, it is important to note that New Institutionalists do not conceive of organizational actors as solely influenced by cultural factors but also recognize the impact of resource flows. But, in contrast to the other theories considered in this chapter, such material factors are regarded as less worthy of study because their impact is seen as modified by institutions. The study of resource flows is not incorporated into the theory as a variable in its own right. This relative neglect of material factors, however, can turn into a shortcoming of this approach as radical changes in resource flows, caused by external environmental factors, may also provide the impetus for institutional crisis and change. If there is a neglect of the growing interconnectedness of individual societies it becomes difficult to understand where external shocks come from, and they tend to be described as emerging *ex machina*. Furthermore, such external influences are usually experienced in common with other capitalist societies and thus exert some homogenizing influence. Some of these factors are better understood by theorists subscribing to the following two approaches.

Institutionalism within a 'political economy' perspective

Authors within this perspective share many of the assumptions of New Institutionalists but accord more importance to class interests and class struggle, both in the creation of institutions and in the analysis of institutional transformation. Thus Hall (1984) views institutions as 'cumulative products of political struggle at a series of crucial historical conjunctures'. But, as he shares other institutionalists' insight that interests and power are partly institutionally shaped, he does not accept the Marxian logic of convergence of institutional structures in all capitalist societies. While Hall is primarily concerned with current outcomes of such historical processes, Crouch (1993) provides us with a very illuminating comparative exploration of such historical institution-building, focusing on the interrelation between state and industrial relations structures. Despite this stronger focus on interests, power relations and struggle, neither of these two authors utilizes this emphasis to elaborate a theoretical elucidation of institutional transformation within an institutionalist framework.

In this latter respect, the work of Thelen (1991) is more instructive. Although her work is primarily an empirical exploration of changing industrial relations structures, she provides some important insights for understanding how change comes about. While most institutionalists pay only lip service to the fact that structures are built and maintained by actors, Thelen again puts actors at the centre of this perspective. She does not simply refer to external shocks as sources of change but concentrates on how actors within institutions utilize such shocks, as well as being concerned with more incremental change. She posits that institutional actors are not completely determined by institutional rules but, given their differential positions within organizations and their differing interests, engage in strategic manoeuvring within set parameters. Such manoeuvring becomes particularly pronounced when external changes of an economic or a political kind challenge the legitimacy of institutional arrangements and bring about a shift in the balance of power between actors. Knight (1992) throws further light on the dynamic aspect of building and transforming institutions by pointing out that all institutions are the unintended consequences of the pursuit of strategic advantage by unequal actors and that their logic is not to fulfil economic efficiency but to make possible the interaction of conflicting interests, via the imposition of rules of the game. It is, however, to be expected that institutional arrangements which reconcile conflicting interests are also more likely to generate economic efficiency.

Whereas most scholars within the institutionalist perspective have been content to study the impact of a limited set of institutional arrangements on specific organizations or related groups of organizations, some recent work in the area of economic sociology has adopted a more ambitious goal. It focuses on a range of institutions, perceived to have an important impact on industrial organization, and seeks to interpret the combined effect of such institutions on firms and markets in systemic terms, positing a societal logic or set of structuring influences, operating at the national level. The societal logic (Orru et al. 1991), business system (Whitley 1992) or social system of production (Hollingsworth et al. 1994), resulting from interaction between institutional framework and industrial organization, is then related to national industrial performance or competitive regimes. Such approaches are very helpful in that they provide a systematic framework for comparative empirical analysis of industrial organization, by elaborating which institutions and cultural configurations impact on industrial organization, as well as specifying how to conceptualize the latter. But they lack the insights of New Institutionalists about how exactly institutions impact on organizations, as well as sharing some of their weaknesses. The explicit or implicit systemic view of these approaches, which emphasizes the interconnectedness of different institutional spheres, is even more prone than other institutionalist approaches to emphasize reproduction and inertia of institutional arrangements at the expense of conflict and change. Lacking the phenomenological perspective of New Institutionalists, these 'systemic' interpretations are also vulnerable to accusations of functionalism in the explanation of organizational reproduction. Most importantly, this approach is prone to emphasize national distinctiveness at the expense of a perspective which highlights the tension between national institutional influences and those impinging on national economies from the wider global economic system.

Although the remainder of this book attempts such a holistic analysis of industrial organization, it tries to avoid both the suggestion of systemic integration and the exclusive focus on reproduction, as well as taking more care to view individual economies as part of a larger economic system. The term 'industrial order' is chosen to refer to interaction between social-institutional structures and patterns of industrial organization.

In sum, institutionalist approaches provide a valuable method for understanding the evolution and perpetuation of distinctive national industrial paradigms and for contrasting the paradigms of different nations in terms of resulting competitive regimes. They also permit a shift away from the exclusive focus on the capital–labour relation and to encompass various relations between capitals, as well as drawing attention to the prevalence of inertia and conformity in patterns of action and social relations. All this provides useful correctives to the Marxist approach but, in the process, loses sight of the Marxist insight that individual societies are inextricably linked with each other in a larger economic and political framework. Institutionalist and Marxist approaches thus can be seen to have complementary strengths. The following two theoretical approaches to be reviewed each attempt, in their own way, to combine these strengths into a unified theory.

FLEXIBLE SPECIALIZATION

General outline

This theory has been advanced by Piore and Sabel in their 1984 book *The Second Industrial Divide: Possibilities for Prosperity* and has been further developed by Sabel (1989, 1990) and others in subsequent articles. The book is a very ambitious work, ranging widely in both time and space and mixing bold theoretical claims with empirical accounts of industrial development in several countries over two historical periods. As the title of the book indicates, it is concerned with understanding the current economic crisis and with elaborating a way out of it as a foundation for a new prosperity. It further signals that we are experiencing times of dramatic socio-economic change and that the way out of crisis will represent an industrial divide with the past.

On a theoretical level, the theory seeks to combine an emphasis on societal institutional contexts with a consideration of general influences, emanating from a world capitalist system. This combination, although innovative in its attempt to transcend Marxism's economic determinism and to develop a more open approach, in the end projects a rather partial and narrow view of the institutionalist perspective and a highly skewed and very partial view of contemporary capitalism.

The authors start off by developing a simple conceptual distinction between two types of production paradigms: mass production and flexible specialization. The 'mass production' type states that firms are concerned with making standardized products on a mass scale, with the help of dedicated machinery and mainly semi-skilled labour. Flexible specialization, in contrast, deals with short production runs of highly differentiated and/or customized quality products, utilizing multipurpose machinery and skilled craft-type labour. As Williams et al. (1987: 406) point out, this simple dichotomy forms the basis for developing a bold argument containing three elements: first, a theory of two types of economy; second, an interpretative meta history of industrial development; and third, an analysis of the current crisis and some proposals for its resolution. Let us look at each element in turn.

The two production paradigms outlined above also form the basis for two types of economy if they are dominant in a given territorial unit at a given historical point in time. But the focus remains narrowly on production. The authors do not presume that each type is totally dominant, and they also allow for the fact that differing degrees of dominance, together with variation in national regulatory frameworks, are connected with different national labour utilization methods which depart from total concentration on one type of labour. But Piore and Sabel never specify the criteria which make it possible to decide when one type has become a challenge to the other.

Each type of economy is connected with its own problems which, to avoid severe economic crisis, each require their own remedies. As mass production is introduced in order to lower production costs through economies of scale, technological innovation is utilized to raise constantly the volume of output. But such constant increase of output requires stable and even expanding markets to recoup the investment in single-purpose machinery. Thus mass production economies can only function if they have a regulatory system which, through political means, creates a 'workable match' between production and consumption at the macro level. One example of this was Keynesianism in the post-war period. If such regulation fails the whole economy is plunged into severe crisis.

Flexible specialization, in contrast, does not depend on stable mass markets. It offers economies of scope and reduces the costs of customized goods. The requirement of perpetual change in products and processes demands an environment which ensures constant product and process innovation. Such innovation can only be achieved if economic competition is balanced by co-operation in such areas as wage determination, design and development.

Economic prosperity and survival, Piore and Sabel posit, depends on firms' ability 'to sustain the innovative recombination of resources'. Co-operation is realizable if flexible producers, working in the same locality, specialize in complementary product segments.

Economic ties need to be supplemented by social ties, based on family, ethnicity, or on common political or religious allegiance, and co-operation is orchestrated in a more or less formal way. To form such co-operative networks, smaller firms forge horizontal links with other firms, and large, vertically integrated corporations split themselves into smaller and more independent business units. Although the Piore and Sabel book concerns itself mainly with networks of smaller firms and their institutional environment Sabel's later articles (1989 and 1990) envisage a role also for large corporations in co-operative, regionally based networks. To qualify for inclusion, large firms enhance their organizational flexibility through internal restructuring and the development of locally based subcontracting networks. The ensuing complexity of production demands greater worker skill, creativity and responsibility and thus calls for management–labour relations of mutual trust and co-operation. The emphasis in their outline of industrial districts is thus very much on economic decentralization and democratization of control.

This type of economy will stagnate if co-operation breaks down and innovation is hampered by market competition between firms on cost grounds, particularly through depressing labour costs. Small firms are particularly exposed to market competition, and the danger of resolving this problem by 'sweated labour' is ever present. This type of economy thus calls for a very different kind of regulatary framework. Although it is described in their empirical accounts of particular industrial districts, the authors remain vague about how such a regulatory environment could be constructed and generalized.

At present, according to Piore and Sabel (1984), only certain countries and regions within them are able to provide such supportive frameworks, due to historically divergent developments. They single out Japan, Germany and Italy, but imply that regions in other nations can learn to imitate environments, conducive to the takeoff of the new production paradigm. Their outline of the institutional environment dwells mainly on institutional complexes regulating labour while other, arguably more important aspects of the institutional framework, such as the financial system and the structure of the state, are neglected. They place emphasis on policy-making at the meso level but do not spell out this policy-orientated part of their theory.

This theory of types of economy is then given a historical and developmental dimension which Williams et al. (1987) have termed 'a meta theory of history'. The latter envisages stages of economic development but, in contrast to previous 'stages' theory, disavows any kind of structural determinism and any simple juxtaposition of a traditional and a modern period. The two types of economies elaborated by them can recur at different times of history, albeit in changed technological and regulatory frameworks. Thus, for Piore and Sabel, flexible specialization is in large part a return to the principles of craft production prevalent in the nineteenth century.

In contrast to the Marxist approach, this meta theory does not connect capitalism with any invariant developmental tendencies, and it also rules out any technological determinism as envisaged by 'industrial society' theory. Although their theory acknowledges the periodic crises of capitalism it sees them as amenable to regulation. Instead, Piore and Sabel (1984) stress the possibility of strategic choice on the part of important economic actors, and the outcome of such choices appear to be shaped by actors' power resources. Throughout the book, there is the assumption that both production paradigms are equal in their economic efficiency and in their wealth-generating capacity. Piore and Sabel (1984: 67) thus present what they describe as 'a branching tree view of history', and the branches are seen to thrive or whither as a result of the outcome of political struggles.

Fundamental choices present themselves at severe crisis points of economic development, no longer amenable to political regulation and lead to what Piore and Sabel term 'economic divides'. Once a decision has been made in favour of one technological paradigm uniformity of production policy gradually develops. Also inertia, together with the deterrent of sunk costs, militates against alternative choices. One such fundamental divide was faced at the turn of the nineteenth century when American firms finally decided against craft production in favour of mass production.

The present crisis, which started in the first half of the 1970s, presents us with another such choice. We can either develop a new international regulatory framework to rekindle market stability and continue with the mass production paradigm, or we can revive prosperity by systematically developing the conditions for flexible specialization. Although Piore and Sabel (1984) claim that both are real choices they do not show how international Keynesianism could be achieved. Their own sympathies lie heavily with flexible specialization, and Sabel's subsequent work has concentrated only on elaborating this concept. In the words of Williams et al. (1987: 412), their avowed neutrality is 'a decorous pretence'.

Their declared openness about routes out of the current crisis is based on an equally open diagnosis of its causes, offering us what they see as two alternative accounts. In one account of the causes of the current crisis, external shocks, such as the oil crises and the breakdown of the Bretton Woods agreement on fixed exchange rates, are implicated. In the second account, structural factors within the economies are seen as the source of our current troubles, particularly the saturation of certain core markets for mass-produced goods and the break-up of mass markets for standardized goods. This is seen to be due to both demand and supply factors, particularly greater differentiation of taste and the entry of newly industrialized countries into world markets for standardized goods.

A critical appraisal

Flexible specialization theory has been extraordinarily influential. It has generated both acclaim and vigorous and comprehensive criticism, as well as stimulating much new empirical research and public economic policy experimentation. It has not only influenced academics but also business managers and policy-makers. The widespread influence, as Nielsen (1991: 16) points out, is partly due to the following characteristics: a clear message, a suggestive line of argument and an optimistic vision of the future. Of the many critical analyses (Williams et al. 1987; Hyman 1988 and 1991; Pollert 1988 and 1991; Badham and Mathews 1989; Sayer 1989; Amin and Robins 1990; Nielsen 1991; Curran 1993) some are more pertinent and constructive than others, and several have already been addressed both by the authors and by sympathizers. Some penetrating, but ultimate overzealous analyses (Williams et al. 1987; Pollert 1988 and 1991) end up by denying the occurrence of any important changes in production paradigm. It is important to submit the many criticisms to careful scrutiny and to avoid throwing out the baby with the bath water.

Of the many specific criticisms of flexible specialization the following deserve particular attention. The first criticism states that there was no complete dominance of mass markets before 1973, nor has there occurred a complete break-up of mass markets since then. Although Piore and Sabel are correct in pointing to significant changes in production policy and organization they leave themselves open to this charge by posing a simple dichotomy between mass and craft production and by failing to spell out clear criteria for assessing change from one paradigm to the other. But this justified criticism, elaborated particularly trenchantly by Williams et al. (1987), should not lead to the denial of any real change but merely towards reworking the typology to embrace intermediate types, such as the notion of 'diversified quality production' (Sorge and Streeck 1987), that is, a new trend to greater product quality and diversity which blends elements of customization into mass production. As this has had significant consequences for innovation, production organization, worker skills and even corporate restructuring, it must be considered an important new development. Also rejection of the Piore and Sable claim that customization has become the dominant production and market strategy should not divert from the fact that these strategies have become more significant in many industries (Sengenberger and Loveman 1988).

A second type of criticism deals with the authors' emphasis on the importance of the actor–structure dichotomy in their approach to historical change. The realization of change through social and political struggles receives scant attention in the empirical account of the current situation, and the very real problems for labour of engaging in such struggles in the current conjuncture is completely ignored – hence the charge of naive romanticism found in many critical accounts. But, at the same time, it would be unjustified to charge them with 'individualistic behaviourist accounts' (Amin and Robins 1990). 'Trust' and 'co-operation', for example, can be conceptualized as collective goods, independent of any given individual actor.

A third line of criticism states that too much weight is put on to the concept of flexibility and that it would have been more appropriate to balance the concept of flexibility with that of rigidity and to indicate new permutations of both (Sayer 1989). But this criticism should not lead us, *à la* Pollert (1988), to throw out the concept altogether but to concentrate instead on more-precise specifications of different kinds of flexibility, as attempted by Badham and Matthews (1989) and Sayer (1989). Many new developments in production organization, labour utilization and corporate restructuring would be difficult to understand without recourse to this concept. To deny the occurrence of any trend towards greater flexibility in, for example, the implementation of the new technology – as do Williams et al. (1987) – amounts to precisely the same sin as that of which they accuse Piore and Sabel, namely to advance one-sided and seriously misleading arguments.

Fourth, Piore and Sabel, in their focus on small and medium-sized enterprises (SMEs) and industrial districts, mistakenly present one element of current change as standing for the whole (Amin and Robins 1990). Furthermore, their conception of industrial districts betrays a naive romanticism about a yeoman democracy and the resurrection of a craft idyll of old which ignore the harsh realities of capitalistic production relations. But such criticism does not imply that the concept of the industrial district is completely useless, nor that there are no tendencies towards local networks of co-operation. It merely suggests that such patterns of economic activity are more exceptional than the authors admit and that the influence of powerful countervailing global tendencies is left out of account. Piore and Sabel's suggestion to take as a political challenge the extension of the flexibility found in industrial districts to other parts of a national economy is an entirely reasonable one, although the difficulty of achieving such a broadening out is clearly underestimated by them.

This last criticism is related to a fifth major criticism about Sabel's conceptualization of large, usually multinational corporations. When dealing with large firms, Sabel (1989 and 1990) concentrates on their production organization and ignores the vital financial and marketing aspects. Large corporations are generally analysed in a superficial manner, and emergent new tendencies in corporate structures and strategies, evident in some large firms, are again presented as the whole picture.

The 'branching tree' model of economic and social development is also open to criticism. Their assertion that, at the first industrial divide, craft and mass production were equally efficient and viable is difficult to believe. They do not indicate what craft production, relying only on manual skill, could counterpose to mass production's economies of scale. They do not make clear why those powerful groups threw their resources behind mass production if the economic advantage was no greater than that held by craft production. Furthermore, it is quite clear that economies of scope in connection with craft methods at the present time could not be achieved without flexible automation – an advantage not available to craft producers at the beginning of this century. Although Piore and Sabel are right to emphasize the overriding importance of co-operative networks in making the new production paradigm viable, it is disingenious to assert that the new technology is only a secondary factor.

A last and very serious charge against Piore and Sable is that they fuse description, prediction and prescription (Pollert 1988). Few analysts can agree with their optimistic vision of the future. But this vision should not simply be rejected on the grounds that capitalism cannot generate any positive developments for labour, but rejection must be based on counterfactual empirical evidence. Most critics point out that, at the very least, there is more openness and uncertainty about outcomes than Piore and Sabel allow for. A consideration of alternative paths of development, such as a neo-Fordist paradigm, although not completely neglected, is not properly integrated into their theory and receives insufficient weight in empirical accounts. Paradoxically, a theoretical position, which insists on strategic choice and on the absence of any structural determinism, in the end effectively leaves room for only one vision of the future. More conviction is carried by accounts, such as Boyer's (1991b), envisaging a plurality of outcomes, of which flexible specialization might be one.

From this review of specific critical points, let us finally move to a more general criticism levelled against Piore and Sabel, relating to ambiguity in the main concepts employed. This should not lead us to outright rejection, as the latter are amenable to clearer specification. The main problem relates to whether we are to regard the concepts of Fordism and flexible specialization as empirical generalizations or as ideal types. If we see them as ideal types which we utilize to guide our investigations and order our empirical evidence, then the criticism about the dominance of specific production paradigms loses some of its force. We then need no longer look for a full realization of either type but merely for a shift along a continuum between the two types. If one further accepts the suggestion of Badham and Mathews (1989: 223) that it is enough for flexible specialization to be seen as a real competitor to the Fordist paradigm to make it a significant phenomenon for study, then the many pedantic and ultimately rather fruitless quibbles about dominance of either paradigm and about the exact timing of a changeover from one to the other become less compelling. This is not to deny, though, that tighter specification of the various concepts, as indicated above, is necessary.

The impressive geographical and historical sweep of the Piore and Sabel theory has led to some unsupported generalizations, to conceptual vagueness and to the proclamation of over-optimistic prognoses and unwarranted certainties about future economic development. But these admittedly serious shortcomings of their analyses should not lead us to deny the considerable merit of their work: it has drawn our attention to some ongoing important processes of industrial change in a highly stimulating way, as well as challenging us to devise more sophisticated and flexible theoretical accounts of such change. It is hardly surprising that such an ambitious task has not been realized at the first attempt. Some of the above criticisms are heeded by the next theory to be considered, although it shares some of flexible specialization's weak spots, as well as having several of its own.

REGULATION THEORY

General outline

Regulation theory is mainly connected with the French Regulation School, containing such names as Aglietta, Lipietz, Leborgne and Boyer. It started from the realization, borne of the current economic crisis, that capitalism's reproduction has been highly problematic and which led to a desire for a better understanding of the different characters and causes of the various historically experienced crises. Regulation theory, according to Jessop (1992: 325), can be seen to strive for a completion of Marx's critique of political economy, as well as making it more applicable to current trends. It is a reaction against the quasi-mechanistic Althusserian Marxist conception of capitalist reproduction, and it is also directed against neo-classical economists' undersocialized and undifferentiated conception of the working of markets, with its emphasis on general equilibrium and the power of the price mechanism.

In contrast to more orthodox Marxist theory, regulation theory repudiates economic determinism and invariant laws of historical development, although its proponents still posit the existence of certain fundamental tendencies within a capitalist mode of production. It differs decisively from other neo-Marxist accounts in its absorption into its theoretical apparatus of an institutionalist perspective which renders it more flexible and better able to appreciate the enduring distinctiveness of individual societies. Regulation theorists seek to combine, in the words of Hirst and Zeitlin (1990: 16), 'openness and contingency ... with a continuing insistence on the systematic nature of capitalism as a mode of production and the centrality of class struggle in its development'. They thus wish to emphasize, at one and the same time, the institutional and cultural diversity of advanced societies and the homogenizing influence of the world capitalist system.

Although regulation theorists differ considerably amongst themselves, it is possible to single out a common core, particularly for the Parisian School. Regulation theory starts from the realization that capitalism, as a mode of production, is unstable and crisis-ridden and that its stabilization and reproduction has to be secured by complex forms of regulation. The theory envisages successive regimes of capital accumulation, allied to congruent modes of regulation.

A regime of accumulation describes 'the stabilization over a long period of the allocation of the net product between consumption and accumulation. It implies some correspondence between both the transformation of the conditions of production and the conditions of reproduction of wage earners' (Lipietz 1986: 19). Such a regime encompasses a pattern of productive organization (use of capital, technology and deployment of labour) – also referred to separately as industrial paradigm – and a pattern of income distribution and consumption. 'Regime of accumulation (RA)' can be defined abstractly and made generally applicable, but it can also refer to a specific national appearance within the international context when it is termed 'mode of growth (MG)'.

Stable regimes of accumulation do not become established automatically but depend on regulation, that is on certain social adjustments to be made. An RA is made viable by a mode of regulation (MR), understood as complexes of institutions, norms and regulating networks which secure the adjustment of individuals and groups to the regime of accumulation. It defines the rules of the game which are applied to the industrial paradigm, the accumulation regime and their articulation (Delorme 1992: 167). Specification of this concept marks out the novelty of the regulation approach and gives it its open and flexible character.

Among the structures and behavioural patterns constituting the MR, some or all of the following are singled out:

1. wage relation (wage–effort bargain, forms of collective bargaining, labour market organization, income distribution and life-styles);

2. form of enterprise (internal organization, source of profit, the regulation of competition and other forms of interfirm relations, and relations with financial capital);
3. banking and credit system (allocation of capital to production, form of money);
4. the state (institutional compromise between capital and labour; form of state intervention, welfare provision);
5. international regime (trade, investment, monetary regulation; political connection of individual states to the world system);
6. social processes which contribute to the construction of ideology, such as education and training and mobilization and persuasion through the media. (Based on Delorme 1992; Jessop 1992; Hirst and Zeitlin 1992).

Forms of regulation may originate at any level of the socio-economic complex, and an appropriate mode of regulation comes about partly by happy chance, partly through class struggle and political strategy; and the connection with a regime of accumulation is best described as a process of historical co-evolution (Jessop 1990: 185). Modes of regulation eventually become destroyed by structural economic crises which slow down productive growth and are expressed in increasing behavioural divergencies between the representatives of capital and labour. The actual working of the MR enters into conflict with the existing institutions and has to be changed.

Although there evolves one global mode of regulation, precise institutional patterns and mechanisms of intervention vary considerably between capitalist societies, due to different historical outcomes of class struggle. This variation between societies has become one major research focus of scholars in the Regulation School. A last concept used by regulation theorists is that of mode or model of development. This term is reserved for the combination of an industrial paradigm, a regime of accumulation and a mode of regulation in one integrated whole.

Regulation theory, like that of flexible specialization, posits a 'stages' model of history; and the motor of history in this model, as in Marxism, is constituted by the development of the productive forces and by the struggle over control of processes of production and reproduction (Nielsen 1991: 25). But in regulation theory periods of economic and social stability are punctuated by crises in a non-determined manner which the theory is striving to understand. As the class struggle is strongly socially influenced, processes of change possess a greater openness than in orthodox Marxist accounts.

Until about the First World War, an extensive regime of accumulation, concentrated on 'the widened reproduction of capital goods' (Lipietz 1986: 25), with a competitive mode of regulation, was dominant in capitalist societies. (It entailed *a posteriori* price adjustment to demand and wage adjustment to prices.) After rises in productivity and a severe crisis of overproduction, this gave way to one of intensive accumulation and monopolistic regulation which, in the USA of the early 1930s, became known as Fordism. The Fordist regime, dominant in Europe during most of the post-war period, is characterized by intensive accumulation and monopolistic competition. The production paradigm has the features of mass production of standardized goods with special-purpose machinery and semi-skilled labour, subjected to a high division of labour and tight managerial control. This pattern of production organization is linked to one of mass consumption, based on high and stable wages and on high levels of welfare, secured by an interventionist state. Trade unions became accepted as legitimate negotiating partners both at the level of the firm and of the state. From the late 1960s onwards, this regime entered a period of crisis, and it is being replaced by another which is as yet poorly defined.

Structural crises which undermine the whole configuration of institutions take different forms at different stages of economic development. Although there is no complete agreement about the causes of the ongoing crisis the following have been identified as important, either singly or in combination: declining productivity and profitability; growing integration into an increasingly unstable global economic system; and, in some accounts, also saturation and fragmentation of markets (see De Vroey 1984 for a detailed analysis of the crises). Whereas Aglietta's early work focused on the USA as the supreme economic power on which international stability depended, more recent accounts are increasingly shifting the focus to Japan as the emerging hegemonic power (see, for example, Boyer 1992b).

Whereas the Regulation School has provided quite detailed accounts of past regimes of accumulation, its members have been very hesitant in defining emerging models of development and specifying the degree of rupture with the Fordist model, let alone making prognoses for the future. This is partly due to the open nature of their theoretical approach, emphasizing contingency rather than determination. This hesitancy is expressed in the absence of any one label for the emerging mode. Aglietta's early work on the USA spoke of neo-Fordism, Jessop (1991 and 1992) uses the term Postfordism, and many regulation scholars avoid the use of any one label. Many British writers, such as Allen et al. (1988) and Harvey (1989), speak of 'regimes of flexible accumulation' and, contrary to Aglietta, see it as an empirical generalization. Several recent works by French regulation theorists, however, informed by a more comparative perspective and being more in tune with the thrust of the open nature of the regulation approach, have emphasized that no one clear model is emerging and have as many as four possible models (Boyer 1988; Leborgne and Lipietz 1988 and 1989, quoted in Nielsen 1991: Boyer 1991b). In a recent paper Boyer (1992b) appears to return to one model of a mainly industrial paradigm – Toyotaism. He treats this very much as an ideal type against which the position of the main OECD countries is measured.

Where various models are given, one of them often approximates to flexible specialization and one to the neo-Fordist paradigm although models incorporating features of the Swedish and Japanese industrial paradigm have also inspired the construction of ideal types. But all versions posit the dominance of differentiated mass-production: a mixture of economies of scale and scope, of continual product and process innovation and emphasize as well the functional flexibility of various aspects of production organization. They focus more on conflict between capital and labour, and the newly emerging production paradigm is seen through less-rosy spectacles than in the flexible specialization approach.

Full specification of consumption patterns and modes of regulation is rarely attempted, because these are believed to be still in flux, but attempts to theorize the role of the state have been made. Recent analyses of this in Demirovic et al. (1992) come up with highly divergent conclusions. Whereas the British contributor (Jessop 1992) characteristically refers to the Schumpeterian workfare state (*Leistungsstaat*) which bears the features of the neo-liberal Thatcherite state, the French contributors to the volume suggest that the incorporated state of the Fordist period has not necessarily outlived its usefulness (Delorme 1992: 175). More general analyses of a model of development (such as Jessop 1991) focus on what is empirically observable – particularly flexibilization and deregulation in labour markets and welfare provision – rather than showing that these features form a constellation, logically connected with the regime of accumulation. Lastly, the regulation approach has found wide acceptance among social geographers (such as Scott and Storper 1987; Sayer 1989) who apply it to the study of regional economies, trying to supercede the over idealistic 'industrial district' model of Piore and Sabel (1984).

Critical evaluation

Although regulation theory covers similar ground and shares many concepts with flexible specialization theory, it has neither had the same wide appeal nor has it attracted such vehement all-round criticism as the latter. Both features can be ascribed to the greater complexity of regulation theory and to its more-ambiguous and less-optimistic message. But even where it shares the weaknesses of flexible specialization – working with simple dualisms and portraying Fordism as more homogeneous and pervasive than it actually was – it does not attract the same frenzied attacks by its largely Marxist critics which they reserve for Piore and Sabel's work.

Among the critical points raised in the literature, the following take up fundamental issues. First, Hirst and Zeitlin (1990) suggest that it is impossible to fit the wide range of regulatory institutions and normative patterns found in advanced societies into one common overarching mode of regulation. They claim that when it comes to the empirical crunch, variety between societies becomes simplified or suppressed in order to hold on to the homogenizing influence of the world capitalist system.

Second, it is not clear how the connection between regime of accumulation and mode of regulation can be conceptualized without falling back on either a determinist Marxism or positing a functionalist integration (see, for example, Clarke 1988). If the latter is asserted, as Hyman (1991: 275–6) points out, it remains unclear why the connection exists; different national trajectories become difficult to explain; and the political implications become fatalistic and social choice redundant. But it should be noted that regulation theorists themselves strongly refute the charge of functionalism (Lipietz 1992a: 52; Jessop 1990: 185), positing instead a process of co-evolution of the two elements in which contingency and 'lucky finds' play a role in the crystallization of the mode of regulation. One does not precede the other but they become stabilized together (Lipietz 1986: 20).

A third criticism of the regulation approach is that it remains very vague about the level at which the three main constructs should be situated and how formation at one level influences that at another. Particularly problematic is the relation between national modes of growth and global capitalism. Does the influence run from the global to the national or vice versa? Empirical accounts often assume a supreme economic power which then shapes national industrial paradigms, while the stress on the national specificity of modes of regulation would lead one to emphasize the opposite route of influence. Lipietz (1986: 22) speaks of reciprocal shaping but wants to give the national level methodological priority. Turning to the national level only, Delorme (1992: 167) sees the industrial paradigm as situated at the microlevel, the accumulation regime at the macro level and the mode of regulation at the meso level. Others, however, assert more variable locations, particularly for the mode of regulation (for example, Jessop 1990). Finally, it is very difficult to envisage how a mode of regulation at the global level could emerge, given the difficulties with the establishment of international Keynesianism which have provided much ammunition for the critics of Piore and Sabel.

Fourth, the conceptualization of the relation between structure and agency, between completed form and class struggle, also remains vague and problematic. While theory continuously emphasizes class struggle, empirical accounts of the current transformation of the accumulation regime are mainly couched in structural terms. Also creation of modes of regulation is said not to be intentionally willed but evolves initially in a 'lucky chance' kind of way, thus excluding the assertion of class interest. The centrality to the theory of class struggle and action is asserted rather than demonstrated. It would be equally plausible to argue that the challenge to the Fordist system did not come from within the system, that is from decline in productivity, but from without. The superiority of the Japanese competitive regime simply made more obvious the weaknesses inherent in the Fordist model. By extension, emerging changes in accumulation regimes are characterized more by the Japanese imprint than by any political action of dominant class forces, although the imposition of the Japanese model depends on a changed balance of class forces.

A fifth point, and one of the most consequential shortcomings of the theory, pointed out by Harvey (1989), is that it does not make clear the mechanisms and the logic of the transition from one regime to another. The deliberate vagueness on this crucial point is defended in terms of the importance of contingency and the socially unique outcomes of class struggle. But it also means that we lack the tools to conceptualize current processes of transformation and instead fall back on a variety of plausible empirical generalizations. As Nielsen (1991: 27) points out, one cannot be sure whether any new trends in industrial paradigm or mode of growth are, indeed, traces of a new order, or whether they are merely transitory phenomena. In the end, the attractive openness and flexibility of the theory is achieved at the expense of conceptual vagueness. This is well summed up by Hyman (1991: 275), who describes regulation theory as 'more confident and coherent as a characterisation of the past than as an analysis of the present, let alone a prognosis of the future'.

One can also raise a criticism, informed by the institutionalist perspective. Although the concept of mode of regulation is strongly beholden to that perspective it is adopted in a fairly superficial way. Regulation theory never makes it clear why institutions assume this regulatory influence, nor do they clarify the mechanisms by which a shaping influence is being exerted. Finally, the issue of institutional inertia and the problem it poses for organizational change is never properly confronted in the discussion of the breakdown and change of modes of regulation. Hence, whether such change starts at the national or the global level also remains unresolved.

The most positive features of regulation theory are that it provides 'a theoretical integration of the dynamics of workplace and society' (Hyman 1991: 272) and that the theory tries to conceptualize, at one and the same time, the distinctiveness of individual modes of growth and the way they are constrained by their insertion into the world capitalist system. The connection between the productive system and the movement of capital is always kept in mind, and hence individual enterprises, regions and national economies are always seen as integrated into the global economy. Also the relation between the state and the economy is integral to the theory. Lastly, in contrast to other Marxist-inspired theories, regulation theory has middle-range concepts and is committed to the 'concrete analysis of concrete conjunctures' (Jessop 1990: 205), as well as encouraging interdisciplinary study which draws on economics, sociology and politics.

CONCLUSIONS

Thus it seems that none of the theories reviewed can satisfy the demands of conceptual rigour and empirical flexibility. Although the latter three are more useful than the first, neither in the end can do justice to the complexities of understanding change of national patterns of industrial organization within a larger capitalist world system. Regulation theory provides the most useful conceptual apparatus, but for an understanding of individual national modes of development one still has to fall back on the more detailed insights of the institutionalist approach. But both flexible specialization and regulation theory are much better suited to the exploration of change. Finally, neither posits a move away from industrial capitalism but merely shows, in different ways, its tremendous adaptability in the face of crisis.

The empirical analysis, in the remainder of this book, of the organizing principles or industrial orders of the three largest European societies will therefore dip eclectically into all the theories. Thus, theories will be used mainly as frameworks, sensitizing us to promising lines of enquiry, suggesting methods of study and providing conceptual tools to organize the empirical evidence. The book draws much inspiration from regulation theory without, however, adopting all its theoretical concerns and concepts. In particular, this study will share its strong focus on mode of regulation or – in non-Marxist language – institutional frameworks as the key to understanding nationally diverse appearances of crises and growth or industrial orders. Like the regulation approach, it also strives to comprehend national patterns of change as the result of the often-contradictory pull of new global influences and deeply entrenched national industrial order.

2. Industrial development in historical perspective

The previous chapter emphasized the point that current industrial organization or competitive regimes are strongly influenced by the institutional framework in which they are embedded and that such societal factors mediate in distinctive ways the impact of forces emanating from the world capitalist system. These social-institutional features, it was further stressed, have frequently deep historical roots which can be traced back to formative stages of the industrialization process. This chapter is concerned to examine these formative stages and to analyse the different ways in our three societies in which entrepreneurs, financiers, workers and state functionaries have interacted, both in the market place and in the firm.

The industrialization process occurred at different times and paces in the three societies, and there is insufficient space to trace each process in detail. Instead, the focus will be on the period between 1880 and 1930 when the so-called Second Industrial Revolution brought about the creation of modern science-based industries and, in their wake, the modern industrial enterprise: the large-scale, vertically integrated firm where owner-management was giving way to a hierarchy of professional managers, and where large numbers of workers were combined with mechanized machinery to produce a wide range of goods. This period has been widely referred to as the beginning of 'organized capitalism', where organization of capital at the top became reflected in the emergence of organizations of labour at the bottom. But, as has already been pointed out by Lash and Urry (1987), the degree and kind of capitalistic organization still differed strongly between the major industrial societies. This period will be discussed under the following headings: the industry–finance nexus; product markets/production strategy; the structure and performance of firms; labour markets and labour organization; and the role of the state in industry.

THE INDUSTRY–FINANCE NEXUS

The way in which capital is made available to the industrial firm has been found to have a crucial impact on its mode of growth and operation, as well as affecting interfirm relations and sectorial development. Britain's early and drawn-out industrialization (1720–1830) allowed gradual expansion of mainly smaller firms. The concentration on the cotton industry required relatively low capital requirements. These combined circumstances meant that most investment could be financed from family savings and/or from retained profits, obviating the establishment of investment banks. During the nineteenth century, lending by regional banks became more common but, after some damaging over-extension, it became confined mainly to short-term credit. Although Britain's status as an empire and important trading nation led to the development of an elaborate, London-based banking system, these banks did not on the whole cater for indigenous industrial firms. Towards the end of the century, when growing enterprise scale and more capital-intensive industries called for higher capital investment, finance began to be raised by the sale of equity, and the stock market soon became the most prominent source of outside finance. The prevention of close bank–industry ties and the development of an active stock market were furthered by the British legal and regulatory environment. It discouraged large bank stakes in non-financial firms and made access to the stock market comparatively easy and advantageous in terms of costs (Prowse 1994: 16f). The number of firms issuing shares rose from 60 in 1887 to almost 600 in 1907 (*The Economist*, 5 May 1990).

What then, were the consequences of this financial regime for British firms and industries? Did British firms have access to sufficient investment capital, and on what terms was access attained? Evaluations of the amount of industrial investment capital available differ between authors. Some authoritative sources, such as Kindleberger (1964) and Best and Humphries (1987), claim that capital export did not starve British firms of capital during this period and that other factors were responsible for the relative economic decline around the turn of the century when the newer industries required high rates of investment. Other sources, however, such as Lash and Urry (1987) and Ingham (1984), hold that the extensive investment and commercial activities of the City institutions abroad had a very negative effect on domestic industry. It is difficult to verify which of these two claims about the quantitative aspect of investment is more credible.

There is, however, a greater consensus on the damaging consequences of the qualitative side of capital provision, namely the terms on which capital was made available, and there is also considerable agreement that the financial system did not serve smaller firms particularly well. In the case of banks, the short duration of loans meant that banks never became closely involved in the business of the borrowing firms and, even less, in the industry in which such firms were situated. Loans consequently never became tied to demands for restructuring or rationalization. In the case of equity finance, the short time horizons of stock holders and their expectations of quick and substantial profits imposed similar constraints on the investment activities of British entrepreneurs.

The situation in France was very different, although equally disadvantageous in its consequences for industrial capital. The much later and more discontinuous industrial development of France meant that neither a thriving system of investment banks nor an active stock market developed prior to the First World War. The few existing investment banks were, on the whole, more interested in speculative investment abroad (Kindleberger 1964). This situation inhibited the growth of firms and accounts for the relatively small size of even the most important firms well into the twentieth century. When requirements of investment capital became urgent from the turn of the century onwards, enterprises in the new, more capital-intensive industries organized themselves to create their own sources of capital supply. They joined together with other firms in loosely knit groups to pool financial resources. The financial-holding companies developing out of these efforts proved very stable and hence very influential in shaping the development of large firms. Lévy-Leboyer's (1980) study of the effects of these holding companies arrives at two conclusions: first, this system further impeded the development of investment banks; and second, holding companies' control over capital allocation prevented a movement towards capital integration and thus impeded the growth and modernization of firms. Smaller French firms tended to be reluctant to become entangled with financial institutions and thus expanded only within the limits of their retained profits.

In Germany, industrialization proceeded within a very short time span, and industrial takeoff occurred in the industries of iron and steel where start-up costs were high. In the absence of accumulated entrepreneurial capital, new institutions had to be created to provide the necessary investment capital. This led to the foundation of a number of private, universal banks, that is, banks which channelled the deposits of small savers towards industrial investment. Both moneyed aristocrats and captains of industry and commerce gave vital early support to the new banks (Esser 1990: 19).

As industry was in need of large and long-term loans, banks had to devise a strategy to minimize their risks. They had to acquire the industrial expertise to help them lend prudently and often made loans conditional on the structural rationalization of enterprises. In addition, they tied their loans to the occupancy of seats on borrowing firms' supervisory boards, which gave some control over business strategy as well as giving enterprises the benefit of banks' wider industrial expertise. Banks also acquired substantial shareholdings in some companies, particularly during the *Gründerjahre*. The close involvement of banks in the affairs of many large companies gave them a sound knowledge of a whole industry and enabled them to influence development in a collectively rational direction. Thus, for example, banks were liable to prevent mutually destructive competition (Tylecote 1982).

In addition to the large universal banks, there were many smaller regional and municipal private and co-operative banks which lent funds to smaller, regionally based firms. The influence of banks over industrial enterprises was highest at the end of the nineteenth century when rapid expansion created a strong need for new capital. This was particularly true in heavy industry, where quick external growth was being pursued, and applied much less to the chemical and engineering industries (Feldenkirchen 1992: 499). Since then large firms have steadily increased their reliance on internally generated funds (Kocka 1975a: 104). This early assumption of a central place in industrial investment by banks was cemented by the introduction of laws and regulations that discriminated strongly against non-intermediated sources of finance and severely hampered the development of an active stock market (Prowse 1994: 24f).

The consequences for enterprises of the German credit-based financial system were, on the whole, very favourable. They assured large firms of capital whenever new opportunities for profitable investment arose and permitted them to take a long view of business development. At the same time, bank involvement forced them to utilize this capital in the most efficient manner, often taking a wider sectorial perspective.

PRODUCT MARKETS AND PRODUCTION STRATEGIES

Industrial structure and production strategy in Britain was strongly influenced by reliance on the markets of its empire. This inclined firms towards labour-intensive, simple and cheap products in the traditional industries, such as food and drink and heavy engineering. At home, too, its chief markets were among lower-income families, with an emphasis on the basic product rather than the highly finished article (O'Brien and Keyder 1978: 177). While this market strategy worked well until the 1870s, it became a millstone during the Second Industrial Revolution. At this time, competition from the USA and Germany became intense, and British firms failed to make the transition towards light machine tools and electrical engineering (Hall 1986). Both the foreign and the home markets were shaped by prominent merchant middlemen who interposed themselves between firms and final customers and retarded product innovation and rationalization – a vital precondition for the containment of costs and for Fordist mass-production (Kindleberger 1964: 148).

In France, production was orientated more towards a regionally highly segmented home market and a concentration on the tastes of the *haute bour-*

geoisie and aristocracy. With the exception of modern industries, which came into being around the turn of the century, production up to 1939 was largely to order, with an emphasis on quality and some concentration on luxury goods. In France, too, the prominence of merchant middlemen in the markets for goods of traditional industries acted as a brake on product and process innovation. Although some French firms made the transition to modern goods and processes – in chemicals, electrical goods and automobiles – they did not acquire sufficient scale in the latter and technological ingenuity in the first two to become competitive on a world scale. Although the car industry outshone British and German efforts in this field, it did not become orientated to mass-production (Kindleberger 1964: 301).

Germany's markets were shaped both by its late and rapid industrialization process and by its insignificant imperial holdings. The speed of the industrialization process did not permit the emergence of a merchant network and inclined manufacturers to internalize the marketing and distribution functions, either individually or through the formation of sales syndicates. Consequently, German manufacturers were able to stay closer to their customers and to adjust products and processes in response to changing customer requirements. The late start on the road to industrialization also meant that Germany was less hampered by investment in traditional products and processes and could thus fully respond to the demands of the Second Industrial Revolution. Its latecomer status also provided an impetus towards developing producer goods and exports. In both products and processes, technological sophistication and quality were at the forefront. But, in contrast to the French case, there has been more mass-production and attention to cost containment, and, in comparison with British industry, more standardization of products.

THE STRUCTURE AND PERFORMANCE OF FIRMS

In Germany, both large and giant firms became established in the then key industries very early in the industrialization process: in the fourth quarter of the nineteenth century. Large size was accompanied by, and partly a result of, forward and backward integration of business activities and by diversification. These modern features were due to a number of influences: the underdevelopment and lack of transparency of markets; the availability of organizational models and management techniques for large, complex units, provided by the developed public bureaucracies which predated industrialization (Kocka 1970); the early dominance of joint stock companies; and last but not least, from the dominance of investment banks, sufficiently strong to finance such growth patterns (Kocka 1975b; Kocka and Siegrist 1979; Best 1990). (This pattern of enterprise growth was similar to that established in the USA at this time and more advanced than the British and French patterns; Siegrist 1980). German enterprises were run in a highly centralized manner (Kocka 1975a), partly due to their rationalized structure and partly due to management orientation.

The increasing complexity of markets and production organization called for changes in managerial control, and professional management teams began to be adopted, regardless of legal form and pattern of share holding (Pohl 1992: 471). Although family ownership of substantial shareholdings and control of corporations was common around the turn of the century (Kocka and Siegrist 1979) it proved much less of an obstacle to modern management forms than in Britain and France. By 1907, personal enterprises (both top and middle management functions are executed by members of the owner's family) had been replaced by entrepreneurial ones (only top management positions were in the hands of owners), and, by 1927, increasingly by managerial enterprises (managers have replaced owners at both levels) in a majority of enterprises (Siegrist 1980). But in many large corporations families retained majority share holdings and control all through this period (Pohl 1992: 471). Two reasons for this reconciliation of family control and modern business management come to mind: expansion financed by bank credit was less likely to lead to loss of family influence; and the bureaucratic management tradition, associated with a moderately high level of education, integrity, and a sense of duty and accountability, checked fraudulent activity and thus lessened the fear of passing control to non-family middle managers, as well as requiring family managers to acquire an adequate level of education.

Expansion of firms occurred both by internal and external growth. Merger movements were distinguished from their British counterparts by two facts: they were followed by rationalization of both capacity and organization (Dascher 1974; Best 1990), and mergers were predominantly horizontal to eliminate competition rather than create conglomerates (Dyas and Thanheiser 1976: 50f) although vertical concentration became more common after the First World War (Pohl 1992: 448). An additional distinctive feature of large firms was their high degree of cartellization from the 1880s onwards. Until the First World War, this was the preferred mode of expansion (Pohl 1992: 447). These efforts to control competition, originally established to gain stability during times of trouble, eventually led to monopolized market domination (Kocka 1975a: 97). Large firms in Germany showed a high degree of interconnection both with other large firms and with small and medium-sized firms – through cartels, shareholdings and contracts. A 1926 government report comments 'it is not the individual enterprise which is now the norm but the complex of enterprises' (quoted by Pohl 1992: 459).

SMEs continued to exist side by side with large corporations, and business ties with larger firms and attitudinal cross-fertilization were common. This survival of the small-firm sector was due to both state support of the artisan sector and to the financial and legal systems which afforded access to investment funds and protection from hostile takeover.

British firms grew only slowly up to 1880, due to the absence of either bank or state involvement and to the predominance of family ownership. The first merger wave during the 1880–1918 period affected mainly firms in traditional industries, such as textiles and brewing. Mergers were not accompanied by rationalization but resulted in loosely federated holding companies, preventing the realization of economies of scale (Hannah 1976a; Levine 1967). The creation of large, publicly quoted multiple-site companies in a cross-section of industries came only at the end of the 1920s (Hannah 1976a). The new ease of raising capital on the stock market led to a rapid expansion of the corporate sector and to the development of the then modern industries. Whereas Hannah (1980) dates the emergence of the large modern company to the early 1930s, Chandler and Daems (1980) point to the underdevelopment of many features associated with modern status and are inclined to postpone it to the post-war period.

As firms were rarely forced to rationalize and modernize, family-dominated large enterprises persisted much longer than in Germany and also resisted modernization of management much more tenaciously (Pollard 1965: 23; Hannah 1976b: 12). In 1919, according to Chandler and Daems (1980: 28), there were few middle and almost no top salaried career managers in British enterprises. Gourvish (1992: 342–3) notes an absence of professional managers in top positions and a clubby, gentlemanly approach to staff recruitment right up to the Second World War.

Large companies at that time predominantly remained loose federations of family firms under a decentralized holding company structure. Vertical integration and diversification remained relatively low, and the absence of a professional management structure, and the lower level of competence associated with it, prevented organizational and technological innovation on the scale experienced in Germany. Although individual companies, such as ICI, began to develop a sizeable R&D facility, most companies lagged behind their main continental competitor also in this respect. All these features left their imprint on performance, which manifested itself in a widening gap with its two industrial rivals: the USA and Germany.

The main structural and managerial transformations in large British companies came about only in the 1960s. Merger waves had led to a level of capital concentration which gave Britain the most highly concentrated large-firm sector in the world, and family influence became much less prevalent than in the German large-firm sector. Although organizational rationalization and technological modernization were now more common, a loose-holding company structure and technological sluggishness still retained an undue weight in industry. Diversification was by now very common and was often of the conglomerate type. The consolidation of large firms from the 1930s onwards led to a strong decline of the small-firm sector which, due to lack of state support, was left exposed to market forces. This decline continued into the early 1970s and left Britain with a very polarized industrial structure.

In France, at the time of the Second Industrial Revolution, large entrepreneurial or managerial firms were exceptional phenomena found in only a few industries, and they tended to be smaller in size than their equivalents in the other two countries. Thus, the two largest in the 1920s – Alstholm and St Gobain – were only 5–7 per cent of the size of ICI or the German IG Farben (Lévy-Leboyer 1980). Many reasons for this slow spread of large firms have been cited: the retarding influence of the financial system; the prolonged influence of family firms; and the large and poor agricultural population and slow population growth, leading to underdeveloped home markets. In 1880, two-thirds of the population still lived in the villages, and by 1911 this had declined to only 56 per cent (Lévy-Leboyer 1980: 122–3).

Mergers of enterprises did occur in the first two decades of the twentieth century, but they were less frequent and substantial than in the other two societies. As in Britain, rationalization of merged units remained insufficient, due to the group structure of industry, discussed above. With a few notable exceptions, such as St Gobain and Renault, large firms failed to integrate, to diversify into new products and to introduce process innovations. In the more traditional industries, as in Britain, distribution and marketing was left to merchant middle men, with comparable negative effects on performance. The 1920s and 1930s brought stronger moves towards large-firm growth and modernization, due to the greater development of a stock market and further mergers. But the decisive steps on the road to modernization were delayed until the post-war period. In the 1960s and 1970s, market changes, combined with government intervention, finally propelled French industry into the modern world.

When we turn towards the small-firm sector, it is notable that its weight remained much greater than in the other two societies and, after 1930, the contrast became particularly pronounced between Britain and France. The dominance in French SMEs of family over business values meant that it became a particularly stagnant sector which, in contrast to its German equivalent, did not interact much with the large-firm sector.

Performance of large French, British and German firms was shaped by their own structural characteristics and by the social institutional environment in which they were situated. An important factor in this environment was the societal system of education and training and the way it interacted with industry. The educational system of a society is prominently shaped by state action, but such action reflects the societal class structure and the demands for a certain type of education made by the dominant classes (Tylecote 1982). Thus the relatively undistinguished performance of British firms during this period is attributed to a number of factors: their fragmented structures and lack of product standardization impeded economies of scale; their technical staff, used to an empirical approach to technical problems, were ill-equipped for the new wave of technological innovation in the chemical and electrical industries which required a science-based approach. Even in the more traditional industries, market structures frequently prevented product innovation (Kindleberger 1964: 302). The British system of higher education, dominated by the traditional universities, eschewed a vocational bias much longer than in the continental countries. They must take a lot of the blame for both the amateurism of British management and for the lack of a strong university–industry nexus in the new industries (Locke 1984). The failure of technical education at university level was replicated at lower levels: technical colleges for artisans were not started until 1900 (Kindleberger 1964: 153). Elitism in secondary education also resulted in insufficiently high levels of competency at the middle and lower levels of enterprise hierarchies. Such an education system reflects the influence of an aristocratic upper class and of an entrepreneurial middle class seduced by, and trying to emulate, upper-class culture (Tylecote 1982).

In German large firms, structural features of both markets and firms, as well as educational qualifications of managers, guided the latter towards more efficient production organization and towards product diversification and innovation. Efficient organization at all hierarchical levels was further enhanced by an early move towards systematic business education, providing the managerial cadres required to run the large and complex enterprises typical of many industries (Locke 1984). Technological innovation in the chemical, electrical and steel industries was being boosted and sustained by the following factors: the early development of ties between the university sector and industry in R&D, resulting in the establishment of firm-internal substantial research laboratories already in the last quarter of the nineteenth century (Kocka 1975a: 105f); the academic education of large numbers of engineers and scientists in management and production; and last, but not least, a relatively efficient secondary and vocational school system, orientated towards the education of lower white-collar and manual workers. The fostering of such an educational system had much to do with the influence of an entrepreneurial middle class which, in contrast to its British counterpart, had fewer opportunities to move in aristocratic circles and to occupy the high political, diplomatic and military positions monopolized by the Junker class (Tylecote 1982). Uncontaminated by aristocratic values, it developed a pride in *Unternehmer* activity and an educational system that provided the technological and commercial expertise to boost such activity.

In France, performance of large enterprises was hampered by the structural features of markets and firms. The French education system was much more highly developed on the technical side than its British counterpart, having a long tradition of excellence in engineering in the *Grandes Ecoles*. But the Cartesian bias of their education and their primary orientation towards producing cadres for the state sector meant the lack of both a research focus and of an affinity with the needs of the private industrial sector for engineers and specialists in business economics. Although graduates began to move into the private sector after 1890, they were regarded as remote from production concerns. A low profit consciousness and a preoccupation with hierarchy, work discipline and leadership were singled out as further characteristics impeding performance (Lévy-Leboyer 1980; Locke 1984). This educational background must have contributed to the fact that, despite some successes in the new industries, the French never reached a competitive position in the period under consideration. The undistinguished performance of both French and British firms during the Second Industrial Revolution meant that both German and American firms began to penetrate their markets and/or established a direct presence in these industries.

LABOUR MARKETS AND INDUSTRIAL RELATIONS

The British union movement at the end of the nineteenth century has been characterized by its numerical strength and comparatively high degree of power at enterprise level but weak national co-ordination, as well as by the much earlier institutionalization of collective bargaining procedures than its continental counterparts. Employers showed an equally weak capacity to co-ordinate their activities on a national level but had organized themselves at the branch level by the end of the nineteenth century (Crouch 1993: 92).

The slow pace of industrialization favoured the gradual transformation of journeymen societies into craft unions and the persistence of remnants of craft organization among the workers. The absence of a sustained challenge from the predominantly small and weakly organized employers and the neutrality of the state permitted unions to build up a system of representation and bargaining which gave workers strong influence over the terms and conditions of their work (Edwards et al. 1992: 4). Although employers frequently challenged union influence over the recruitment and deployment of labour, such challenges consisted mainly of local squirmishes rather than all-out confrontation. Enduring economic expansion, their own disunity and lack of state support for an anti-union offensive made employers disinclined to challenge customary union rights in a sustained manner. Control over workers was mainly exerted through the piece-work system, and more direct forms of control over workers were not implemented (ibid.: 5). Although early unions were craft unions, unions of the semi-skilled began to evolve towards the end of the century. The expansion of the population and the continuing movement of labour from the countryside into the towns brought into the developing factories large numbers of unskilled and lowly skilled workers, well suited to the market strategy outlined above (O'Brien and Keyder 1978: 173). New kinds of occupational groups and types of workers were gradually absorbed into the union movement in an incremental way, and this led to the creation of a highly segmented union movement and to competitive multi-unionism at plant level.

The system of industrial relations evolved at the work-place, and the state did not attempt to regulate it through the imposition of legal rules. Work rules and rules of bargaining and the definitions of rights and obligations of both sides of industry developed through daily practice at the work-place and, through long usage, acquired authority as 'custom and practice'.

Another feature of the British industrial relations system – its adversarial style – also had its origins in the early phase of industrialization. The occurrence of harsh confrontation between small master-craftsmen and journeymen on the one side, and the indifference to production matters on the part of larger, commercially orientated merchant-owners on the other, put their indelible stamp on industrial relations (Landes 1969; Fox 1985). It shaped the development of a style which is characterized by minimal involvement and 'arm's-length' relations on both sides, as well as by an adversarial approach, resorting to industrial action as the first rather than the last resort. Opportunistic behaviour on both sides has also been encouraged by the lack of regularity in bargaining processes and the ensuing absence of long-term horizons. Adversarialism was expressed in a comparatively high level of industrial conflict, measured in working days lost per thousand workers (figures for 1900 are quoted by Crouch 1993: 100).

When Fordist production methods finally began to make some impact on large British firms from the 1930s onwards (Littler 1982) the efficiency gains that were connected with it in the USA could not be realized in British firms. But this was not only due to union obstruction but also to the organizational and managerial factors outlined previously.

In France, the union movement evolved at the end of the nineteenth century but did not engage in collective bargaining until much later. The discrepantly slow evolution and recognition of the French union movement, relative to other countries with a similar degree of economic development, is explained by Crouch (1993) by the peculiar relation between the post-revolutionary liberal state, the Catholic Church and economic interest organizations. After the 1789 Revolution there occurred a confrontation between a 'jealously secular state and a determinedly activist Church' which had become the rallying point for anti-modernization forces. Among these were the ancient corporate economic associations of the guild system (Crouch 1993: 301f). Legislation in the wake of the Revolution outlawed any form of collective organization of both employers and workers. Although this decree was revoked in the nineteenth century it influenced French political culture until at least the First World War. Lack of accessibility of the state by the labour movement bred hostility and political opposition which, in turn, led to an escalating spiral of hostility and alienation. Politicization of unions and organizational fragmentation resulting from ideological rivalry made unions unattractive to employers and greatly delayed the institutionalization of collective bargaining. Employers were also slow to combine into associations able to conduct co-ordinated bargaining. These features, together with the long dominance of the economy by owner-managed SMEs, traditionally hostile to unions, have gravely undermined the influence of French unions in the enterprise and in the polity. Despite union weakness, levels of industrial conflict were relatively high (Crouch 1993: 99).

The antagonistic style of French unions dates from the early dominance of the first anarcho-syndicalist tendencies in the *Confédération générale du travail* (CGT) and the original *Force Ouvrière* (FO) and, later, from the alliance between the CGT and the Communist Party. This influence has resulted in ambiguity as to whether political or economic goals should take precedence (Goetschy and Rozenblatt 1992: 404). Antagonism has been reinforced by the marginalization of unions by both employers and the state, and has frequently spilled over into the political arena. During the twentieth century, it has forced the state to make concessions in the form of a piecemeal strengthening of the system of labour representation.

Due to the drawn-out nature of the industrialization process, French labour grew only slowly. Until the First World War, skilled labour predominated. Although the apprenticeship system was destroyed, together with the guild system, there occurred no continual dilution of skilled labour from rural migrants, as had been the case in Britain. Rural migration assumed significant proportions only from 1890 onwards. Production continued to take place in workshops rather than in factories right into the twentieth century, and mechanization of processes occurred significantly later than in Britain and Germany (O'Brien and Keyder 1978: 178f). Recruitment and training of the labour force continued to occur on the basis of kin relationships (ibid.: 193). In the early twentieth century, when some larger firms began to develop, the solidly upper-middle-class managers expected and got a docile labour force with little control over production organization and none over recruitment and training. Although leading industrialists, such as Renault and Citroen, became very enthusiastic about Fordist production organization, the insufficient scale of production in most industries severely limited the usefulness of this production model.

In Germany, the quick pace of industrialization and the early formation of large enterprises led to the creation of a sizeable working-class movement from the 1870s onwards. Organization at the bottom of the hierarchy was paralleled by strong organization of industrialists at the top – both as a response to labour and facilitated by the high prior degree of organization of business owners in trade associations. The extensive cartellization of industry from the 1890s onwards gave further impetus to employer co-ordination and solidarity.

Both industrialists and the government were greatly alarmed by this emerging working-class movement. To contain it, Chancellor Bismarck introduced a two-pronged offensive: a ban on the unions and the related Social Democratic Party, and the introduction of rudimentary welfare legislation. Neither measure was successful in containing the working class in the longer run.

When the ban was lifted in the early 1890s the unions developed rapidly in membership and organizational terms. Their development was fuelled both by the poor social conditions, attendant upon rapid urbanization and population growth, and by the repressive tactics of autocratic employers and government (Geary 1991). On the eve of the First World War, three million workers were unionized, and the movement is said to have been the largest and best-organized in Europe (Berghahn and Karsten 1987: 144). The union movement was, however, divided into the Social Democratic and more militant wing and the smaller and more acquiescent Christian wing. While one group of employers in the modern industries wanted to accede to the union demands for the institutionalization of collective bargaining, the vocal and well-organized reactionary heavy-industry wing remained vehemently opposed, reacting to strikes with industrial lockouts. The government gave moral and practical support to this latter group. The progressivism of German industrialists in production organization was not replicated in labour relations, where autocratic treatment remained the order of the day. The level of industrial action was relatively high in this early period.

During the First World War, some concessions towards the unions began to be made. But only during the social and political turmoil, following defeat in 1918, did employers finally recognize the right to association of workers, with the conclusion of the Stinnes–Legien Agreement. This year also saw the beginning of worker–employer co-operation with the founding of the bipartite Central Working Group. In 1920 came the legal introduction of works councils, elected organs for worker representation and consultation at the level of the firm. But the conservatives among the employers were only in temporary retreat and re-emerged in strength during the later 1920s when workers were weakened by the Depression. By their repressive tactics, they paved the way for the political events of the 1930s and the total destruction of the union movement.

This rapid and turbulent development of the German union movement in a politically and industrially hostile environment explains why, despite impressive numerical strength and the existence of a large component of skilled workers, German workers did not come to possess the same shop-floor power as British workers. Nor did the unions ever develop the organizational features of the British craft unions which, in the end, hampered industrial innovation and productivity in British firms. In contrast to French unions, German unions' organizational strength won them some crucial rights and concessions after the First World War which, although short-lived, nevertheless provided the experiential base on which they could build after the Second World War.

THE ROLE OF THE STATE

Although direct intervention in industrial organization by the state was not systematically exercised at this stage of capitalist development, European states nevertheless played a more or less important role in economic life, with significant consequences for industrial organization. This role was shaped by political ideology and state structure but also by the timing of the onset of industrialization.

Germany

Germany's status as a 'latecomer' to the industrialization process prompted more extensive intervention in economic life than in the other two countries, and the state was both more visible and controversial (particularly, with the benefit of hindsight, after the Nazi period) than it was amongst its two most important European neighbours. State influence over the economy (both in Prussia and in imperial Germany) consisted both of the provision of relevant infrastructure – especially of a transport system and a system of education well attuned to industrial needs (Locke 1984) – and of more direct intervention, such as help to industry in its early stages (Supple 1983: 179), although direct intervention had been more frequent in Prussia than in the German empire.

But the German state was not as directive as is sometimes asserted in the literature, nor did it have an industrial blueprint that it sought to implement. First, it is notable that intervention in economic life under Bismarck was more often guided by political motives of balancing class interests in a way which would preserve and strengthen the established political system than by economic considerations (Rosenhaft and Lee 1990). Second, although the German imperial state was very authoritarian – the executive was not elected by, nor accountable to, parliament (the *Reichstag*) – state influence in the economy was also circumscribed in significant ways. Even at this early stage (around 1870) German industry showed a significant degree of self-organization which increased steadily during the period under consideration (Puhle 1970). This was due to the fact that institutional structures of the guild stage of economic development – organized interest associations, exercising both lobbying and public order functions – had been carried over into, and adapted to, the industrial stage.

Such incorporation of organized interest associations came about in Germany, but not in Britain or France, for a number of reasons: the late industrialization and greater temporal proximity of the industrial to the guild stage; the weak development of political liberalism and bourgeois individualism which encouraged the long survival, first, of guilds, and then, of corporate principles of economic organization (Lane 1991); and last, the late emergence of the German state and the consequent problems of state-building encountered (Crouch 1993). Thus trade associations and chambers of trade, formed prior to German unification in 1871, were important from the very beginning of the German state. Banks, although not formally endowed with public-order functions, nevertheless became important organs of industrial self-administration and frequently implemented what amounted to industrial policy (Esser 1990: 20). Given the weaknesses of the political parties, these associations were also powerful political lobbies and managed to exert considerable influence over the executive in economic questions (Puhle 1970; Rosenhaft and Lee 1990: 19). Thus the existence of these bodies of self-administration/political lobbies placed important limits on the influence the state exerted over the economy. Further limits were placed by the fact that imperial Germany and the Weimar Republic were federal states, delegating some important economic resources and functions to the constituent regional states (*Länder*) and also to municipalities. Last, the central role of the highly professional civil service must be emphasized. This went beyond economic policy-making and manifested itself in 'the hegemonic force of the ... bureaucratic ethos within German society as a whole' (Rosenhaft and Lee 1990: 16) and, one might add, particularly in the management of large industrial firms.

Thus, in conclusion, German industrialism was not state-directed, but it did receive more state sponsorship than the other major European economies. It is notable that German industrial modernism was achieved within a political framework with many survivals from a more archaic political age.

France

The French state, in contrast, seen as *dirigiste* and entrepreneurial in more recent decades, played a very limited economic role in the period under consideration in this chapter (Kindleberger 1964). The French economy, prior to the First World War, was run according to a *laissez-faire* pattern which, although similar to the British pattern, differed from it in some crucial respects. Although the state had been active in providing the social infrastructure for industrialization earlier in the nineteenth century, by the end of the century it had largely retreated from economic life. The space left vacant was not occupied by active economic lobbies or functional associations devoted to self-administration, as in neighbouring Germany. The French state tradition, forged during the Revolution, had created a distinctive brand of secular political liberalism which did not tolerate the intrusion into the political economy of either the Catholic Church or of any organizations of the corporate type.

The abolition of the guild system in the wake of the Revolution and the prohibition of collective organization of both business owners and labour, embodied in the 1791 Law d'Allarde and the Decree Chapelier, influenced political culture and economic association well into the twentieth century. Even after these laws had been abolished there were few nationally coordinated associations of trade or employers, let alone of labour (Crouch 1993). (The *Confederation générale du patronat français* was only founded in 1925, at the instigation of a government which needed to send a representative to the International Labour Organization (ILO) in Geneva (Crouch 1993: 141)). Nor was the inactivity of industrial capital, still highly dispersed at this period, compensated for by organized intervention from financial capital. The high degree of political centralization also put limits on the development of local economic action and even private initiative (Kindleberger 1964: 197).

Thus the combination of an inactive central state, the underdevelopment of local political power and the absence of intermediate economic interest associations go some way to explain the economic stagnation and industrial backwardness characterizing France during this period. Political liberalism of the French kind did not prove conducive to the achievement of economic modernization.

Britain

The highly developed *laissez-faire* doctrine in nineteenth-century Britain prevented substantial interference of the state in economic matters. This was altered to some degree after the Second World War, but even then government intervention remained piecemeal. Although the British state did not guard its sovereignty as jealously as the French state, it too had outlawed guild principles of economic organization in 1835. The early onset of industrialization had, in any case, destroyed the main structures of the old corporate system by the middle of the eighteenth century, although there remained remnants, particularly in the organization of labour (Crouch 1993: 314, table 10.1). Thus, in Britain, too, intermediary functional interest organizations of capital were slow to emerge to fill the vacant space left by a liberal state, and the tradition of corporatist self-administration was never to take root.

The lack of national business organization in the period under consideration, however, was no longer due to state prohibition but was more connected with the deep entrenchment of voluntarism among business owners and with the fragmented nature of industrial capital. In contrast to the situation in France, however, more local business initiatives were undertaken.

CONCLUSIONS

This examination of a formative period in the industrialization process of the three largest European societies has shown how the development of different social-institutional frameworks shaped the evolution of the modern industrial enterprise and influenced the ways in which it obtains and utilizes capital, labour and technological know-how. Many of these structural characteristics, it will become clear in subsequent chapters, have endured up to the present day and continue to shape performance in nationally distinctive ways. Others have been transformed over time by external events, such as the World Wars, by determined and prolonged state intervention, as has been the case in France in the 1960s and 1970s, or, more gradually, by internal struggles and accommodation between capital and labour, or by the impact of market processes. The social-institutional frameworks in which firms are embedded should thus not be seen as iron cages which impose immutable constraints. But, at the same time, they remain highly influential forces, channelling globally generated economic influences into nationally distinctive industrial orders.

3. The relations between financial and industrial capital

Chapter 2 briefly examined the differing relations between financial and industrial capital in the three largest European societies at a formative stage of the industrialization process. This examination indicated that the relation is of considerable importance both for industrial organization and performance. This chapter will focus on the post-war period and highlight both continuity and change in the industry–finance nexus. Here the role of the financial system in relation to both large and small firms will be examined. Globalization of financial markets, European integration and deregulation of national markets during the last decade have wrought considerable transformation in financial sectors, and national patterns of the industry–finance nexus will come under strong adjustment pressures. The largest part of the chapter is devoted to drawing out the implications of enduring national divergencies of financial systems for individual firms, sectors and the whole industrial structure. Here the focus will be on the following aspects: the differing national self-conception of firms and the way in which this shapes investment behaviour; the ownership structures of large firms and the forms of control associated with them; implications for performance and growth of smaller firms and the way this shapes industrial structure in terms of firm size; and lastly, the effects both on sectoral restructuring and on the transfer of investment capital to new industries and/or innovative activities. The concluding section will examine more recent changes in financial systems and attempt to assess their transformative potential for finance–industry relations.

THE ROLE OF THE FINANCIAL SYSTEM IN INDUSTRIAL FINANCE

In Britain and Germany, the fundamentals of the financial systems and the structure of the industry–finance nexus have changed relatively little since the end of the last century. In France, in contrast, there have occurred considerable changes in this relation during the post-war period. Although both British and German large firms now mainly finance investment from retained profit new capital is still raised predominantly in the old way. The British system is still strongly equity-based and centred on the stock market although bank credit is also significant, and the German system remains credit-based and centred on the universal private banks, and the issue of equity has remained a minor instrument to raise finance. Legal and regulatory mechanisms – which were abolished or relaxed only in 1992 – have continued to discriminate heavily against the development of the stock market and have left it dominated by universal banks (Prowse 1994). The less stringent requirements for large companies to disclose their financial accounts have acted as an additional impediment to the activity of investors (ibid.: 28–9). Thus in Britain in the early 1980s, shares quoted on the stock market represented over 4,000 companies whereas the equivalent figure for Germany was only 500 companies (Bayliss and Butt 1980: 180), and in 1985 adjusted figures for stock market capitalization as a percentage of GNP contrast a British share of 81 per cent with a mere 14 per cent for Germany (Prowse 1994: 30, table 6). In both societies, share ownership is no longer predominantly in the hands of individuals or families but either in the hands of financial institutions (Britain) or, in Germany, is vested in other non-financial companies and, to a much lesser extent, in the hands of banks. In Britain in 1990, 4.3 per cent of common stock was held by banks, 45.2 per cent by other institutions, and 10.1 per cent by non-financial corporations. The figures for Germany are 10 per cent, 12 per cent and 42 per cent, respectively (Prowse 1994: 21, extract from table 2). Moreover, in Britain the overwhelming majority of shares held by financial institutions are held in their capacity as agents for other investors, whereas in Germany ownership on their own account is substantial (ibid.: 23). Whereas in Britain, laws and prudential rules have led to a very high degree of dispersal in share ownership, in Germany ownership remains exceptionally highly concentrated (Prowse 1994: 35). Majority ownership and control by other corporations and, to a lesser extent, by individual families has, however, remained very pronounced in German large joint-stock companies (ibid.), and German medium-sized companies remain predominantly family-owned (Tylecote 1991; Quack and Hildebrandt 1994). In Britain, in contrast, majority and/or family ownership is much rarer in both categories of firm.

These different positions of English and German companies *vis-à-vis* financial institutions are reflected in contrasting philosophies about their role and responsibilities. Whereas British companies are run primarily in the interest of shareholders, German companies do not see the maximization of profit to shareholders as their prime purpose. Managers are more concerned to safeguard the long-term stability of the company which is seen 'as "a social institution" within a local community, providing wealth and employment' (Anglo-German Foundation 1993: 18).

Small and medium-sized enterprise (SMEs) in both countries are strongly reliant on bank credit. In the highly concentrated British banking sector,

SMEs rely on the same banks as large firms and suffer severe disadvantage in access to finance. This disadvantage does not flow primarily from lack of availability of bank credit but from the terms on which such credit is available (Small Business Research Centre 1992).

In Germany, in contrast, there exist two alternative banking systems which are especially attuned to the needs of SMEs and, with state support, can compensate them for the disadvantages of small scale in the credit market. The two additional banking sectors are respectively publicly and co-operatively owned, are incorporated into a tiered system and have a large number of small, locally embedded banks with a relatively high degree of independence. These banks have access to long-term, fixed-rate (LTFR) capital which is re-lent to them by a number of national financial institutions, underwritten by the state.[1] Additionally, these local banks have access to the superior financial expertise of higher tier banks at *Land* or federal level, belonging to the same banking system. Legal and structural mechanisms enable or compel these local banks to lend in a way which takes into consideration the special interest of the locality and its industries. The tendency of German banks to see the customer–bank relationship in holistic terms has resulted not only in their more local orientation but also in a markedly lower default rate of firms than in Britain (Bannock 1994).

At the level of the *Land*, the savings banks have increasingly been used to finance industrial restructuring and to administer funds made available for such purposes by the federal state. These two banking systems – the savings and co-operative banks – account for over half of total assets of the German banking system (Vitols 1994: 1), and they are of immeasurable importance to the economic health and high performance of German SMEs – the so-called *Mittelstand*. Whereas in Britain, credit to SMEs is mainly available for the short term and, if fixed-rate, at a significantly higher cost than to large firms on money markets, German SMEs are not exposed to these crippling disadvantages (Small Business Research Centre 1992: 36f; Vitols 1994: 5; Quack and Hildebrandt 1994).

This second German banking system is highly important in both the scope of its industrial activity and its qualitative effects. It provides an excellent illustration of German collaborative networks, where state involvement is channelled through lower tier (both *Land* and municipal-level) banks which are better able both to recognize local needs and to make sure that state subsidies are utilized in an efficient manner. This system is now being extensively used in the Eastern Länder to regenerate local entrepreneurship (Deeg 1994).

In France, the post-war period saw the introduction of a new system of investment finance which stayed in place until the mid-1980s. France moved from reliance on financial holding companies to a credit-based system of bank financing. But this system has not been based on a free market for credit, as in Germany, but on a regulated market with administered pricing and credit ceilings (Syzman 1983). The state, through the *Trésor* in the Ministry of Finance, plays a central role in this system by directing both the allocation of funds and by determining the prices of credit. Credit has been made available on a long- and medium-term basis, and provision of credit has often been linked to restructuring demands for both firms and whole branches of industry. Industrial sectors targeted for expansion or restructuring were given favourable access in terms of both the amount of funding and of borrowing costs. This system of allocating capital became the means and, indeed, the precondition of active state intervention in the economy, which made it possible to restructure and modernize manufacturing industry from the late 1950s onwards. Although many important banks were nationalized to ease state control, more indirect mechanisms of state influence over banks have been equally influential. The relation between banks and firms is not as close as in Germany, but there is more involvement than in Britain.

French firms also raise capital by issuing equity but, as in Germany, this is handled by banks. Between 1961 and 1982 the stock market has been stagnant (Cerny 1989: 148) but, due to financial deregulation and other government action, has significantly increased its importance in the last decade. Many new financial services have been created. Reforms have transformed Paris 'from a financial backwater into a modern, efficient and competitive financial centre' (Boucek 1993: 80). Stock market capitalization rose from 9 per cent of GNP in 1978 to 25 per cent in 1986 (Cerny 1989: 149). The increased opportunity for French firms to go the stock market has been paralleled by a decline, since 1984, in the practice of administered credit through the banking system, and the role of the state in the financial system has been significantly reduced since the mid-1980s. Banks no longer have access to previously almost unlimited refinancing from the Bank of France, and the ensuing increase in the cost of bank credit has given large firms an incentive to go to the stock market instead. The banking sector has also been changed by the 1984 Banking Act which abolished the old system of specialist banking sectors (Quack and Hildebrandt 1994). Family ownership and control has retained some importance even in large firms, and up to 1986 a comparatively large number of firms were under state ownership.

Until the early 1980s, state involvement in credit allocation was mainly aimed at large firms. But since then SMEs have received more consideration, and a number of subsidized schemes have been especially targeted at them (for details, see Quack and Hildebrandt 1994). But a number of circumstances still make the quality of provision problematic for SMEs: first, the large number of very small and weak firms makes them very risky debtors for banks and has led to cautious and restricted lending by banks which, unlike their German counterparts, do not belong to 'pooling networks'; secondly, lending is very fragmented, with a large number of small firms sharing an insufficiently high volume of subsidized loans; thirdly, despite a variety of types of bank engaged in lending to SMEs, none serves the spectrum of SME needs. Consequently, the latter often have to consult several banks and do not develop close ties with any of them (ibid.)

Thus, despite recent improvements in the financing of SMEs French SMEs still perceive bank services as unsatisfactory. They mainly finance their new activities through short-term debt, and the terms of their borrowing are significantly worse than those of large firms (Vickery 1986: 39f).

THE IMPACT ON PERFORMANCE

Britain

In Britain, neither shareholders nor banks become closely involved in the management or supervision of firms, nor do they identify with them. If the fortunes of a firm decline, shareholders simply sell, while banks might become involved when the crisis is fully developed but not necessarily to rescue the firm. This lack of direct involvement in and influence over firms on the part of shareholders is expressed in the fact that they are rarely present on the company board. As board members are usually picked by the management team and the chief executive frequently also holds the position of board chairman, internal control over top management is perceived to be very weak (Charkham 1994; Prowse 1994). The board is thus unable to influence company strategy, or to prevent developments inimical to shareholders' interests, such as high salaries and huge golden hand-shakes to top managers in the case of takeovers, or to prevent fraud, as in the Guinness case or – worse – in the Maxwell defrauding of pensioners. The high degree of dispersal of British share ownership – financial institutions rarely hold more than 5 per cent of a company's shares – is both source and consequence of this low degree of active control and involvement, and also makes it easy to reallocate investments. Nor are financial ties to other industrial firms common, with cross-shareholding being relatively rare.

This large measure of freedom from direct outside control for British managers is, paradoxically, coupled with a considerable degree of indirect control over management decision-making which, in the end, limits their manoeuvring space more than the German version of bank control. Every major financial decision has to be taken with an eye on the movement of the stock market. Quick returns on investment and high dividends have to be achieved to keep the confidence of shareholders. Reinvestment of earnings is significantly lower than in France and even more so than in Germany. Industrial managers complain that stock market pricing does not adequately reflect expenditures for innovation and future profits (Tylecote 1991: 67) and thus inhibits relevant investment. The ultimate sanction is the threat of hostile takeover which, in the British financial system, is relatively easy and frequent: in the 1980s three out of four takeover bids in the EC occurred in the UK (Porter 1990: 503). As takeovers occur in a cyclical manner and are also a costly way of exerting control, there is widespread doubt about whether they represent an efficient means of external management control (Charkham 1994; Prowse 1994).

Those who favour the British market-based system point out that it guarantees a genuinely free and flexible capital market which gives greater transparency to investors and acts to discipline management (Stelzer-O'Neill 1994). They claim that the share market does adequately reflect future profitability from R&D investment and thus cannot be charged with encouraging short-termism. But, as Tylecote (1991: 68) points out, market efficiency depends on the availability of adequate information about the prospects of innovative activity, and he argues that investment analysts are insufficiently qualified to have such knowledge. Franks and Mayer (1992), quoted by Prowse (1994: 67), argue in contrast that the Anglo-Saxon system is well-suited to making assessments of the future prospects of firms and is thus more likely to encourage innovative activity than is a credit-based system. Even if this generalization is difficult to substantiate in empirical terms, it seems clear that innovative activity has received more support from the British financial system in one specific respect. The existence of a vigorous stock market has, in turn, favoured the development of other capital markets, such as that for venture capital which has eased conditions for new innovative firms.

The many long-time critics of short-termism further charge that it influences strategies of labour utilization and prevents the transition from a low-skill, low-wage economy to one making long-term investment also in labour. Furthermore, the ensuing necessity by managers to prove constant financial performance makes for a concentration of accountants in top management positions and keeps firms focused on financial rather than on production performance. The strong orientation on financial gain both by stakeholders and managers and the speculative actions resulting from it has led to the coinage of the term 'casino economy'. A share in a company no longer signals an ownership psychology – loyalty to the firm and care for and interest in what one owns – but has become a mere betting slip (*The Economist*, 5 May 1990: 7). Moreover, the lack of stability in ownership terms influences managers' and other employees' orientations towards the company, undermining feelings of identification with, and loyalty towards, the employing firm which come to undermine performance (Franks and Mayer 1990; Hughes 1992: 23).

The claim that British short-termism has its origin in the industry–finance nexus, although widely accepted, is difficult to substantiate and often denied by incumbent managers. But the head of Siemens-Plessey Electronics, a British company recently transferred to German ownership and now enjoying much increased R&D spending as well as longer pay-back periods, has no doubts about British short-termism and German long-term investment horizons:

> What Plessey did most of the time was respond to the City of London's need for quarterly profit increases. The British electronics industry hasn't done well globally because they have had their eyes on the wrong ball. Sensible long-term plans were disrupted constantly by short-term operations. (*The Financial Times*, 13 April 1994).

The British financial system shapes not only the individual firm but also whole sectors, as well as the size distribution of firms. The lack of involvement in business matters by both banks and large investors means that there is no private-sector agent to plan and co-ordinate any major sectorial restructuring programme, and the predominance of a *laissez-faire* governmental ideology in the post-war period has also precluded consistent government activity in this area. The result has been the gradual death of whole sectors, such as shipbuilding, machine tool manufacturing and, eventually, indigenous car manufacture as well. Furthermore, the reluctance of many financial institutions to make long-term investments in smaller companies and the relatively high cost of bank credit has put British SMEs at a severe disadvantage (Skidelsky 1993; Vitols 1994). It results in severe capital constraint, keeping down both labour and capital productivity and preventing expansion (ibid.; Alford and Garnsey 1994). SME disadvantage is further compounded by the constant threat of acquisition and takeover, leading to a size distribution of firms where the proportion of medium-sized firms is much smaller than in both Germany and France (Hughes 1990), as well as undermining the independence of small, innovative firms (Hughes 1992: 30).

Germany

In Germany, in contrast, the relations between banks and industrial firms have remained close, although the relationship has changed from one of bank dominance to one of interdependence and mutual support. This applies also to the situation in the new East German states. Let us examine more closely the nature of this relationship and its consequences. Every major firm has a house bank, that is one bank with which the firm has a long-standing and close business association, and any given bank may act as house bank to a number of enterprises. At the present time, long-term bank loans are still the most important source of external financing but far less important than internal financing (Edwards and Fischer 1990). Given that, between 1986 and 1990, 78 per cent of gross finding came from retained profits (Prowse 1994: 32, table 8), it no longer makes sense to depict large German firms as credit-dependent (ibid.; Esser 1990: 23; Anglo-German Foundation 1993). The argument has more force, however, in relation to SMEs (ibid.), and the large private banks are increasingly shifting their business focus in this direction. Bank lending has a number of advantages for firms: it does not dilute ownership; bankers usually accept lower dividend payments than shareholders and they do not seek rapid capital gains (Smyser 1992: 88–9).

Furthermore, the large number of regional, municipal and co-operative banks, which have access to LTFR credit at comparatively low interest rates, assures SMEs of a comparatively predictable and reasonably priced supply of capital (Skidelsky 1993; Vitols 1994; Bannock 1994). It enables SMEs to reduce the capital-constraint gap relative to large firms and achieve a relatively high rate of both capital and labour productivity, as well as of export and innovation activity (ibid.). Lastly, the publicly and co-operatively owned banking system gives small, efficient firms an opportunity to expand. It accounts for the comparatively large and competitive sector of medium-sized firms, as well as explaining the high degree of family ownership and control of these firms, in comparison with their British and French counterparts.

For the large private banks, ties of ownership, both through banks' own shares in enterprises and through their representation of small investors, creates another link and potential source of influence. But the proportion of share capital owned by banks has fallen over time and now consists of only 9 per cent of shares in circulation (Deutsche Bundesbank 1984: 16). But potential bank influence rises considerably through their share of voting capital, that is, that of small scattered owners for which the banks have a proxy voting right (Esser 1990: 24). Their share of voting capital gives them not only a strong voice but often the decisive veto right over management decisions: they sometimes own up to 25 per cent of shares and can vote an even higher proportion (in the ten largest companies over 50 per cent, according to Cable 1985; see also Edwards and Fischer (1991: 27f; Prowse 1994: 37). Such substantial ownership rights make them committed to a given firm, and they are able to block hostile takeovers, although these are also prevented by the highly concentrated ownership of non-financial corporations and remaining family majority ownership (Prowse 1994). Involvement as both lender and owner is preceded by a close analysis of firm performance – not merely of retrospective financial performance, as in Britain, but by prospective analysis of markets and of performance on all aspects of business, such as management qualifications or the state and trend of current orders (Bayliss and Butt 1980: 43). The same rigorous analysis applies to lending by savings and co-operative local banks to SMEs. Bankrupts rarely get another chance to start their own business. Because of their greater knowledge, German banks are prepared to lend where British banks might not become involved, and they also accept higher ratios of debt to equity.

An additional important way to maintain influence is through the occupancy of seats on supervisory boards. A study by the Association of Banks revealed that in 1986 of the 1,466 seats on the supervisory boards of the 100 largest firms, private banks held 114 seats and other credit institutions held a further 51 seats. Many more seats, however, were held by representatives from other firms and by representatives of labour (Esser 1990: 26). It is worth noting, though, that bank representatives are frequently the chairmen of boards and thus exercise a disproportionate influence (Boehm 1992: 206).

These combined circumstances give banks a large stake in given firms and also a high degree of potential influence and control. The literature is divided on how much this potential is actually utilized. Boehm (1992: 206), after considering all the bases of bank influence in detail, is convinced that in many cases banks have a definite effect on managerial decision-making. Usually they assert this informally rather than through the supervisory board. Strong interference in internal management affairs, like the recent forcing out by Deutsche Bank of one chief executive at Daimler Benz to replace him with one more sympathetic to diversification into aerospace (*International Management*, March 1990: 29) – is, however, rare. There is other evidence, though, that German management in large corporations enjoys a high degree of autonomy as long as the firm stays competitive in the long run (*Manager Magazin*, **6** (1989): 252f; Esser 1990). Esser asserts that supervisory boards have passively followed the strategies of their top managers (ibid.: 27). For Esser (ibid.) and Eglau (1989) the true influence of bank representatives lies in other areas. They sensitize managers to their competitive environment by sharing their wider sectorial perspective and knowledge of financial markets with the executive board (ibid.). Most firms even welcome the presence of bank representatives on their supervisory boards and see it as enhancing their status (Eglau 1989: 192). If business deteriorates, banks do not pull out but try to improve the firm's fortune – some very costly recent rescue operations were those of the giant AEG and of Klöckner Steel and Hoesch. This does not amount to a propping up of lame ducks but is always allied to restructuring injunctions. Other sources infer collusion, facilitated by extensive cross-holdings of shares, as well as negligence due to the holding of too many directorships by individual bankers (Eglau 1989: 138f; *Manager Magazin*, **8**, 1993: 35–51). They explain why many cases of management error and incompetence have not been detected by supervisory boards in recent years (ibid.). But for many analysts the German board is still held to exert stronger internal control than its British counterpart, due to the fact that membership is not determined by management and no members of management are represented on it (Charkham 1994; Prowse 1994). The following conclusion by Prowse (1994: 55) sums up well the situation on bank control: 'while it is likely that banks in Germany ... play some role in the corporate control of firms, it is not at all clear that they play the primary role'.

A more indirect effect of the financial system on German managers has been a lesser concern with short-term performance and a willingness to strive for satisfactory rather than large profits (Porter 1990: 375). This, in turn, accounts for the much lower importance accorded to financial specialists in top management positions than is the case in Britain. However, in recent years many large multinational companies have become more preoccupied with financial concerns than with technical leadership (ibid.: 376–7).

Lastly, the structure of the industry–finance nexus gives banks the knowledge and opportunity to act as a guiding and co-ordinating influence at sectorial level, and banks have, indeed, been prominently involved in the restructuring of traditional and crisis sectors. But even in this area banks are no longer all-powerful but, like industrial firms, are now partially at the mercy of turbulent international markets. Thus, to conclude this section, in Germany the interests of both fractions of capital are very much in tune with each other, and government financial and fiscal policy does not run the risk, as in Britain, of favouring one fraction while damaging the other.

The system is, however, not without its critics, who are to be found in industry, in the Bundesbank, in government and, increasingly, abroad. The latter accuse German large companies of being 'owned by banks, unbothered by share holders, secure from predators and heedless of profit' (*The Economist*, 23 May 1992, German Survey: 14). While this is a caricature of bank influence on German firms, some of the implied criticisms deserve closer attention: first, that banks are too powerful and that a misuse of that power could have disastrous consequences; second, that banks undermine competition; third, that they impede innovation; fourth, that by protecting firms from hostile takeover banks shield managers from market discipline; and fifth, that bank domination has prevented the redistribution of capital, entailed by mass share ownership, and that small shareholders are treated badly by the banks which handle their shares.

The accusation that banks are too powerful has already been touched upon. The investigations by Esser (1990) and Prowse (1994) show convincingly that, in the case of large firms, banks no longer play a prominent role as providers of credit nor as share owners, and that large firms increasingly finance investments from their own resources, are substantial share owners in their own right, and rival banks in their influence. Hence it is more appropriate to speak of mutual dependence. In concert with many other commentators, Esser concludes that banks' prominent presence on supervisory boards seldom leads to a usurping of management functions (ibid.). This was also confirmed by a recent survey of 954 joint stock companies, investigating the degree of outside influence on management board decision-making (*Industrie-magazin*, June 1989: 252f), as well as by an in-depth study of the activities of Deutsche Bank (Eglau 1989). Both established that bank influence was absent in nearly all areas of strategic decision-making, except that of financing new activities.

There is more substance to the claim, reported by Cable (1985: 1), that banks function 'as a self-appointed planning commission, and [dominate] the stock market as investors, stock brokers and advisors'. Their dominance of the capital market makes that market less open and free, as well as making access to the stock market more costly for firms (Stelzer-O'Neill 1994; Prowse 1994). In contrast to the situation in Britain and France, until 1992 banks had almost a monopoly on capital allocation to industry. But banks counter this criticism with the not totally convincing argument that the large number of German banks ensures competition. In 1980, there were said to exist 3,465 clearing banks (quoted in Bayliss and Butt 1980: 182).

Banks are not only said to restrict competition on capital markets but are also charged with limiting competition in other ways. Thus Kocka (1975a: 103) suggests that short- and medium-term bank support for temporarily failing companies loosens the immediate connection between a firm's market success and survival chances, and Eglau (1989: 194) provides examples of rescues by Deutsche Bank of ailing firms which would have perished without such bank intervention. Tylecote (1982: 50) claims that competition between firms, leading to mutual destruction, would be prevented while one or two banks had an interest in the same industry. It can be argued, however, that both these limitations on competition are more likely to be beneficial than harmful in the longer run.

More serious is the third charge that banks impede the transfer of capital into new, more innovative industries and firms. Banks, in contrast to stock market investors, are said to be orientated towards assessing firms through an evaluation of the quality of managers and employees in performing certain fairly standard tasks (Franks and Mayer 1992, quoted in Prowse 1994). It is, however, not clear why German banks, with their intimate knowledge of firms and industries, should be so reluctant to invest in innovative activity. Nor is it obvious why firms, which are highly capitalized themselves and have access to foreign money markets, should be shaped in their investment behaviour by banks. It is, however, true that banks develop a stake in certain industries and that they would not act as investors and innovators independent of firms. It has also been shown that delay in developing markets for venture capital has affected the creation of small innovative firms (Anglo-German Foundation 1988).

The suggestion that banks have protected German firms from hostile foreign takeover is not generally denied, although company law also plays an important part in resistance to takeover. Such protection has been strongly attacked by British advocates of free markets (see John Redwood quoted in Hughes 1992: 22) who connect takeovers with the enforcement of greater managerial efficiency. But the correctness of this assumption is doubted by many British economists (such as Hughes 1992). A representative of German capital defends such protection on the grounds of the incompatibility between British and German conceptions of the role of the firm, shaped by the different financial systems and by company law. Thus the president of the Federation of Germany Industry (BDI) endorsed such blocking action in the following terms: 'we like to maintain a certain protection against pure investors who come to exploit a company, distribute the liquidity and then try to hand it over to another investor. We would not like to see this happen in our country' (Anglo-German Foundation 1993: 5). Hughes (1992: 31) recommends a standardization of European company law which would curb both the worst excesses of the open British system and those of closed, finance-group-dominated European holding companies.

A last criticism is that banks have developed a cosy relationship with managers at the expense of small shareholders' interests in dividends (Boehm 1992: 156f; Steinmann and Jehle, quoted by Tylecote 1991: 68). But this is countered by Cable (1985), who finds that bank-controlled companies perform significantly better than other firms. More recent work by Elston and Albach (1994) shows that firms with closer bank ties are less sensitive to liquidity constraints than firms with weaker ties, due to better access to information of various kinds. It is, however, notable, that share ownership has low popularity in Germany and that small personal investors have a very low stake in industrial firms.

The striking underdevelopment of the stock market is partly a consequence of bank dominance but is also due to other reasons. Financing on the share market is reserved to public limited companies. Only between 2,000 and 3,000 of Germany's 2 million enterprises fall into this category (Deutsche Bundesbank 1984: 12; Anglo-German Foundation 1993: 9), and a mere 619 of the latter were quoted in official dealings on the stock market in 1990 (*The Economist*, 27 April 1991: 42). On average, over a 15-year period, non-financial enterprises met only 5 per cent of their external financing needs by issuing equity (ibid.). This low involvement becomes even clearer when viewed in comparative terms. Whereas in Britain the value of shares in circulation is equivalent to about one-third of GDP, in Germany it is well below one-tenth (ibid.).

The growing popularity of the private limited company and the fall in popularity of the public limited company is connected with the rigidity of the latter's legal form. It compels management to give co-determination rights to employees even if the firm falls below the normal cut-off point of 500 employees, and it enjoins all public companies to disclose their results. But this does not explain why enterprises which have this legal form do not trade on the stock market. Here it is thought that banks may play an inhibiting role, as entry into the stock market is dependent on active bank support, and the cautious banks will only recommend well-established firms. A further reason for low participation in the stock market is that share holding has not been popular with individual investors due to an alleged low profitability, as compared with bonds (Deutsche Bundesbank 1984: 16). Nor has there developed a sector of institutional investors, as in Britain. In consequence, the bulk of shares is owned by other enterprises, contributing to an unusually high degree of interlocking ownership among companies.

What are the alleged effects of this underdevelopment of the stock market? Foreign buyers complain that the narrow German share market offers few possibilities of diversifying (Deutsche Bundesbank 1984: 17). Domestic critics say that bank dominance undermines competition as banks might not lend to competitors of firms in which they already have a strong investment, and such constraint of competition would undermine the economy as a whole (Smyser 1992: 87). But the banks could counter this accusation by pointing to their relatively low proportion of all share ownership. The underdeveloped stock market also impedes the flow of investment into private venture capital funds for the start-up of new innovative but risky firms if investors are unable later to divest themselves of these companies in the stock market. More generally, a more developed stock market in Frankfurt could reduce the cost of trading and could provide more liquidity to the Germany system (Smyser 1992: 91).

In sum, the predominance of banks in the German financial system has given enterprises many advantages and has provided a very stable environment, but this very stability is also interpreted as staidness and a lack of entrepreneurialism. It is clear, however, that the advantages outweigh the drawbacks for enterprises and that, despite some recent technical improvements in the Frankfurt market and an increase in stock market trading in the 1990s (Smyser 1992: 91), we cannot expect a drastic change in the German industry–finance nexus in the near future. Smyser's suggestion (ibid.: 92), that access to capital for the purposes of production and not, as in Britain, for trading in capital, will remain a securely entrenched notion among bankers and industrialists, is very persuasive, but powerful global influences may eventually overide even these strongly held convictions and well-proven practices.

France

In France, as in Germany, banks are the most important source of investment finance. Up to the mid-1980s, relations between industrial firms and banks were distinctive in three respects: first, they were state-influenced and lending thus occurred not only according to business criteria but also according to political ones, such as the maintenance of a domestic computer industry. This government domination is reflected in the composition of top management where former civil servants, particularly those from the Ministry of Finance, are popular. This makes for a more pronounced technocratic than ownership influence in large companies. But a reduction of state involvement in credit allocation, together with large-scale privatization, will probably reduce the degree of elite circulation or *pantoufflage* in future. Second, the French banking system was more specialized than that of either Germany or Britain, some financial institutions lending only to certain sectors of the economy, and long-term and medium-term credit being handled by different institutions. This made the system more inflexible and, for smaller firms, more complex to deal with. But deregulation in the early 1980s made the banking sector more flexible and competitive, but also, due to a substantial reduction in state subsidies, more expensive, especially for SMEs. Third, French banks have a high degree of industrial expertise and also pool their knowledge with other banks to gain an understanding of different industries. This makes lending less risky and, as in Germany, longer-term and less conservative. Their relations with clients are not as close, though, as in Germany, and they have less control over firms. It is not clear whether or how French banks exert control over large firms. They do not enjoy the close ties with firms of their German counterparts, yet they seem to give more medium- and long-term loans than do English banks. One suggestion is that the close ties between individual members of the financial and industrial elite and the influence exerted by the former over top managerial appointments serve to discipline chief executives and hold them personally accountable for the economic success of their enterprise (Hanqué and Soskice 1994). Shareholders have only a low level of influence over the board, and the company chairman preserves a high degree of autonomy (Gordon 1990: 99–100).

The effect of the banking system on SMEs has not been beneficial. The introduction of several subsidized loan schemes in the early 1980s appears to have been 'too little too late'. The many very small and weak family-owned enterprises have not been able to take sufficient advantage of them, and the majority of medium-sized companies have become subsidiaries of larger groups and depend on centralized company finance (Quack and Hildebrandt 1994: 15–16). Consequently, there remains a much larger gap in performance between large firms and SMEs than in Germany (Stoffaes 1989).

During the 1960s and 1970s, the French financial system and its ability to restructure the economy in the direction of larger-scale and modern industries found many admirers in Britain. This admiration declined during the 1980s when state intervention became less fashionable and, given the growing globalization, also less feasible. Since the mid-1980s, there has occurred a move away from administered bank lending in favour of a stronger development of the stock market. Between 1983 and 1986, total subsidized loans dropped by about a quarter (Cerny 1989: 156). State dominance of investment finance is now connected by some influential policy-makers with uncompetitive over-investment and delayed adjustment in traditional sectors, as well as with hasty mergers and unnecessary integration, damaging to medium-sized firms (Stoffaes 1989: 122f). Stoffaes directs his criticism not merely at the administered nature of bank financing but at any kind of bank financing. He claims that it has favoured material investment, considered as assets on the balance sheet and providing banks with guarantees, while neglecting immaterial investment and more risky innovatory activity.

Stoffaes even infers that this system of financing has impaired French competitiveness and pleads for a stronger development of capital markets which he associates with greater flexibility (ibid.). But this position is by no means generally accepted, and, according to Cerny (1989: 157), there is still a fierce debate about whether the move to the stock market is desirable or harmful for the 'real economy'. After the partial withdrawal of the state from the financing of large firms 'the Achilles heel of capital – lack of private finance – has become more obvious' (Boucek 1993: 75–6).

CONCLUSIONS AND PROSPECTS

The above analysis of the three European financial systems and of their impact on industrial structure and company performance has shown that, in the early 1990s, significant differences between them still justified a distinction between a British financier-dominated capitalism and a German producer-orientated capitalism. France could be portrayed as a weaker version of the latter, due to the prominent role of the state in capital allocation.

But it is also becoming evident that, in response to European integration and growing globalization, there have occurred some efforts to change aspects of the financial system in all three societies, and a modest degree of convergence can be observed. In recent years some of France's biggest banks have begun to imitate German banks and have started to acquire large portfolios of shares in French companies, in the hope of becoming favoured house banks. Companies, in their turn, expect privileged access to investment funds and protection against takeover from other European companies (*The Econo-*

mist, 4 September 1990). But as French banks do not benefit from German banks' right to proxy voting, their influence is unlikely to rival that of the big German banks although their closer direct involvement could lead to the development of higher trust relations in the future. The French government, elected in 1993, is planning to make the Bank of France an independent bank, on the model of the Bundesbank. As indicated above, there has also occurred a significant shift towards the British equity-based system of investment finance, and it is difficult to predict whether the bank-credit or the equity-based market system will win out in the longer run.

Ironically, French imitation of German banks comes just at a time when the latter are coming under increasing pressure at home to change their practices. The Monopolies Commission, wishing to curb the power of the banks over firms, wants to impose a 15 per cent limit on banks' shareholdings in any individual firm; to restrict the number of seats individual bank directors can hold; and to reduce the overlap in ownership of shares in firms in related industrial segments. But, as Deutsche Bank has pointed out, the ensuing sales of its shares – it has, for example, 28 per cent of the shares in Daimler-Benz – would open the doors wide to foreign buyers: an occurrence strongly opposed up to now. More generally, the large private banks are said to be losing some of their influence over industry: firms depend more on retained profits and on pension funds, and some of the largest firms now have their own internal banking department. Large firms are also said to go more frequently to foreign capital markets, but this has not been documented by any of the sources consulted. The recent election by Daimler-Benz of a non-banking chairman to their supervisory board is seen to be a very significant symbolic indication of the lessening importance of the bank–industry nexus. In addition to reforming the banking system, there has also been more emphasis on developing the stock market, in preparation for the introduction of the single market in 1992 (*The Economist*, 5 May 1990). Since then the market has seen a notable increase in trading but the shift appears to have been less pronounced than in France.

The British financial system has also seen important changes during the last decade. These do not, however, signal convergence with the Continental pattern but a perfection of the existing system. Changes have been designed to abolish restrictive regulations and thereby strengthen the international position of the City but, at the same time, restructure the system 'to create a framework in which the financial institutions and markets would contribute to a transformation of the economy's productive base' (Coakley and Harris 1992: 56). The hallmark of these changes was deregulation, bringing an end to specialization in financial services and functions by certain institutions and eroding the old division between City institutions and the rest of the banking system. But, as so often in the past, the interests of the financial and the industrial sector could not be combined. Some of the measures introduced led to a dismantling rather than to a regeneration of large parts of manufacturing industry and brought no change in the markets' and banks' short-termism and lack of interest in production (ibid.).

But two recent developments are bound to force more pronounced adjustment processes in the future. The first is the huge increase in international trading and investment of money rather than goods and the huge profits which can be made from speculative investment. To participate fully a country needs a highly developed stock market. The second notable development comes from European integration. The 1992 project's European Financial Area is meant to bring about a common market in financial services by means of a harmonization of the operations of financial intermediaries and markets. This means that credit institutions lending to industry can operate freely across the European Union. Equity trading would also assume a European dimension although it is not yet clear whether this would occur in one centre or in several national exchanges.

These developments also entail the removal of existing regulatory and institutional impediments to takeovers which are perceived to distort the competitive process. There is widespread expectation that the integration of capital markets is likely to bring about the domination of the British financial model and the tendency towards hostile takeovers associated with it (Franks and Mayer 1990: 192). It remains an open question how these two developments would change the up to now highly distinctive national patterns of acquiring investment capital for productive purposes. While there is some indication that bank financing has hampered certain aspects of business development, particularly some aspects of innovation, there is little assurance that a move to a system based on the stock market would lead to an overall improvement. On the contrary, there is much evidence from the British case that harmful effects would outweigh beneficial ones. It remains to be seen whether German firms and banks can go on to resist the 'free market' rhetoric and the temptation of easy gain from financial speculation. Prowse (1994: 70) predicts that the German system may be quite impervious to recent and planned changes, due to the substantial financial independence from banks of large firms. He suggests that if Germany continues to ease access to the securities market but maintains its current policy of not placing restrictions on active investors, it may even prove to be the most viable financial system in the long run.

NOTE

1. The savings and co-operative banks receive their LTFR funds from three sources:

(a) special publicly owned federal-level credit institutions which issue bonds on national markets; the most important among these are the *Kreditanstalt für Wiederaufbau*, the *Deutsche Ausgleichsbank* and the *Industriekreditbank*. They do not usually deal directly with firms but through house banks at the local level;
(b) risk-pooling and refinancing mechanisms within the savings and co-operative banking sector;
(c) funds from insurance companies.

Roughly two-thirds of long-term bank lending to SMEs is refinanced through these three mechanisms (Vitols 1994: 12).

4. The restructuring of large firms: towards neo- or post-Fordism?

Although large corporations have been characteristic of advanced European economies for the best part of this century the trend towards capital concentration and the dominance of large, often multinational corporations has greatly intensified during the post-war period. During that time, the growing internationalization of trade and the resulting growth in markets, together with technological progress and a general increase in prosperity, all favoured industrial concentration; that is, an increase in the proportion of assets, turnover and employment in the hands of a decreasing number of large and giant productive units. An example from German industry – the firm of Mercedes-Benz – illustrates the scale of this phenomenon and indicates the power implied by this concentration: its turnover during the late 1980s was no less than half the GDP of Austria, and its employees constituted about two-thirds of Austria's total industrial employment (Tichy 1990: 61).

Capital concentration was accompanied by integration of all stages of the productive and distribution process and led to a high degree of centralization of control. The large, vertically integrated firm, devoted to mass-production, was seen as the epitome of Fordism. Both employment and production relations in post-war Europe were shaped by this type of firm.

Until the 1970s, it was widely believed that economic efficiency could only be obtained in large units and that a country's international competitiveness depended on a highly concentrated large-firm sector. From about the mid-1970s onwards, belief in the economic supremacy and virtue of the large firm began to waver, and the trend towards industrial concentration came to a halt. Rising scepticism about superior economic performance of large firms became reinforced by a revival of the ideology of entrepreneurial capitalism. Changes in world markets, economic recession, rapid technological change and the emergence of the Japanese challenge all contributed to a search for new organizational forms, both within the large corporation and in the place of it. The Fordist model became associated with rigidity and was pronounced to be unable to respond to the new problems and challenges. Some analysts predicted that the large firm had had its day. One of its earliest and most scathing critics (Bannock 1973: 4) describes the mature corporation as 'a blind alley in the evolutionary process, like the dinosaur'.

New demands began to face large firms: existing production models became undermined by new market demands, entailing both higher quality and versatility and perpetual innovation, and by the competitive challenges, issuing both from the more efficient Japanese and the rising East Asian economies and from the advent of the single European market. Before we can examine the impact of all these challenges on large corporations in the three largest European societies and assess their varying responses, it is necessary to establish their different starting positions. The following will, therefore, outline the main structural characteristics and modes of operating of large firms during the earlier post-war decades – the period now described by the short-hand term Fordism.

LARGE FIRMS DURING THE EARLY POST-WAR PERIOD

Britain attained significant concentrations of large, managerial enterprises in a cross-section of industries relatively late in the twentieth century but finally surged ahead in the post-war period. After several large merger waves during the 1960s and 1970s, Britain achieved the highest degree of capital concentration of any advanced society, outpacing even the USA (Chandler and Daems 1980: 3). Ease of takeover afforded by the British financial system contributed in no small measure to this outcome. Thus, during the 1970s, the 100 largest British firms accounted for around 50 per cent of UK manufacturing output and employment (Williams et al. 1983: 32).

Germany's early evolution of a powerful large-firm sector was temporarily reversed after the Second World War, when anti-trust legislation, imposed by the American victors, led to the dissolution of some giant firms. But during the 1960s, the process of concentration resumed with renewed intensity, raising the share of the 50 largest manufacturing firms of turnover and employment to 47 and 37 per cent respectively by 1977 (Claessens et al. 1989: 217). This gave Germany the second most highly concentrated manufacturing sector in Europe. But, in contrast to the situation in Britain, Germany has been left with a stronger sector of family-owned SMEs to counterbalance the giants. Due to a relatively permissive regulatory system for active investors, ownership concentration in large German manufacturing firms has remained much more pronounced than in Britain (Prowse 1994).

In France, a significant concentration of large firms in a cross-section of industries was first created in the post-war period. Only from the late 1950s onwards, under pressure and guidance from a modernist state, were holdings consolidated to form a number of 'national champions' in all the modern industries. By the early 1970s, there existed 18 giant industrial groups which employed 11 per cent of the industrial workforce (Lévy-Leboyer 1980: 117).

Further mergers occurred in the early 1980s, in the train of nationalizations under the first socialist government. Nine major industrial groups remained, and 55 per cent of the work-force were employed by enterprises with more than 500 employees. France is no longer a country of petty entrepreneurs although its large-firm sector remains smaller than in the other two countries and the weight of its small-firm sector heavier. Family control has also remained more entrenched than in the other two societies. According to data quoted by Mayer and Whittington (1994: 4, fn 3), 42 of the top 100 French firms are still under family control.

The following figures will put the degree of concentration into a comparative perspective for the 1980s. Of the 100 largest firms in Europe (in terms of turnover), 28 were British (including the two Anglo-Dutch), 24 German and 17 French. Of the 20 biggest, four were British, seven German and four French (*L'Expansion*, Dec. 1989–Jan. 1990: 149). These figures show Britain leading in large firms, Germany in giants and France coming third and joint-second respectively.

Large corporations are unevenly distributed between industrial sectors, and the distribution differs between our three economies. While concentrations of large companies were once indicative of the competitive strength of a sector this is now only partially the case. In Britain large firms dominate in some low-technology sectors, such as food and drink, footwear and clothing, but also in oil, chemicals, electrical engineering and aerospace. In Germany they are found mainly in technology- and science-intensive sectors, such as chemicals, cars, electrical engineering, but also in steel and producer goods. Significantly, some highly successful sectors are still dominated by SMEs, such as mechanical engineering, printing and precision optics. France has large firms concentrated both in highly traditional industries, such as food and drink and cosmetics, and in high-tech sectors, such as weapons technology, nuclear industry, chemicals and automobiles.

Degree of capital concentration tells us only part of the story, and we also need to examine structural characteristics of large firms, such as employment concentration, degree of centralization and form of governance or control structure, as well as vertical integration. Such analysis of structural features has been found to be a very difficult task, due to the highly complex ownership structures of French and German firms (cascades of holdings and subholdings with external minority shareholders) and the lack of transparency about the locus and manner of control in all countries. Hence the evidence on some of these aspects is only fragmentary. In Britain, capital concentration has not usually been accompanied by employment concentration. Growth through merger and the frequent failure to rationalize acquired units has led to a steadily increasing number of establishments per company – a rise from 27 to 72 in the 1958–72 period (Prais 1976: 62). A comparison of the British pattern with the German showed that during the 1970s the top quartile of British plants were significantly smaller than the top quartile in Germany (Prais 1976). A more recent comparison of British-owned companies with foreign-owned ones of similar size within Britain has shown that by 1985 British-owned companies still had many more and smaller establishments (Marginson et al. 1988: 46). In France, as in Britain, hurried merger waves were not followed by production rationalization (Telesis 1986), and the proportion of the working population employed by large establishments was only about half that in such employment in Germany (Scott 1985: 202). In both Britain and France, horizontal and vertical relations with other firms have largely been of the 'arm's-length' type.

German corporations show a relatively high degree of vertical integration in some industries; that is, they internalize many upstream and downstream functions, such as making their own components or having their own distribution networks. This high degree of integration and closure, particularly in the steel and chemicals industry, leads one commentator to speak of autarkous enterprises (Grabher 1988). In many other industries, however, the establishment of long-term and close vertical and horizontal relations with other firms has always been a significant feature (Porter 1990; Bannock and Albach 1991). Although production is highly diversified, diversification is mainly in related technologies or products, although conglomerate mergers became more frequent in the early 1980s (Bühner 1990: 4). Britain's lesser propensity towards vertical integration (Hannah 1976b: 199) and greater leaning towards conglomerate structure shows diametrically opposed structures and strategies. Thus, in 1980 47 per cent of companies had diversified into related businesses and 18 per cent were conglomerates (Goold and Campbell 1987: 295). If the main advantage of large production units lies in economies of scale and scope and the ability to operate a large distribution and/or service network, then it becomes clear that only German corporations were designed to reap the benefits of Fordist production methods.

Patterns of diversification do, in turn, influence the forms of corporate governance. Here the literature distinguishes between the following forms: the traditional unitary form – the U-form – with a functional organization and a high degree of centralization, informed by bureaucratic rationality; the decentralized holding company – the H-form – with weak central control and no separation of operational from strategic functions for central management; and, lastly, the multidivisional company – the M-form – where a high degree of decentralization by product or region is accompanied by financial and strategic control from central management. A progression from the simply U-form to the sophisticated M-form, it has been posited by American scholars, will accompany the growth and modernization of companies, and European firms would follow American ones on this path towards convergence. Dyas and Thanheiser (1976) and Mayer and Whittington (1994) have found that European firms, particularly French and German ones, have not *generally* followed this path, and the latter also suggest that the claimed superiority of the M-form is not proven.

Companies of a conglomerate type are much more likely to assume a decentralized form of decision-making; that is, a holding-company form or, more frequently in recent decades, a multidivisional form (M-form), as pioneered by American corporations before the Second World War (Goold and Campbell 1987: 295). Most large British corporations in the 1980s had assumed some form of divisional structure, but a large minority were still holding companies (Marginson et al. 1988: 48). In other words, British companies have highly decentralized governance structures but, in most cases, centralized financial control. French and German companies retained their U- and H-forms much longer and adopted the M-form to a much lesser degree (Dyas and Thanheiser 1976). In Germany, the M-form not only became adopted more slowly but even experienced a partial reversal during the 1980s (Cable and Dirrheimer 1983: 49). It has been suggested that German companies neither need the centralized financial control, having better owner control through banks and families (ibid.), nor would their managements tolerate the pressure towards short-termism flowing from the centralized financial control of the M-form (Tylecote 1982).

But the large, vertically integrated and centralized corporation, found still relatively frequently in Germany and France, has also been associated with many negative features: excessive bureaucratic hierarchy and control; failure of communication; and rigidity. Detailed comparative research on organizational structure and functioning by Maurice et al. (1980), however, has shown German firms to possess relatively short hierarchies, large spans of control and a relatively high degree of organizational flexibility. This was seen to be due to flexible forms of labour deployment, but it may also be related to the fact that large production units are often internally decentralized into a number of relatively independent workshops (Grabher 1988). French firms were shown to be in all respects at the opposite end of the scale and British firms occupied an intermediate position between the two on most counts. But British firms were also considered as being very compartmentalized in horizontal ways and hence inflexible. This research focused quite strongly on production organization. Other work with a wider focus on all areas of management control (Horovitz 1980; Child and Kieser 1979; Stewart et al. 1994), in contrast, sees less flexibility in Germany and more in Britain. The picture is thus by no means clear.

A last feature of large corporations to be examined is the geographical distribution of head offices, as these have a decisive multiplier effect on the industrial activity and employment profile of towns and regions in which they are situated. In Western Germany this distribution is very decentralized over 11 industrial agglomerations and, for the very large companies, over five geographical areas. In France, in contrast, distribution is highly concentrated, with 85 per cent of all headquarters situated in the Paris area during the 1980s (Krätke 1991: 259). Although France has experienced some decentralization of firms during the 1980s this has mainly affected low value-added activities whereas R&D, design and marketing activities have predominantly remained located in the Île de France (Dubois and Linhart 1994: 68–9). The British pattern shows a moderately high degree of headquarters concentration, with 65 per cent situated in the London area during the first half of the 1980s (Krätke 1991: 259).

This brief review of the size distribution, organizational structure and forms of control of large corporations in the three European societies has revealed very diverse patterns. Only German large firms approximated to the Fordist type in structural terms, but, due to other organizational measures and the functional flexibility of employees at all hierarchical levels, rigidity in production organization was avoided. New theoretical approaches of the 1980s, however, ignore any such national distinctions and advance a general indictment of the large Fordist firm: it is no longer associated with efficiency but with all manner of rigidities in the face of demands for diversified quality production and constant technological innovation. The perceived need for flexibilization and reduction of hierarchy is no longer postulated merely in academic publications but has also become a widely accepted management creed. It is clear from the preceding discussion that it is often difficult to determine the boundaries of firms, and hence it will be highly problematic to assess the degree and manner of recent transformation.

RECENT TRANSFORMATIONS OF THE LARGE-FIRM SECTOR

The challenges which began to face large firms from the mid-1970s onwards forced them to search for new strategic orientations and organizational structures. Resulting transformations in structure and strategy have been variously conceptualized as the need to adopt a new regime of accumulation (regulation theory) or a new production model, best suited to smaller units (flexible specialization). The common denominator in the two theories is the perceived necessity to achieve greater flexibility in all aspects of enterprise activity and to engage in some organizational fragmentation. But whereas flexible specialization theory posits a general shift in favour of smaller units and decentralization of control – a move away from the Fordist corporation – many theorists following the regulation approach see the Fordist large corporation as persistent and deny deconcentration in terms of ownership and market control (Amin and Dietrich 1991, taking up the position of the Grenoble School of regulation theory). But there are no hard and fast divisions on this issue between representatives of the two theoretical schools. Thus many Parisian Regulationists envisage a mixture of both tendencies, and some scholars, favouring flexible specialization theory, such as Sengenberger and Pyke (1990), emphasize that the trend towards smaller production units does not signal the end of the large corporation.

Even Sabel's more recent publications (1989, 1990) no longer posit the demise of the large corporation, merely its organizational transformation. But his argument does imply a move away from the Fordist type of corporation in countries like Italy, Germany and Japan, and also differs fundamentally from that of regulationists in its interpretation of corporate control. Market fragmentation, he argues, has made many large firms abandon mass-production and economies of scale. The ensuing necessity to react flexibly to constantly changing demand has been met by a downsizing of production units, a decentralization of corporate decision-making, as well as by a process of vertical disintegration, achieved by a new form of subcontracting to smaller and more specialized firms. These fragmentation processes have been facilitated by the new flexible technology. Sabel further claims that responsibility for design, production, sales and, in many cases, R&D as well, has been assigned to quasi-independent operating units. Corporate headquarters have been much reduced, and top management concerns itself mainly with strategic planning, accounting and some research. 'Thus the corporation becomes more of a federation of companies than a single organizational unit' (Sabel 1990: 10). Such decentralization within ownership units is then accompanied by processes of vertical disintegration whereby manufacturing of the greatly increased number of components or modules is externalized to independently owned subcontractors. This new 'collaborative manufacturing' is designed not only to enhance flexibility but also to save costs and to gain access to the innovative capacity of mainly smaller subcontracting firms (ibid.: 10f). Sabel never investigates the possibility of whether radical vertical disintegration leads to deconcentration of capital and control and to the creation of smaller ownership units although such an outcome might be seen as strongly implied by his analysis.

Amin and Dietrich (1991), in their critique of flexible specialization theory's conceptualization of large corporations, assume such an implication. Their work is concerned to show that, despite much organizational decentralization and vertical disintegration, there has occurred no deconcentration of capital and control. They argue that, on the contrary, large multinational corporations have not abandoned their mass-production models and are as concerned as ever to achieve economies of scale and market control. If anything, they are now aiming to extend their market dominance across national boundaries and to this end pursue corresponding strategies of capital concentration, as manifested in the growing movement towards international mergers and strategic alliances. Consequently, for Amin and Dietrich (1991), organizational decentralization does not lead to decentralization of control which, in most industries, has remained firmly in the hands of a few oligopolistic firms and has even been strengthened by the new subcontracting relationships. They rightly point out that the flexible specialization approach concentrates one-sidedly on flexibility in production and fails to consider other factors, such as R&D, marketing and finance, where scale and oligopolistic advantage remain important to large firms. They undertake a useful detailed analysis of mergers and alliances and the professed motives for undertaking them, both within and between European countries, as well as on an international scale, to support their theoretical points.

The following sections will systematically examine the available evidence on corporate fragmentation tendencies, to explore how far actual developments support the various theoretical positions set out above. The theorists discussed above assume general fragmentation or concentration trends and do not consider the different national starting positions, resulting from the divergent national business structures and strategies, that were established historically. This investigation, in contrast, will systematically consider the pre-existing national diversity in structural forms and cultural dispositions, demonstrated in the first part of Chapter 4. Three fragmentation tendencies, variously labelled within the literature, will be examined here under the following headings: decentralization, vertical disintegration and capital deconcentration.

Decentralization is internal change of a structural or organizational kind, resulting in the breakup of large units into smaller ones or merely in decentralization of operational decision-making and responsibility and a reduction of the management hierarchy. The net result of decentralization strategies would be more and smaller organizational subunits and/or flattened managerial hierarchies, as well as a reversal of the trend towards centralized decision-making.

Vertical disintegration involves the externalization of activities, previously done in-house, without any transfer of ownership. Most analyses focus mainly on subcontracting, but this account will also include strategic alliances as they result in a partial externalization of functions, without a change in ownership. Subcontracting involves the externalization of production tasks, services and design activities to legally independent firms, often controlled via market power. The greater use of subcontractors has been coupled with a transformation of the buyer–supplier relationship, often referred to as relational or partnership subcontracting. The buyer demands quality assurance, cost reduction through constant efficiency improvement, technological know-how and just-in-time (JIT) delivery. In return, the supplier gains longer-term contracts. The result of this strategy would be substantial down-sizing and fragmentation of operational units, but the consequences in terms of de- or reconcentration of control and capital must remain open questions to be answered only by empirical investigation. Strategic alliances with legally independent firms are entered into in order to co-operate on R&D, product development and marketing. They involve the partial externalization of previously wholly integrated functions. As such alliances are commonly set up between firms who are leaders within their industry (Vonortas 1990: 201), the resulting relationship is less likely to be a hierarchical one. It is more likely to entail a sharing of control rather than a one-sided extension of control, as implied by Amin and Dietrich (1991) and Walsh (1991b). But the exact nature of the control relationship can only be determined by empirical investigation.

Deconcentration involves the breakup of larger units into smaller ones in ownership terms. It may take the form of management buy-outs and/or of the unbundling of conglomerates through the sell-off of areas of activity or of whole units. The latter then enables the large firm to concentrate on what is defined as core business and to follow the imperative for innovation on a more manageable scale. The net result of deconcentration would be a halt or even a reversal of capital concentration and the abandonment of the large and giant Fordist corporation, provided these processes are not outweighed by counter trends in mergers and acquisitions. What then is the evidence from our three European societies that one or more of these fragmentation processes have been occurring?

Decentralization

There is widespread agreement in the literature, regardless of its theoretical bent, that due to the necessity for speedier and more flexible reaction to constantly changing market demands, decentralization of decision-making to operating units and a flattening of managerial hierarchies has been a notable development of the 1980s. There is, however, little systematic evidence about what form decentralization has taken and which levels of management have been affected. There is no agreement on whether this has led to a decentralization of managerial control, or whether Fordist centralized management control is being maintained even in spatially decentralized units, due to the development of the new control technologies. Whereas followers of the regulation approach posit the continuation of centralized control through technology and internal markets, proponents of flexible specialization are more inclined to stress the independence, or at least the interdependence, of decentralized units.

Concerning the reduction of hierarchy, it is unclear to what extent responsibility has been pushed downwards to production staff. Different levels of qualification among such staff in the three countries (for details, see Chapter 8) lead one to expect different outcomes in this decentralization process.

Observers of a decentralization trend refer to a proportional decline in the employment share of large firms (see, for example, Sengenberger and Pyke 1990: 5). Aggregate data for the mid-1970s to the mid-1980s show clearly that concentration, measured in employment terms, has come to a halt and that the larger firms in all three societies have been shedding labour disproportionately (ibid.). Comparative figures for the 1981–7 period show, however, that this employment loss has been very pronounced in Britain whereas it has been more moderate in France and only very slight in Germany (Eurostat figures, quoted by Hughes 1992: 11). But it remains unclear to what extent this employment reduction indicates a simple reduction in manning levels, due to either recessionary pressures or to the introduction of new technology, and to what extent it signals genuine corporate decentralization strategies. A more detailed country analysis will establish more clearly what is involved.

For Britain, many sources point to the growing number of establishments per company, together with a decrease of their size in employment terms. Thus, between 1979 and 1983 the number of establishments per company increased from 37.5 to 40.7 while average size declined from 644 to 429 employees (Marsden and Thompson 1990: 101) – an indication of considerable decentralization of operations. Edwards's (1987) survey of larger plants (more than 200 employees) in a cross-section of industries in the mid-1980s confirms both decentralization and growing operational autonomy, but also notes the existence of a 'loose–tight' relationship with headquarters through the setting of performance standards in the majority of cases (ibid.: 91f). A similar survey by Marginson et al. (1988) confirms this pattern, and Storey and Sisson (1990: 62) see decentralization as 'near commonplace'. But this appears to be largely decentralization within the company, which merely constitutes an intensification of old patterns of organizational control. There is no indication that it has entailed a dramatic reduction of hierarchy and a shift of responsibility to production departments, as envisaged by 'lean production'.

Evidence from France also shows this trend towards a reduction of employment in larger units. Thus, between 1976 and 1988, the employment share of large companies (with more than 500 employees) declined from 20.7 per cent to 14.6 per cent (*Le Monde*, 13 June 1990, quoted by Sengenberger and Pyke 1991: 5). Data for the large *groupes* indicate a similar reduction in the size of production units between 1974 and 1986, but no increase in the number of branches (*Economie et statistique*, 229, Feb. 1990). It is thus not clear whether this development signals decentralization or merely shedding of labour during the recession. In some cases, trends towards decentralization have been counterbalanced by renewed moves towards centralization, following acquisition or merger (Mayer and Whittington 1994) – a very frequent recent occurrence. Although French firms, too, have experimented with the shortening of hierarchies, pluridisciplinary project teams and horizontal relationships, the long legacy of Taylorism and Fayolism is hard to dislodge. The situation is well summed up by Dubois and Linhart (1994: 83): 'there are not everywhere integrated, interactive, transparent and homogenous firms ... but some significant changes here and there, impelled by managers of good will'.

Given the previously high degree of centralization in German firms, one would not expect from their managements the same eagerness to tread the decentralization path, but the evidence is somewhat mixed and inconclusive. Weimer (1990) quotes a leading management consultant who claims the continuation of a relatively centralized management style. This is confirmed by Kern (1994: 35) who points to the following enduring features: 'enterprise units are too large and hierarchies too long and rules of competence too exclusive', suggesting both vertical and horizontal rigidities. But against this evidence, it is noticeable that the concept of 'lean production' has had a strong resonance among German managers and that a number of large firms have begun to decentralize activities to operational units and to reduce the hierarchy (Faust et al. 1994). This exercise is not another rationalization wave to shed labour, but is explicitly designed to ensure more flexible and speedier responses to changes in market demand. Faust et al. (1994: 110) speak cautiously of 'the first steps towards institutionalizing a new vision', but show that these organizational changes are being undertaken systematically in various industries. They are having very significant consequences for patterns of work organization and control in production and production-related departments, but they also entail big reductions in managerial employment and promotion chances (ibid.). Other analyses also detect an emerging trend towards decentralization, without, however, providing documentation (Wittke 1989; Pries et al. 1990: 14). Jacobi (1991) quotes case-study evidence that such decentralization has become pronounced in two sectors: the machine tool and electro-technical industries. In sum, it seems that, although centralization of control is still prevalent in large German firms managements now have begun to tackle this problem in a systematic fashion and, in a significant minority of cases, have created more flexible corporate structures.

Vertical Disintegration

The literature from all three countries puts a strong emphasis on both the growth in subcontracting and on its changed nature and purpose. This assists buyer firms to reduce demand, innovation and efficiency risks, as well as cope with the great increase in parts resulting from the move towards diversified quality production. It is generally inferred that computer linkages still guarantee integrated production and that market power secures hierarchical control. This development is thus seen to represent a simultaneous reversal of vertical integration and an assumption of a new form of quasi-integration.

But there is no agreement in the literature on the magnitude and breadth of such increase. Whereas the French and, to a lesser extent, the British give statistical data which support a moderate increase in the subcontracting of production tasks during the 1980s (ACAS 1988: 12; IMS 1986; Morris and Imrie 1991; *Enjeux*, 62, 1985; Bonneau et al. 1989; Dubois and Linhart 1994), the literature on Germany argues mainly on the basis of case-study evidence from a limited number of industries (Grabher 1988; Semlinger 1989: 95) or firms (Sabel 1989: 33). More generally, it has been shown that contracting out of services is much more prevalent than that of production tasks (Weimer 1990: 127). An increase in the subcontracting of production operations, moreover, remains confined to assembly-based sectors, such as cars and consumer electronics, whereas there is little scope for subcontracting in process-based industries and in industries producing perishable consumer goods (de Smidt and Wever 1990: 9).

It is equally problematic to generalize on the quality of the new division of labour between firms. While there is some evidence for Piore and Sabel's (1984) claim of a more collaborative partnership relation, there is other evidence that the large firm retains control by virtue of its superior market power. The nature of the relationship differs both between sectors within societies and between societies. In the first case, Japanization of subcontracting has proceeded furthest in highly globalized industries exposed to intense competition, such as the automobile and electronics industries. In the second case, pre-existing structural and cultural characteristics of industrial organization have mediated more recent attempts to remodel outsourcing in significant ways. (For more detail, see Lane 1991). In each economy tendencies towards both co-contracting and relational contracting will be found, as well as networks entirely dominated by the financial power of large firms, but the degree of relational contracting will vary. While in France and Britain the dominance of large industrial groups or firms respectively remains an important factor (Dubois and Linhart 1994: 66f; Imrie and Morris 1992), in Germany there remains more scope for SME supplier firms to preserve their autonomy, except perhaps in the car industry.

Another form of externalization of business activity which indicates simultaneous vertical disintegration and quasi-integration are the many recent strategic alliances and joint ventures between large firms, seeking to share innovation risks, as well as gain access to scientific knowledge and markets.

There is evidence that this path is more often adopted by continental than British firms and that it may be a strategic alternative to acquisition (Amin and Dietrich 1991).

Deconcentration

Deconcentration can come about in a variety of ways: divestment due to rationalization after a takeover; unbundling in the move from conglomerate structure to greater product specialization; and management buy-outs of parts of companies in financial difficulties. Although all these developments are said to have been prevalent in the 1980s, particularly in Britain, it is necessary to counterbalance them with movement towards reconcentration, due to vigorous merger activity.

The evidence from Germany suggests that fragmentation of large units through splitting-off, unbundling or buy-outs has been insignificant to date. The only notable exceptions have been spin-offs by Siemens and Loewe Opta (Weimer 1990: 129). This is in contrast to the British pattern, where divestment activity became very prevalent during the 1980s (Shutt and Whittington 1984: 16; Wright et al. 1989: 116; Chandler 1990). Thus the volume of leveraged buy-outs in Britain in the second half of the 1980s was double that of the rest of Europe (Prowse 1994: 49). Weimer persuasively attributes this absence of German deconcentration trends to institutional and attitudinal characteristics: impediments posed by the financial and legal systems, as well as by managerial attitudes (ibid.). In addition, the greater homogeneity between large and smaller firms in employment conditions and industrial relations systems provides less of an incentive to fragment into smaller units. Also, German large firms have not experienced the same labour control problems as British firms, and they have been more able to achieve flexible production arrangements within large units. A last important reason for the higher incidence of fragmentation in the British context is, of course, the greater proportional importance of conglomerates during the Fordist period (Chandler 1990: 626) and the partial reversal of this diversification strategy during more recent years. The extent of divestment in Britain has led to a market for selling and buying enterprises which has no equivalent on the continent (ibid.).

An investigation of divestment and acquisition activities of large French firms in the 1974–86 period found that, in order to achieve greater specialization, firms have rid themselves of numerous activities while at the same time investing in new activities. Divestment seems to have been greater than reinvestment in terms of *'postes de travail'* affected (*Economie et statistique*, 229, Feb. 1990). Dubois and Linhart (1994), however, see a deconcentration process, indicated by the expansion of the 'small firm' sector, as more apparent than real, because a majority of these new small firms remain financially controlled by the large *groupes* (ibid.: 66f). They identify a growth of concentration during the 1980s and posit a 'hegemony of the big firms' (ibid.: 85). In the French case, moreover, capital concentration is accompanied by extreme geographical concentration in the 'Megapole of the Parisian region' and, more recently, a few metropoles in the southern regions (ibid.). The extremely high degree of concentration in the industrial groups is indicated by the following figures for 1989: 20 per cent of all industrial firms, 66 per cent of employment, 75 per cent of turnover and investment and 90 per cent of exports are ascribed to the *groupes* (ibid.: 67).

To what extent have deconcentration trends been counterbalanced by renewed trends to capital concentration? Such opposing trends might result from technological change and the imperative towards innovation in some industries but also from trends towards European integration and globalization in many industries. The first trend has been documented by van Tulder and Junne (1988), while reconcentration due to globalization has been highlighted by Amin and Dietrich (1991). The two trends are, of course, often complementary.

From the 1970s onwards, three radical new core technologies have appeared simultaneously: microelectronics, materials technology and biotechnology. The wide applicability of these technologies in both products and processes, their combined application in several industries and the much-increased pace of innovation have confronted firms with demands which only the large multinational companies can cope with. Although this development has prompted greater specialization in core areas and hence has given some impulses towards unbundling, it has also prompted new diversification strategies and integration processes, leading to increased concentration (van Tulder and Junne 1988). A good example here is that of the Daimler-Benz group's acquisition of MTU, AEG and Dornier. These help to control strategic inputs for profitable core business in automobile production: AEG's radar technology to detect obstacles in a car's path and Dornier's materials technology for devising new car frames (ibid.: 29).

The high cost of technological innovation, necessitating a much increased R&D facility, and the risks associated with it have driven firms to find new ways of getting access to technological and scientific knowledge. Some, such as strategic alliances, obviate increased capital concentration, while others, such as the acquisition of innovative small high-tech firms, favour it. The latter is reported for the pharmaceuticals industry in Germany (Weimer 1990; Grabher 1988) and more generally in Britain as a preferred route for quick access to innovation (Saxenian 1989; Walsh 1991b). Thus, on balance, activities in the field of R&D, including access to government support, are favouring large firms, rather than deconcentration and the creation of small units.

The advent of the single market and the increasing globalization of markets have provided further impetus towards capital concentration. Attempts to secure a favourable position in this enlarged market have brought about a flurry of mergers in all three societies, and such mergers are increasingly crossing national boundaries. But merger activity has been far more pronounced in Britain than in Germany (Hughes 1992: 21), and it is more appropriate to see the merger boom as an Anglo-Saxon rather than a general European phenomenon. Thus, while the average annual volume of completed domestic mergers and corporate transactions during 1985–9 had a value of US$107.6 billion in Britain, it amounted to only US$4.2 billion in Germany (Prowse 1994: 47, table 12). For Germany, a further push towards concentration has come from reunification and the resultant marketization of the East German states. Thus many large Western firms have taken over viable parts of the mainly large firms in the East, such as the merging of the largest steel combine into the already giant firm of Krupp.

The intensification in national, inter-European and international merger activity by European firms during the 1980s has been well documented by Amin and Dietrich (1991), who claim that this activity signals increased capital concentration and oligopolistic tendencies and a lack of decentralization of corporate control. For them, all this proves that scale economies are still very important and that the large Fordist corporation remains very prevalent. Furthermore, its power has become even greater now because strategic control extends beyond corporate boundaries (the new subcontracting) and because of a heightened degree of co-operation between oligopolistic firms (strategic alliances) (ibid.: 69). Examination of similar data by Hughes (1992: 23), however, leads to the contrasting conclusion that no general increase in monopoly power has taken place. Given that this trend has been much stronger among firms based in Anglo-Saxon countries, this development has a lot to do with the nature of different national financial systems and should not perhaps be posited as a universal trend.

How do we evaluate these claims? In the light of other evidence on concentration and in view of the earlier discussion about pressures towards globalization, the claims of Amin and Dietrich are plausible. But their data provide by no means unambiguous support for a general trend towards reconcentration of capital and control, and some of their own points also qualify the claim about an undifferentiated trend in this direction. First, they completely ignore the trends towards deconcentration detailed above and neglect to offset divestment against merger activity. Second, their strong emphasis on a merger boom during the 1980s never provides comparative figures for earlier decades to substantiate this claim. Here it is notable that, although merger activity during the 1980s was strong in terms of the expenditure incurred, the number of mergers accomplished in Britain in 1986 –

the peak year of merger activity – was below that of any year between 1963 and 1973 (Gray and McDermott 1990: 71). Fewer companies have been acquired, but they have become larger and more expensive. Third, the reasons for merger cited by Amin and Dietrich (ibid.: table 3.4) by no means unambiguously bear out their claim that strengthening of market position has been the chief motive (ibid.: 57). On the contrary, rationalization/restructuring received the highest proportion of mentions in all years, except 1987–8, and strengthening of market position came top of the list only in that year. In fact, motives for merger are highly diverse, differing according to strategy prevalent in industries and countries.

The puzzle of simultaneous tendencies towards large-firm concentration and the trend towards deconcentration, indicated by the marked growth of smaller firms, is solved by Dubois and Linhart (1984: 67f.) in the case of France. They talk of a 'double evolution' due to opposing external influences. While the trend towards greater internationalization and mounting R&D expenditure pushes towards concentration, the development of niche markets and the high variability of demand compels fragmentation. Fragmentation, however, does not lead to deconcentration, as large French firms generally have maintained financial control over their SME subcontractors (ibid.).

CONCLUSIONS

The foregoing has shown above all that there are still many unresolved questions in this area of corporate restructuring. It must, therefore, remain an open question whether 'the principle of giantism' (Dubois and Linhart 1984: 59) and the Fordist paradigm continue to be important aspects of corporate structure and strategy. Ambiguity comes from divergent developments between firms in different industries and countries, from the variety of fragmentation strategies adopted and from the as yet poor empirical evidence in several of these areas. On the one hand, the need for greater organizational flexibility and for spreading risk have led to strategies of decentralization, vertical disintegration and even some deconcentration in ownership terms. Such fragmentation trends appear to have gone furthest in Britain – a country which has always been characterized by greater decentralization of its organizational structures. On the other hand, however, the necessity for constant technological innovation on a broad front and the ensuing push to increase the global reach of companies is only within the capacity of large firms which, moreover, benefit disproportionately from governmental R&D support. The single market, too, largely favours the larger firm. Statistical evidence points more strongly to enduring capital concentration though not necessarily to an increase in monopoly power. Moreover, organizational and financial integration can be combined with fragmentation of production, and the latter should not be confused with fragmentation of capital and control (Martinelli and Schoenberger 1991: 128). Thus, the large and often global company is not only here to stay but, in the longer term, will weather the turbulent business climate much better than the supposedly more flexible SME because it has a greater range of organizational strategies at its disposal.

But this is not to deny the incidence of widespread adoption of more flexible and decentralized corporate structures and of new ways of spreading risk and gaining access to technological know-how. Attempts to achieve some vertical disintegration and to reduce hierarchy have occurred in all three societies, and horizontal relations between large firms are increasingly assuming the form of temporary alliances, without the merging of ownership. There have been widespread efforts in all three societies to create relations of greater trust both within and between firms, as well as encouraging greater initiative and commitment from both employees and subcontractors. Central control has become less detailed and immediate but has nevertheless been retained and, in the case of subcontractors, perhaps has even been increased. Thus there has occurred operational decentralization within and between firms but, at the same time, integrated management of the entire value-added chain.

These structural and attitudinal transformations are still emergent and as yet poorly documented so that it would be premature to herald the arrival of the post-Fordist corporation. But, at the same time, it would be wrong to deny the occurrence of any kind of structural and strategic change, and it is easiest to agree with the Parisian Regulationists that the current situation is a very mixed one in which old Fordist principles of organization co-exist with neo-Fordist ones, combining economies of scale with economies of scope and quick responses to the market (see, for example, Boyer 1991a: 23f).

While there has been a considerable degree of convergence in the ways in which large firms in our three societies have adapted to new risks and opportunities there is also much evidence that old national features of an institutional and cultural kind have endured and have, indeed, crucially shaped the transition process towards a new regime of flexible accumulation. As pointed out by Lash and Urry (1987), companies in previously highly organized economies have shown a much less notable trend towards fragmentation than the always loosely organized British corporations. Britain remains in many ways a very special case within Europe, and it is totally unjustified to generalize from the British case, as many theorists are inclined to do.

Whereas this chapter has been concerned with structural change of large corporations in general, the following chapter will explicitly deal with the fact that such restructuring usually has an international dimension.

5 Internationalization or globalization of large firms?

The last chapter has repeatedly referred to an intensification of internationalization or even globalization of economic activity and alluded to the attendant transformation of multinational companies. What is meant by these terms, and how far have we experienced a global shift (Dicken 1992)? Has such a shift finally swept away remaining national distinctiveness of business organizations, as well as rendering irrelevant the social and political contexts which have moulded them? This chapter will answer these questions by systematically examining how far and in what ways large corporations in different European societies have responded to an alleged global shift.

Internationalization refers to an increasing spread of economic activity across national boundaries. This has been achieved in two ways: the first and very traditional way has been for large firms to extend their markets across national borders by exporting a significant share of their production. In this case production remains in the home country but distribution networks may be built up in foreign countries; a second way to internationalize has been for large companies to place a significant proportion of direct investment in foreign countries (FDI). A company which operates in many different countries but retains a clear home base in one particular country is called a multinational company. Such a company will retain all the high value-added elements of the value chain in the home country, and its foreign subsidiaries remain predominantly assembly operations. Such a process of internationalization became established at the turn of the last century but has become highly significant only in the post-war period. Recent decades have witnessed a further intensification of FDI, the emergence of new investor countries and a wider geographical spread of both outward and inward investment. Reasons for FDI are various and have received different weights in different periods of time: gaining better access to and reducing the costs of raw materials; reducing labour costs; gaining entry into or enlarging markets; and spreading risks. The strategy pursued in placing FDI, then, has an obvious bearing on the choice of investment site, and the changing strategies over time explain the shift away from FDI in developing countries to developed ones.

The concept of globalization refers to a qualitatively new development in the interconnection between national economies and has given rise to the

82

emergence of companies which transcend national borders – namely, transnational companies. The international economic system is no longer an aggregate of nationally located functions but becomes autonomized as production
and markets become truly global (Hirst and Thompson 1992: 361). Transnational companies no longer have a national home base but source, produce
and market on a global scale, as dictated by their business strategy. Economic
activities thus become fragmented and globally dispersed and reintegrated to
capture linkages between countries (Dicken 1992). Globalization affects all
stages of the value chain, from R&D to distribution. The emerging transnational company frees itself from any specific national dependency and is
no longer regulated and controlled by a national state; it also transcends the
influence of other national institutions, such as banks, trade associations and
trade unions (Hirst and Thompson 1992). Finally, this type of company has a
much wider geographical reach than the mere multinational, operating on a
truly global scale. The degree of globalization aimed for varies not only
according to business strategy but also in line with organizational and technical factors that differ between industries. Instead of having a presence only in
a few foreign countries, the global company has a global presence. This
process of globalization is said to be accompanied and, indeed, facilitated by
the emergence of new technologies in transport and communication, as well
as by a greater homogenization of tastes and of production methods across
national boundaries.

Let us now turn to the empirical evidence from our three societies and
examine first the extent and nature of internationalization and then enquire
whether and to what extent recent transformations point towards marked
globalization trends. The three countries are examined as both the home base
and the host to MNCs. In the latter respect, increasing volume of inward
investment, the changing national origins of investors and the varying economic and social effects on the host country will be considered.

The analysis of European MNCs will put a strong emphasis on their
embeddedness in the institutional environment of their home country and on
how this has shaped their internationalization strategy – a focus which has
received insufficient consideration to date. Exceptions to this rule are the
work of Porter (1990) and Sally, who comments:

> The implantation of MNEs in national policy networks invests them with a politi-
> cal identity that factors into their capacities to leverage advantage in international
> competition and cooperation.   (Sally 1994: 172).

Focus on the home base, however, will be accompanied by the recognition that
companies increasingly become situated also in global structures and hence
must manage the constant tension between the two in a productive way.

INTERNATIONALIZATION

The development and growth in importance of MNCs has been connected with multiple economic and social effects and has been interpreted in both a positive and a highly critical manner. But it is very difficult to generalize about these effects. Outward investment may be, but is not necessarily, connected with insufficient investment and employment creation at home. Inward investment is more often associated with benefits but is also seen to carry grave risks. On the one side, it is argued that foreign competition for domestic assets ensures that they will be used in the most efficient way and that consumers will benefit. Local managements may learn from the superior technological capacity and/or management skills of foreign MNCs, and the state may have to improve infrastructure to attract such investment against competitors. On the other side, negative influence can ensue if foreign companies drive out domestic ones which had a higher R&D intensity or technology transfer. Economic damage and social costs will arise if foreign firms make insufficient use of indigenous supplier firms or fail to create a large number of higher skill jobs.

Impact of inward investment is also far-reaching in social terms, as foreign MNCs have a large influence over the location and quality of employment, over industrial relations and over the environment. Charges of footlooseness and lack of loyalty to any one country, as well as of job exporting and creating unemployment, are frequently levelled against MNCs. Whether or not any or all of these positive and negative influences occur cannot be decided *a priori*. Outcomes will depend both on the particular business strategy, guiding either inward or outward direct investment and on the economic and social context provided by the host country. Although MNCs are considered to be highly autonomous economic actors Sally's definition points out that many features of their business operations are strongly influenced by their home country. Let us now focus on actual developments in the three countries, first on processes of internationalization during the earlier post-war decades, and then explore tendencies towards globalization during the 1980s and 1990s.

Britain

British FDI started at the end of the nineteenth century. Taking advantage of Britain's political status as an international power, British MNCs were the biggest investors, locating mainly in the relatively protected markets of Commonwealth countries. Even on the eve of the Second World War, British FDI still constituted 40 per cent of overall FDI (Hood 1986: 79). Since then, the USA has overtaken Britain in the volume of investment, but Britain remains, with a large gap, second in the international league table concerning stock of

Table 5.1 *Foreign direct investment outflows from the larger industrial countries as percentage of total outflows[a] (annual averages), 1975–91*

	1975–9	1980–4	1985–9	1990	1991[b]
United States	47	24	19	15	17
Britain	18	24	21	8	12
France	5	8	7	16	15
Germany	9	9	8	11	14
Japan	6	11	17	22	20

Notes:
[a] Extract from a larger table. Totals will not add up to 100.
[b] Preliminary figures.

Source: IMF, quoted by *The Economist*, 19 September 1992, World Economy Survey: 17.

FDI, and outward far exceeds inward investment. Table 5.1 gives an indication of outflows of FDI over time, and affords comparisons with other advanced countries. During the 1980s, increases in the outflow of FDI have also been accompanied by a much increased outflow of purely financial portfolio investment and a general globalization of financial dealing.

A profile of British MNCs must emphasize the following points: the degree of concentration among MNCs is very high and, in the early 1980s, the 70 leading ones had a significantly higher foreign than home output (Stopford and Turner 1985: 3). They also have an unusually high proportion of their employment abroad – some 40 per cent, as compared with only 25 per cent for Germany and 20 per cent for France (United Nations 1988). Investment is spread among a number of locations, with the lion's share going to the USA and the lowest proportion to the developing countries (ibid.: 10). In recent years, Europe has assumed increased prominence as an investment site, but the absence of significant investment in South East Asia and Africa indicates that British FDI does not have a truly global reach. This pattern of investment is consonant with a strategy driven by either market considerations or risk distribution, rather than by calculations of labour cost-cutting, as suggested by the thesis about the New International Division of Labour (NIDL). Case studies, such as Walsh (1991a) on the textile industry, have also shown that MNCs can now reap greater cost advantages at home through restructuring and the introduction of new technology.

MNCs perform better than purely national companies but, apart from a handful of leading companies, British MNCs at the aggregate level have declined in world status (Hamilton 1987: 169). In terms of sales, they came fourth, after West Germany (ibid.: 173), but well before France. Investment occurs mainly by acquisition, reflecting Britain's advantage in the financial field, as well as its relative technological weakness (Hood 1986: 88). In terms of target industries, investment is heavily skewed towards industries with low-research intensity and, more recently, increasingly towards services. The bulk of investment is still in the industries of food, drink, tobacco, textiles and clothing, leather and shoes, paper and wood products (Hamilton 1987: 172) but also of chemicals. In the late 1970s, R&D-intensive industries accounted for only around 10 per cent of total investment (Hood 1986: 83). Generally, British companies perform better in marketing-led than in technology-led industries.

Evaluation of British MNCs and of outward FDI differs according to what aspect is under consideration and is also influenced by the political ideology of the investigator. The main concerns about British MNCs are, first, that they have a weak 'headquarters' spin-off effect in terms of technology and, second, that the high proportion of their sales abroad has a negative impact on their export performance at home (Hamilton 1987: 178). Given that their outward investment is frequently bigger than their home investment, there is also concern about the export of jobs. Such net export is believed to have increased from about 1974 onwards (ibid.: 177). During the last recession, the leading MNCs contracted employment more strongly at home than abroad (ibid.: 175–6), although there were marked differences between sectors. Deteriorating home markets and, in some cases, lower costs abroad were cited as the main reasons (ibid.). An example of this trend to escape ailing home markets is the recent expansion abroad (USA and France) of the engineering firm GKN which concentrates on auto components (ibid.: 180).

As indicated by Table 5.2, Britain is the second most popular investment site after the US. Such inward investment increased greatly in the 1960s and the first half of the 1970s, began to decline in the 1980s, due to disinvestment by US firms (Hamilton 1987: 183) but has risen again in the 1990s. During the 1980s, inward investment was significantly higher than that into France and Germany combined (*The Economist*, 23 June 1990: 89).

The most important investors, in terms of the volume of funds, are the Americans, followed by the Europeans. The Japanese come a long way off third, although Britain attracted by far the largest proportion of all Japanese investment in Europe (Young and Hamill 1992: 16). By the end of the 1980s, Japanese investment amounted to 10 per cent of the book value of all FDI in Britain (Auerbach 1989: 272), but the impact of the Japanese on the British economy has been much greater than suggested by this relatively modest share. Reasons for Britain's popularity as an investment site are, first, language and culture-based, particularly for American investors. Of equal importance, however, in comparative European terms, are the discrepantly low corporation tax, wages and social charges (Eltis 1992: 5), together with the

Table 5.2 *Foreign direct investment inflows into the larger industrial countries as percentage of total inflows[a] (annual averages), 1975–91*

	1975–9	1980–4	1985–9	1990	1991[b]
United States	33	53	51	29	14
Britain	23	15	14	21	25
France	10	7	6	8	18
Germany	7	2	2	2	3
Japan	0.5	0.8	0.4	1	2

Notes:
[a] Extract from a larger table. Totals will not add up to 100.
[b] Preliminary figures.

Source: IMF, quoted by *The Economist*, 19 September 1992, World Economy Survey: 17.

availability of skilled workers and highly educated professionals. There are signs that Britain is losing some of its popularity as an investment site to countries like Ireland and Spain (Young and Hamill 1992: 11).

In the early 1980s, one in seven of British workers in manufacturing worked in a foreign-owned company (Stopford and Turner 1985: 4), and of the 1,000 largest firms in Britain, 402 were foreign-owned (ibid.: 133). In 1991, 13 per cent of all manufacturing jobs were in foreign-owned companies (Confederation of British Industry (CBI) 1991: 15) – a very similar proportion. The British economy is thus dominated to an unusually high degree by MNCs, which accounted for over 70 per cent of corporate profits in the early 1980s (Stopford and Turner 1985: 3).

Foreign MNCs tend to concentrate in high- to medium-technology industries – in motor vehicles, drugs, electronics, mechanical engineering and paper. But there has been a worrying tendency among US and European MNCs in some industries to use lower capital and higher labour intensity (semi-skilled labour) than in their home countries and to treat the UK as a location for mere assembly operations (Hamilton 1987: 184; Auerbach 1989: 273). In the words of Hamilton, 'foreign-owned multinationals tend to bring to the UK product and process technology which is "intermediate" between that of lagging British firms and that of lead multinationals'.

Foreign investors have been both suspected and welcomed, and their welcome has increased during recent times of high unemployment. What, then, has been their effect on the British economy in general and on manufacturing industry in particular? On average, according to Stopford and Turner (1985: 4), foreign MNCs are more profitable, use their employees more productively, invest more and are bigger exporters. Recent figures published by the CBI (1991) show this gap to be considerable. Thus value-added per employee in UK-owned large firms (with net output of more than £200 million) of £24.400 can be contrasted with £35.400 in foreign-owned ones, and respective figures on capital spending per employee are £2.889 and £3.999. This all-round superiority becomes less striking when one compares them with companies in the same industrial segment: that is, export-prone ones (Stopford and Turner 1985). But the fact remains that, for the economy in general and in terms of offering a demonstration effect to British companies, they are good news. Auerbach (1989: 272) puts this even more strongly when he says: 'the weight of inward investment in the UK is undeniable, as is its overall beneficial effect for British capitalism'. Some industries, such as the car industry, would no longer be in existence if it were not for the Japanese presence.

But some negative effects of inward investment must be noted, particularly in the area of R&D and in some aspects of employment. Usually R&D and design activities have remained at the national headquarters of foreign MNCs, so the danger arises of Britain becoming a so-called 'branch plant' economy – an effect also manifested in the tendency towards lower skill intensity and insufficient spin-off effects for the local economy of supplier firms. Such an economic region experiences insufficient technology transfer and boosts to human resources development. It may become technologically dependent on foreign firms and thus enter a downward spiral in the field of technological innovation.

The effect of foreign MNCs has been largely positive in terms of employment creation. During the last recession, they cut employment less than their UK equivalents (Hamilton 1987: 192), although two caveats must be raised. First, employment may be more insecure in MNCs with 'branch plant' characteristics in as far as they are easier to close down and, hence, more likely to relocate to more profitable sites or activities – accounting for the accusation of footlooseness. Second, the absence of many 'headquarters' functions, including R&D, and the strong concentration on semi-skilled activity means that they do not create as many skilled and top-level jobs as would their British equivalents, nor do they boost skill development more generally. Although Japanese companies must be exempted from the latter charge, they have been accused of curtailing managerial promotion chances by filling top management positions with Japanese nationals.

In the field of industrial relations foreign companies are sometimes less willing to compromise than British ones, but cannot generally be said to have a bad industrial relations record. There is, however, a greater indirect control over labour by MNCs in that the threat to relocate production to another country serves to dampen labour militancy and increases performance pressure. Such a threat is more real if the above-mentioned 'branch plant' syndrome prevails, and/or when the company practises dual-sourcing, as is the case, for example, with the car companies Ford and General Motors. Actual relocation, however, has been extremely rare. Lastly, trade union negotiators find it much more difficult to deal with local managers who take their orders from a remote parent company.

The Japanese are again a special case in the field of industrial and employment relations. On the one hand, they have been associated with a more egalitarian and more consultative personnel policy. On the other hand, their predilection for green-field sites and areas not associated with labour militancy, together with their insistence on single union representation or even 'no-strike' deals, has begun to undermine British union leverage. More recently, some concern has been expressed about the impact of their subcontracting methods – particularly the JIT regime – on supplier firms, particularly about the much-increased work intensity and control it is said to have brought for production workers (Delbridge et al. 1992: 97f). During the last decade, however, the positive demonstration effect of Japanese organizational innovativeness has received more attention than any negative effects their production methods and sourcing practices might have.

The negative impact mentioned above is often highlighted by political commentators who contrast the openness of the British economy to foreign investors with the much more closed nature of economies in continental Europe, including France and, to a greater extent, Germany. This lack of reciprocity is becoming more worrying with the development of the single European market (SEM) and is seen to contradict its basic principles.

Internationalism, it was suggested earlier, is not only indicated by a company's FDI but also by its foreign trade. Historically, Britain has been a very important trading nation, and its large companies have been international in this second sense as well. More recently, however, the British share of world trade in manufactured goods has steadily declined, and Britain now has a negative trade balance. The activities of MNCs have contributed greatly towards this trend. Thus in 1990, the UK had only 8.7 per cent of exports of the world's 11 most advanced countries, as compared with Germany's 20.2 per cent and, less spectacularly, France's 9.8 per cent (CBI 1991: 13). During the 1980s there occurred no detectable movement towards international markets (Millward et al. 1992: 17). Moreover, the composition of export destinations is not sound. There is still too heavy a concentration on developing countries, where the demand structure does not encourage technological updating and where demand tends to be unstable. At the same time as export activity has declined, FDI has notably increased. Hood (1986: 89) sums up this situation well when he says that 'the UK displays an unusual combination of highly aggressive international business, emerging from sectors in sharp domestic decline'.

Germany

Many large German firms also have a long tradition of internationalization. Thus, large firms in the chemical and electrical engineering industries were already important foreign direct investors by the First World War, but the Second World War destroyed these foreign links which were revived again from the 1960s onwards. Due to these political contingencies, the German route to internationalization after 1945 became predominantly one of exporting, and FDI developed more recently and more hesitantly than in Britain. In several recent years, Germany was the largest exporter in the world. In 1986, German firms exported five times as much in value terms as they allocated to FDI (Julius and Thomsen 1989: 20), and the bulk of exports has been going to developed countries. From the mid-1970s onwards, however, FDI has increased at a notable rate (Olle 1985: 1). Although the exporting route was still dominant for most large companies in the 1980s, the rate of FDI has grown more strongly than that of exporting (ibid.: 7). Germany now occupies the second place in Europe in volume of outward FDI and has a higher annual outflow of capital than Britain, but in terms of accumulated stock still comes well behind Britain (see Table 5.1). Investment occurs both on green-field sites and by acquisition.

Investment abroad is concentrated on industrial segments of domestic strength, such as vehicles, machine-building, chemicals, electrical engineering, and iron and steel, and also shows a steadily increasing share in high-tech industries. As in Britain, concentration among MNCs is high: in 1981, 57 per cent of all FDI was owned by only 128 large companies and, of these, 16 owned more than one-third (Olle 1985: 2). German MNCs are among the largest in Europe.

If we look at FDI in relation to all investment by German MNCs, then it is notable that it has not changed much in proportional terms between 1974 and 1982, although production abroad accelerated significantly in the same period. According to Williams et al. (1990: 6), in 1988 FDI was only one-ninth of domestic investment. Also a large proportion of FDI is directly connected with exporting and is in the areas of distribution and servicing rather than in manufacturing.

Among the biggest foreign investors in terms of absolute volume VW came top, followed by Bayer, Hoechst and BASF, and then by Siemens, Daimler, Bosch and Mannesmann (Olle 1985: 3). When FDI is regarded in relation to domestic investment, only some of the big chemical companies (Bayer, Hoechst and Beiersdorf) invested as much or nearly as much abroad as at home. For most of the other big investors, however, foreign investment was far less than domestic. Seen in such relative terms, multinationalization is relatively low in such high-tech or high-skill industries as automobiles and precision optics. Thus in the late 1980s, VW had less overseas production than the American car producers, and BMW and Mercedes had no foreign subsidiaries (Dicken 1992). In addition, high-value, technologically advanced VW cars were produced only in Germany. Streeck (1989: 148) speculates that the German industrial culture, supporting a combination of high-skill labour with high-tech production, is indispensable to car manufacturers, and Porter (1990: 369) quotes the manager of Zeiss, a precision optics company, as confirming this argument for this skill-intensive industry. The picture, however, has begun to change during the 1990s. Severe recession, increased international pressure on cost structures, together with the opening up of the low-wage countries of Eastern Europe, are inducing more and more companies to relocate production or start outsourcing to firms in Poland, Hungary and Czechoslovakia (*The Economist*, 24 October 1992: 91; personal communications from German managers during field work in 1993).

Table 5.1 shows the overall volume of FDI in recent years. FDI is placed predominantly in developed countries. In 1988, 52 per cent of investment was in Europe (41 per cent in the EC), 40 per cent in the Americas (28 per cent in the USA), 2 per cent in Japan (Smyser 1992: 201) and only a small proportion in developing countries. Few German corporations are as large and as globally orientated as the giant American and Japanese companies, and some German politicians are becoming concerned that the global economic system is being taken over by the dual power of the USA and Japan (ibid.: 201–2). Only a few of the chemical giants and Siemens are making a concerted effort to become global players (ibid.). Germany has, however, an historic advantage in Eastern Europe and Russia, and changes in this part of the world will stimulate FDI in years to come.

The German debate on outward FDI has concentrated on its impact on employment. There has been no unequivocal answer to the question of whether FDI always leads to job exporting. Very generally, it has been found that this is not necessarily the case among German MNCs. Their FDI, it is suggested by Olle (1985: 88f), has predominantly been motivated by considerations aimed at the expansion of markets and not by substitution of home production. This optimistic evaluation may, however, be less applicable in the 1990s.

Inward investment by foreign MNCs has always been far less than Germany's outward investment and, as shown in Table 5.2, it is low by comparison with other advanced countries. German MNCs make a far bigger contribution to total turnover than foreign ones which, in 1980, were responsible for 23.6 per cent of annual turnover (Olle 1985: 11). During the 1970s, both the share of production and of employment of foreign MNCs fell appreciably: a trend contrary to that experienced by most other advanced societies (Wohlmuth 1985: 24). In the 1980s, FDI stagnated and was lower in volume than that located in France (*The Economist*, 23 June 1990: 89). Between 1982 and 1991, foreign direct investment constituted only 1 per cent of domestic investment (*Blick durch die Wirtschaft*, 31 May 1994). But despite this seemingly lower foreign involvement, the proportion of those employed in foreign-owned companies was, in 1986, nevertheless at the same level as that in Britain: 13 per cent of all manufacturing employment (figures quoted by Amin 1992: 8). Investors are mainly American and European but there has also been a gradual increase in Japanese investment. Thus, in 1990, about 7.5 per cent of Japanese investment went to Germany (Smyser 1992: 203), and in 1992 there were around 110 Japanese manufacturing enterprises, as compared with about 125 in France and 190 in Britain (Eltis 1992: 7, chart 4).

Willemsen (1989) attributes this stagnation in inward investment to a lack of attractiveness of Germany as an investment site. He blames comparatively high direct and indirect labour costs, energy costs and the high costs arising from rigorous environmental legislation. In addition, he bemoans the excessively high tax burden in comparison with other European countries. Total German tax burden of 70.4 per cent, according to a recent study by the *Institut der Deutschen Wirtschaft*, compares with a French and British burden of only 53.5 and 37.9 per cent respectively (Willemsen 1989: 116). Other commentators, such as Julius and Thomsen (1989), see the German system of employee co-determination as a deterrent for investors. But an additional reason for the underdevelopment of inward investment into Germany must lie in the great difficulty confronted by would-be investors contemplating acquisition. Takeover can only occur if a firm is quoted on the stock market, and, as pointed out in Chapter 3, only a minority of large firms is quoted. But even where firms are quoted, takeover is often prevented by the highly concentrated ownership structure, by legal arrangements giving certain shareholders more voting rights than their share merits or by bank protection (Anglo-German Foundation 1993). If we consider that the other two advanced countries with very low inward FDI are Switzerland and Japan, low amounts of FDI may be as much connected with a country's industrial strengths as with its shortcomings as a production site. Whatever the main reason for this stagnation in FDI, there is now concern in some circles about the imbalance between outward and inward investment (Dierkes and Zimmermann 1989).

Social and economic consequences of inward investment are not widely discussed in the literature. This may be due to the lesser overall weight of foreign MNCs in the German economy and, with notable exceptions, to the lesser threat they pose for domestic firms, in comparison with the British situation, in employment, industrial relations and technology transfer terms. A worrying economic consequence may be that low amounts of FDI mean few technological and organizational stimuli and insufficient opportunities to learn from superior foreign examples.

France

In comparison to the other two societies, France has been lagging as an international foreign investor (Julius and Thomsen 1988: 22). In the earlier post-war decades, the volume of French outward FDI was well below that of Germany, and a relatively high proportion was in the developing countries of North Africa and parts of the Middle East where France had a political influence. Even in 1980, 30 per cent of foreign subsidiaries were still in such countries, with former colonies in Africa being particularly prominent (Macharzina 1986: 3), but the lion's share of investment has gone to the USA (Julius and Thomson 1988: 22). Since the 1980s, FDI has greatly increased and France become a truly international investor, as indicated by the growing volume in Table 5.1. Investment has been mainly in the energy sector, and FDI in manufacturing has been relatively underdeveloped.

Concerning manufacturing, Ghertman (1986: 46) describes French MNCs as doing well in industrial segments where good engineering is combined with state diplomacy, as in military equipment. But he is less sanguine about their competitiveness on world markets where cost effectiveness becomes an important consideration. Evidence from the car industry shows that French production strategy has remained highly localized (Dicken 1992: 304). More generally, the capacities of French MNCs reflect their strong dependency on the state and bear witness to the weakness of horizontal institutional connections with trade associations, banks, research institutes and SME supplier firms. French companies cannot draw strength from the dense networks enjoyed by German companies, but neither are they as weakly embedded as British MNCs.

Traditionally, France has been hostile to inward investment, and the relatively high level of public ownership has also precluded it. But attitudes began to change in the later 1980s, and privatization has given some scope to FDI, although this has been strictly controlled by the state. In recent years greater efforts have been made to attract foreign investors, sometimes in fierce competition with the UK, and inward investment notably accelerated in the 1980s. During the mid-1980s, enterprises with foreign participation accounted for 21 per cent of industrial employment, 26 per cent of industrial investment (*Service des Statistiques Industrielles* 1988: 46) and 26 per cent of total sales (Julius and Thomsen 1988: 23). According to Julius and Thomsen (1989: 23), France now has the highest participation by foreign investors in manufacturing industry of any G5 country. The biggest investor is the USA, and Germany occupies second place (ibid.: 50). France has also begun to attract Japanese investment and, by the beginning of the 1990s, had over-taken Germany but still received far less than Britain (Eltis 1992). Its attraction for Japanese investors is its central European location and its moderately high wages.

The second internationalization strategy – exporting – is not much more developed than in Britain. Although the overall volume is relatively high, its composition is not sound, and France has been running a trade deficit in recent years. Exporting cannot be considered an alternative to FDI but, rather, a complementary strategy.

GLOBALIZATION

To what extent do the national patterns of internationalization reviewed suggest that, during the last decade or so, changes in international economic integration have reached a qualitatively new stage which is best described by the label globalization? There has certainly occurred a marked quantitative increase in both outward and inward investment, an entry of new investors, the opening up of new investment sites in Eastern Europe and a much increased global competition. Increased growth and complexity of FDI has been accompanied and facilitated by growing global financial integration and by the development of global communication and co-ordination networks. But all these developments do not in themselves constitute sufficient criteria to talk about globalization in the sense of a qualitatively new stage of internationalization.

When we examine the patterns of international trade and of outward FDI we can see the following: first, the globe is increasingly being divided into trading blocs, based on South East Asia, North America and Western Europe, and that European countries trade primarily with each other and only marginally with the rest of the globe; second, in terms of outward FDI, Japan and the USA are the only genuinely global economic powers but have remained only lightly affected by inward FDI. Thus, only 6.5 per cent of American equities and 4.3 per cent of Japanese were being held by foreign investors in the late 1980s (*The Economist*, 19 September 1992) – hardly a sign of global integration.

In contrast, the outward investment activity of our European societies has remained confined to traditional investment sites in Europe, and international mergers and acquisitions have not grown over the 1980s (Amin 1992: 8, table 2). France and Germany in particular are lagging in this respect. Germany, moreover, still gives preference to the export rather than the FDI route, and its industry appears to remain highly reliant on domestic industrial infrastructure for its production strategy. For France, too, both exports and FDI strategy show a high degree of dependence on domestic factors, particularly state intervention and support for selected industries. This is perhaps less true of Britain, whose MNCs are less technology-based and hence less reliant on domestic infrastructure which, in any case, has received less state development than in the two continental countries. Concerning inward FDI, the British and French manufacturing industries are now penetrated to an unusually high degree, but Germany remains dominated by domestic firms. Thus, few European firms have the global reach to contemplate global business strategies.

Is globalization perhaps increasing in terms of European companies' adoption of globally integrated production strategies? Fragmentation and global dispersion of corporate functions to the main trading blocks according to an integrated business strategy, is said to be a notable new development, particularly in industries experiencing rapid technological change and/or intensified competition (Amin 1992). Whereas Amin (ibid.) sees this development as replacing the old model of corporate organization with a clear division of labour between metropolitan headquarters and branch plants in less-favoured regions, Dicken's (1992) investigation of trends shows that European firms are largely absent among these new global operators. Dicken (1992: 196f) also sees little evidence that high value-added activities in the production chain have been moved away from the home country. Thus headquarters are only rarely moved away from the home country and key staff are still recruited predominantly locally. In the field of R&D, there are emerging a few international interdependent research laboratories, but the predominant position remains one of R&D being concentrated in the home country (ibid.: 199). This continued reliance on the educational, research and general institutional infrastructure by the vast majority of large MNCs is also emphasized by Porter (1990) and by Hirst and Thompson (1992). Even such a strong advocate of globalization as Ohmae (1990) unwittingly shows the continued relevance of national institutional and cultural features to companies' competitive strategy. But there are differences between industries and the firms within them in the degree to which they have been affected by globalization. Thus, it is notable that globalization trends have been quite pronounced in the chemical industry and that the British firm ICI has gone much further down the globalization route than the German chemical giants Bayer, Hoechst and BASF (Grant and Paterson 1994).

There is more evidence that a decoupling of the production process and a strategic dispersion over different national locations has been occurring. But, according to Dicken (1992: 202), there is no single and simple trend or pattern of dispersal emerging, whether at the global level or within countries. Also, dispersal has remained confined to some, predominantly assembly-based, industries and there is insufficient data to judge whether this practice has been increasing during the last decade. It would be unwise to exaggerate the ease with which corporations undertake relocation of production activities from country to country according to cost considerations. Although the threat of such relocation is sometimes employed, actual relocation is much rarer than is implied by the phrase about the footlooseness of large MNCs.

Although considerations of labour cost remain important in location decisions, changes in technology and in production policy have reduced their importance. The changed production paradigm, with its emphasis on diversified quality products and the use of skilled labour, has made investment in developing countries less attractive and, due to the demand for quick and flexible responses to market changes, also less viable (Schoenberger 1989). Hence production activities are now more confined to economically weaker areas in advanced, rather than developing, societies but may set in motion the same vicious circle of technological dependency. Of FDI into developing countries during the 1980s, the lion's share went to the newly industrialized South East Asian countries (*The Economist*, 19 September 1992, World Economy survey: 17), many of which no longer have lower wages than Britain.

To summarize the position on the dispersal and global integration of corporate activities, one can concur with Dicken (1992: 144), who concludes that emergent globalization co-exists with an enduring high degree of local differentiation and that MNCs have to manage an internal tension between globalization forces on the one hand and localization forces on the other.

But globalization has also been understood in terms of the rising prominence of a variety of qualitatively new processes, as outlined at the beginning of this chapter. There is no doubt that global integration in financial terms has greatly increased. New modes of communication and co-ordination across continents have assumed growing importance, in both the financial and the manufacturing sectors, but these have accompanied rather than caused globalization. A more significant new phenomenon is perhaps the growing trend towards new modes of cross-national horizontal integration. Thus joint ventures and strategic alliances of both an inter-European and an international kind have increased during the 1980s as a result of both technological change and intensified global competition. Vonortas (1990: 192) conceives them as an alternative to FDI which provides firms with higher flexibility in global technology acquisition and more effective marketing and distribution but may involve a partial loss of control. Such quasi-integration has occurred both between European firms and with American and Japanese firms (ibid.; Amin and Dietrich 1991; van Tulder and Junne 1988; Hamilton 1987: 193). It is notable, however, that such alliances are much more frequently undertaken by American and Japanese than European companies (Vonortas 1990). Interfirm co-operative alliances are formed to achieve the following objectives: sharing the costs and risks of R&D; gaining access to new areas of technology, as well as to new markets and new skills (Walsh 1991b: 121). One example of European collaboration in what Child (1987: 41) calls the co-contracting mode is Airbus Industries. Another, focused only on R&D, is the establishment of an information exchange on materials technology between European mass-producers of cars (van Tulder and Junne 1988: 3). In addition, collaboration between large firms and small innovative high-tech firms is also on the increase (Walsh 1991b). Such non-equity-based horizontal quasi-integration across national boundaries is certainly a qualitatively new phenomenon. It denotes both a more globally integrated business strategy and more interdependence across national boundaries, but at the present time it must still be regarded as a strategy complementing rather than replacing a domestically based R&D strategy.

When we turn to examine the claims about a growing homogenization of tastes and product markets, and, following from these, of converging production practices, the picture is complex and the evidence is not at all straightforward. On the one side, there is the claim about growing homogenization of tastes and product markets (Vonortas 1990: 189), and on the other side, there is talk about growing instability of consumption patterns and of shortening product life-cycles, constant innovation (Amin 1992: 18) and growing customization (Young and Hamill 1992: 5).

While there is a lot of support for the Piore and Sabel thesis that domestic markets have become more highly differentiated or multi-niche markets (ibid.), particularly in some industries, at the same time there is occurring some homogenization of taste and demand between countries (McGee and Segal-Horn 1992: 29). Companies are said to have adopted global marketing strategies 'designed to penetrate simultaneously the world's major markets with new or updated products' (United Nations 1988: 57, quoted by Amin 1992: 17), although, as I have shown, European companies do not yet trade in all parts of the globe. This more global reach is said to be particularly pronounced in markets for such durable consumer goods as cars, electronic entertainment equipment and selected branded foods and drinks, while tastes in other goods, such as most fashionware, most foodstuffs, many drinks and furniture, as well as many producer goods, remain nationally differentiated.

Despite some convergence towards a new 'flexibly automated' production regime, there remain distinctive national forms of capital investment, production organization, personnel practices and industrial relations which shape a more or less pronounced and coherent move away from a Fordist production paradigm (for further details, see Chapters 7 and 8). These differences between national production regimes are not only perceived and exploited by investing MNCs but are also reinforced and perpetuated by them. Although MNCs certainly absorb some of the features of their host country and may become a hybrid, their influence rarely spreads out to the rest of the economy. Also control and reward patterns continue to reflect dominant patterns in their home countries, due to the fact that managerial careers and access to key resources remain shaped by the dominant institutions of firms' home countries (Whitley 1994: 177).

While increased global integration has certainly restricted the autonomy of some national institutions, it has not eliminated them in the way suggested by the globalization thesis, as outlined by Hirst and Thompson (1992). Although the transnational corporation has become a rival of the nation state it has not rendered it completely impotent and ineffectual. The nation state still has an important role to play in both the domestic and the world economy. Intensification of global competition has, in some ways, made it more important for the nation state to keep its economy competitive although the means to achieve this have had to change in the face of growing global interdependence. Thus Porter (1990: 19), one of the foremost students of competitive strategy, concludes that:

> competitive strategy is created and sustained through a highly localized process. Differences in national economic structures, values, cultures, institutions, and histories contribute profoundly to competitive success. The role of the home nation seems to be as strong as or stronger than ever.

Sally (1994: 177f) sees the relationship between MNCs and governments as one of growing interdependence. Intensified world economic competition makes governments more dependent on strong MNCs, and the latter come to rely more on infrastructural facilities and the knowledge base of their home country. (For further discussion of the relationship between national states and MNCs, see Chapter 9.)

Thus German firms still raise their external finance predominantly through bank loans, and their British counterparts continue to rely on the stock market. In Germany even the highly internationalized chemical giants maintain strong relations with their national trade associations, while the much less embedded British ICI has severed its national connections to a far greater extent (Grant and Paterson 1994). There is still plenty of scope for a national policy supportive towards industry, particularly policies relating to the creation of social infrastructure and to education and research capacity. The French state has gone much further than this and has actively intervened to shelter its domestic industries against global competition. More generally, national institutions are still firmly in place, and international arrangements to replace them are slow to evolve. Even where international governance structures exist it is notable that they bear the strong imprint of the nation which was hegemonic at the time of their creation (Whitley 1994: 177). Thus the European Commission, Whitley suggests, tends to operate in a predominantly French and German, rather than a British or American way (ibid.).

There have also been some counter-tendencies to the expansion of globalization. Both the new production paradigm and the Japanization of subcontracting have brought moves towards a national reclaiming of production activities and towards the regionalization of subcontractor networks. Thus stages of the production process which were previously decoupled and sited in low-wage countries are now increasingly returned to domestic manufacturing; for example, production of clothing in Germany and Britain (Walsh 1991a) and electronic wafers in Britain (Henderson 1989: 158f). New demands in terms of quality and new technological capabilities make such a return more viable. New tendencies towards regionalization of supplier networks, connected towards the large buyer firm by JIT methods, joint design of products and the purchase of multicomponent subassembly, have been reported particularly in the car industry. Stipulation by the EC of a proportion of local content in products made by non-European firms has stimulated the development of local or, at least European, supplier networks. Another impulse towards regionalization has been noted in the German machine-tool industry where increasing demands for customized systemic solutions to process restructuring and innovation demand close consultation and geographical proximity. Thus growing globalization may well be combined with some regionalization, although no clear picture has as yet evolved. MNCs have tried to adjust to these dual developments by creating an optimum balance between strategies of centralization and decentralization.

Thus, to conclude, there has been a notable increase in world trade and an escalation in FDI, accompanied by new forms of international integration and by some weakening of national institutions. But globalization, however defined, is as yet only an emergent rather than a completed process, which has resulted in various geographical blocs rather than in one global sphere. Moreover, it has engulfed different advanced economies to differing degrees and has affected them in different ways: European MNCs have taken the globalization route much less avidly than American and Japanese companies. National industrial order is still very important for MNCs, both for the selection of markets and investment sites and for the competitive strength and strategy of global companies. Porter (1990) goes so far as to claim that the nation state has become more rather than less important for the global company.

The globalization process has interacted in complex ways with changes in the production paradigm and consequent corporate restructuring, which have led also to some renewed moves towards regionalization. But there is no doubt that an acceleration of globalization must be expected during the 1990s and that further impulses towards capital concentration and a weakening of the nation state will accompany it.

6. The small-business sector: source of economic regeneration or victim of economic transformation?

Small and medium-sized enterprises (SMEs) form the overwhelming majority of firms in the three largest European societies. But until the 1970s, both academic and general social interest in them was scant, particularly in Britain. It has been held that the size of an economy's small-business sector stands in an inverse relation to a country's degree of economic development (judged by GDP). It was, therefore, argued that the small-firm sector was an archaic remnant from an earlier stage of capitalism and that its decline should be considered as both inevitable and desirable.

More recently, it has been realized that these assumptions are unwarranted. The small-firm sector became regarded as an integral part of advanced industrial economies. During the 1980s, opinions shifted even further in favour of small firms, and academics and policy-makers at both ends of the political spectrum began to connect small firms with economic and social regeneration and a new economic strategy, pointing the way out of economic crisis. On the political right, small owners are presented as culture heroes – creators of an enterprise culture which would not only regenerate the economy but also revive the moral backbone of society. Among social scientists on the reformist political left, the work of Piore and Sabel (1984) articulated and inspired a new faith in small firms as the agents of economic and political regeneration. In their own and in much subsequent work (such as Hirst and Zeitlin 1989 and 1992; Sengenberger and Loveman 1988), small firms are not viewed in individualistic terms but rather as being embedded in a dense structure of both interfirm ties and social and political support systems. They are viewed as parts of regionally based networks of specialized and innovative firms, achieving a new balance between competition and co-operation. Both these analyses see the SME as an independent economic agent, performing a role which is complementary to that of large firms.

But this paradigm has not found favour among all political economists, and receives particularly harsh criticism from British scholars, inspired by regulation theory. Such analysts have continued to view the capabilities and economic role of small firms with wary scepticism (see, for example, Shutt and Whittington 1984; Rainnie 1991 and 1993), and connect its current resurgence firmly with the fragmentation tendencies in the large-firm sector, as discussed in Chapter 4. Their view of the small firm stresses above all its dependence on, and domination by, large corporations and denies it any economic or social regenerative role. Dubois and Linhart (1994), while also stressing the importance of 'large-firm' fragmentation strategies, leave more room for the emergence of networks between large firms and SMEs.

Evaluations of small-firm performance have, on the whole, payed very low attention to national differences in the overall profile of the SME sector. Such differences are much more pronounced than in the large-firm sector, as SMEs are more dependent on the socio-institutional framework in which they are embedded. Hence any conceptualization of the role of SMEs must supplement universal types of explanations by an institutionalist perspective. It is, therefore, useful to start with an examination of national historic records of the decline of the small-firm sector up to the early 1970s and relate these to social-institutional frameworks. But before such historical analysis, some of the problems of definition and measurement need to be addressed.

DEFINITIONAL PROBLEMS

A small business is said to be distinguished by the following characteristics: it utilizes a small amount of capital and a small labour force; it has a small share of a given market; it is often owner-managed and has a simple form of business organization (no layers of bureaucracy); and, lastly, it is legally and financially independent from other firms. This four-point definition still begs a number of questions, such as: what is a small amount of capital or a small labour force? Cut-off points differ both within countries, according to economic sector, but also between countries, and they are to some extent arbitrary. Comparisons between countries define size almost invariably in employment terms, and German and French statistics have a significantly lower

Table 6.1   Definitions of size of industrial enterprises in terms of the number of employees

	Britain	France	Germany
Small firm	200 or less	(1) – 50	(1) – 49
Medium-sized firm	No definition	51 – 300	50 – 499

Note: Both German and French statistics exclude the smallest firms with up to 10 (France) and 20 (Germany) employees.

cut-off point and distinguish more clearly between small and medium-sized firms than do British ones. These differences are shown in Table 6.1.

Because of these discrepant definitions, international comparisons usually employ the following OECD definitions:

Very small	< 20 employees
Small	< 100 employees
Medium	100–499 employees
Large	500+ employees

In Germany and, to a much lesser extent, France, the craft or artisan sector is still very important and is often included in statistics. In Britain it is considered very insignificant and is omitted. In the early 1980s, the German craft sector contained 70 per cent of all manufacturing firms, had 20 per cent of employees and accounted for 11.5 per cent of GNP (Doran 1984).

HISTORICAL DEVELOPMENT OF THE SMALL-FIRM SECTOR AND CURRENT STRENGTHS

Britain has long had the smallest small-firm sector, not only of European but of all advanced industrial societies. The decline started in the 1930s – at the same time as large-firm concentration became significant – and continued until the late 1960s/early 1970s. Table 6.2 shows the outcome of this relatively strong decline during the 1960s in international comparative terms.

Table 6.2   The proportion of employed in small (<200 employees) manufacturing enterprises (%)

Britain	31
France	45
USA	39

Source: Bolton Report (1971).

More recently, the decline has not only been halted but has been reversed. The 1980s have witnessed a veritable boom in small firm development in Britain. In Germany, the decline of the small-firm sector has proceeded more gradually and has not advanced quite as far. As in Britain, the decline was reversed from the mid-1970s onwards. If, however, the small and the medium-sized sectors are considered together, then they stayed fairly stable at around the 40 per cent mark during the period 1963–84 (Sengenberger and Loveman

*Table 6.3   The distribution of the number of industrial enterprises[a], of
               employment share and of gross value added[a] by employment size
               (%)*

| | No. of Units | | Employment | | Value added | |
	1981	1983	1981	1983	1981	1983
Small enterprises (20–99 employees)						
France	75.5	75.8	19.7	20.2	17.1	18.0
Germany	69.1	69.8	14.7	15.2	12.5	12.6
UK	76.6	77.4	13.8	14.9	10.5	11.5
Medium-sized enterprises (100–499 employees)						
France	19.9	19.7	25.4	27.1	22.8	23.3
Germany	25.1	—	24.6	25.6	22.5	—
UK	17.5	17.1	14.5	15.7	13.0	13.8

Note: [a] As a percentage of enterprises employing more than 20 people.

Source: Eurostat, *Structure and Activity of Industry*, various issues, quoted by Dunne and
Hughes 1990.

1988: 58). In France, the proportion of SMEs stayed almost constant up to the
middle 1960s, reflecting the late development of France's large-firm sector.
From the early 1970s onwards, the number of SMEs, including tiny firms,
began to grow again. Table 6.3 shows the comparative European strength of
small firm employment and turnover in the manufacturing sector, stating the
position separately for small and medium-sized firms. It shows that the small-
firm sector is now of similar magnitude in Britain and Germany, while France
still retains a larger proportion of employment and output in small firms. When
we examine the proportional strength of the medium-sized sector in the three
societies, however, France and Germany both have a larger sector than Britain.
But the German economy contains larger enterprises in both the small-firm
sector and the medium-sized sector than that of the other two countries, and a
far higher proportion of its medium-sized firms remain under family ownership
and control.[1] This has obvious implications for stability, performance and
entrepreneurialism. Other comparisons show that Germany has far fewer self-
employed concerns without employees than both Britain and France (Bannock
and Albach 1991: 4; OECD 1992: 159); this is, of course, the most vulnerable
end of the small-business spectrum (Hakim 1988).

   This revival of small firms at the aggregate level, it must be remembered,
hides the very high chance of mortality at the individual level. In France,

almost 50 per cent of new small firms disappear within four years (Dubois and Linhart 1994: 67). In the UK, 12 per cent of businesses newly registered for VAT are deregistered within a year, and 35 per cent within three years (Johnson 1991: 247); and in Germany in 1985, 37 per cent of insolvencies were in firms less than four years old (Sengenberger et al. 1990: 32). But generally, the incidence of bankruptcy is much lower in Germany than in Britain, due to the much closer involvement of local banks in the general affairs of the firms they lend to. Bankruptcy rates have grown significantly during the 1980s (Vickery 1986: 32; Sengenberger and Loveman 1988: 19), and even more so, in the 1990s (OECD 1992).

Two questions arise. First, why did the British small-firm sector decline disproportionately strongly in the early post-war decades? Second, how do we explain the recent resurgence of this sector in all three societies, as well as in most other advanced societies, across a whole variety of economic sectors?

REASONS FOR DIFFERENTIAL DECLINE

Small firms are very dependent on their environment: both on their relations with larger firms and with social and political institutions. Where this environment provides a dense network of support structures the stability of the SME sector is much greater than in societies where small firms are relatively institutionally isolated. We shall briefly analyse the nature of this environment in our three societies in the earlier post-war period and beyond (a more extended discussion can be found in Lane 1991).

Political environment

In the political sphere, three aspects are important for enabling small owners to express their interests *vis-à-vis* the state: the system of political representation and the degree of political decentralization, as well as the size and organization of the small-business lobby. In Germany, the system of proportional representation, the federal political structure and the relatively high degree of self-organization of the industrial craft sector, supported by the system of Chambers, have combined to provide reasonably effective representation of small business interests and to ensure that, despite the dominance of a highly concentrated large-firm sector, SMEs have enjoyed remarkable stability over time. In Britain, none of these political conditions have prevailed, and SMEs have not been protected from the impact of market forces. This difference between the two countries is well illustrated in Doran's (1984) book on the craft sector and in the more general comparisons by Bannock (1976 and 1981) and by Bannock and Albach (1991) of the two small-firm sectors. The French sector of SMEs shares some features with that of Germany, except for the high degree of political centralization up to the 1980s and the lesser survival of an industrial craft sector. Hence support systems have been provided not so much by formal institutions but more by informal neighbourhood networks and have been less effective. Politically, the French system has been conducive to the representation of organized minority interests. Historically, the weight of the French SME sector, backed by the large petit-bourgeois peasant sector, has made it a very important political lobby, which politicians ignored at their peril.

The economic environment

Among economic factors impinging on SME viability, the financial system must be given pride of place. In Britain, the concentration of the banking sector has made access to capital more problematic than in Germany, and lending occurs on much more disadvantageous terms. Credit is mainly short-term with variable interest rates, and the cost is well above that incurred by large firms (Skidelsky 1993; Vitols 1994). Availability and cost of finance was still seen by SMEs to be the most important constraint on ability to meet business objectives in the early 1990s (Small Business Research Centre 1992: 27), and lack of capital is believed to account for the much lower rate of British small firms growing into medium-sized companies (Bannock 1994). Once a company has reached a certain size and is quoted on the stock market, acquisition or takeover is always a hazard.

French SMEs are less exposed to this hazard, but their access to bank capital has also been both problematic and costly (Lévy-Leboyer 1980: 122f; Vickery 1986: 38f), due to state influence over bank lending which, in the 1960s and 1970s, was strongly biased in favour of large firms (Stoffaes 1989: 123). Since the early 1980s, however, there has been some improvement in business financing for smaller firms, due to the greater availability of state-subsidized funds, channelled through various financial and other local institutions (Vickery 1986: 40).

In Germany, the financial environment has long been more favourable to SMEs. The banking system is more decentralized, and both municipal and co-operative banks lend to SMEs on a long-term basis at comparatively low cost and often at fixed rates of interest. This is due to banks' access to state-subsidized funds (for details, see Chapter 3).

These differences in access to finance and business advice by SMEs in the three countries have far-reaching consequences for expansion, performance and relations with larger firms. They result in different levels of investment and capital and labour productivity (Vitols 1994) which, in turn, influence technological innovation and export activity.

In both France and Germany, family ownership and management prevailed much longer than in Britain. Many commentators connect the relative economic vitality and entrepreneurial spirit of German craft enterprises with its ownership status. A second economic factor, reinforced by cultural habits, which sustains small firms in certain domestically orientated industries in France and Germany, but not in Britain, has been the greater regional segmentation of the home market and a more pronounced consumer prejudice against high-volume goods.

THE REVERSAL OF DECLINE: SOME EXPLANATIONS

Whereas some studies of the resurgence of the small-firm sector seek explanations mainly in the inherent characteristics of small firms and their alleged superior or inferior economic capacities and social conditions, other analyses see the answers in the new structures and strategies of the large-firm sector, as outlined in Chapter 4. Five different types of explanations will be examined here:

- government 'small business' promotion programmes;
- influence of recession;
- inherent advantages of the small firm;
- the 'flexible specialization' thesis;
- the fragmentation strategies of large firms.

Government 'small business' promotion programmes

In Britain, a turn-about in governmental and academic thinking on the small-firm sector can be dated to 1971, the year of publication of the Bolton Report. This report evaluated the contribution of smaller firms to general economic health very positively, and some economists began to wonder whether there was, perhaps, a connection between Britain's undistinguished economic performance and the underdevelopment of its small-firm sector. Political enthusiasm for the sector escalated in the 1980s when the Conservative government began to propagate the idea that a revitalization of capitalist society – not only economically but also morally – could be achieved through the development of the small-firm sector. This complete change of attitude was accompanied by a host of political measures (Johnson 1991: 241f). On the one side, these measures tried to provide the supportive environment which had been lacking, and, on the other side, they eased and eliminated regulations of various kinds. Government-sponsored agencies offering advice and training, such as Small Business Services and the New Enterprise Programme, and schemes offering financial assistance or better access to capital, such as the Business Start-up/Business Expansion scheme and the Loan Guarantee Scheme, tried to kindle the entrepreneurial spirit. Relaxation of various tax demands (particularly in enterprise zones) and employment and health and safety regulations attempted to ease the life of entrepreneurs once their businesses were established.

In Germany a policy on SMEs had been an integral part of economic and social policy (*Mittelstandspolitik*) throughout the post-war period. After 1977, there occurred some change in government policy towards a stance of more active and sustained support for small businesses (Bögenhold 1985: 85; Neumann and Unterwedde 1986: 183), but there never developed quite the same 'small-firm' euphoria and the celebration of an enterprise culture as in Britain. It is, however, notable that government policy on the economic and social regeneration of the former German Democratic Republic has made the creation of SMEs one of its cornerstones (Wassermann 1992: 115). In the case of France, despite much political rhetoric in favour of SMEs, actual policy has long discriminated against them in favour of large firms. A proactive new policy on small firms arrived only in the early 1980s. (For details on agencies and policies assisting small firms, see Vickery 1986: 40f).

A recent comparison of government promotion of small firms in Britain and Germany (Bannock and Albach 1991: 10) established the following: Germany targeted a much higher proportion of spending specifically towards SMEs; German funding aimed at growth whereas British subsidy supported start-ups; Germany's funding was much more decentralized than Britain's; the German, but not the British government channelled significant resources into R&D (20 vs. 2 per cent of funding). Whereas German policy was interventionist but offered 'help for self-help', British policy was mainly concerned to remove, or compensate for, market imperfections (ibid.: 13). Lastly, government support for smaller firms in Germany has not entailed much relaxation of regulations in social legislation or wage determination (Weimer 1992: 314).

Such changes in government policy, Sengenberger and Loveman (1988: 45) point out, are premissed on the belief that small firms are innately dynamic and, in the past, have either been impeded by too much government regulation or been the victim of imperfections in the capital market. Although such changed government policies undoubtedly contributed to the revival, particularly in Britain, they do not explain it (ibid.; Johnson 1991: 243).

Influence of recession

The fact that a comparable small-firm revival also occurred in the recession of the 1930s has led various commentators to connect the present expansion of the 'small-firm' sector with the business cycle. While some analysts single out unemployment as the push factor behind individual entrepreneurship, which is further stimulated by the availability of government start-up schemes, by cheap bankruptcy stock of machinery and premises and by the greater availability of cheap and docile labour, those believing in the innate virtue of small firms claim that its inherent flexibility permits it to adjust better to recessionary conditions than do large firms.

Sengenberger et al. (1990: 44) argue that the recession alone cannot explain the revival, as the latter occurred in a very large number of countries with widely variant macroeconomic conditions. They see the business-cycle downturn as merely coincident with a major institutional crisis and hence expect the revival to outlast the recession. Other analysts, in contrast, have made a strong case for the importance of recession and unemployment as at least partially important explanatory factors, particularly in Britain. Thus there is substantial evidence to show that for a significant proportion of new British business founders, actual or anticipated unemployment was a reason for the start-up (Hakim 1988; Johnson 1991; OECD 1992; Small Business Research Centre 1992: 7). It seems that Sengenberger dismisses this explanation too indiscriminately. It is of considerable importance in countries where high levels of unemployment coincide with government start-up schemes for the unemployed – as in Britain and France – and with a superficially successful simulation of an enterprise culture, as in the British case. Such a prominent presence of the unemployed among new business founders also explains the discrepantly high representation of the precarious category 'self-employed without employees' among British as compared with German and, to a much lesser extent, French small-business owners. (The figures for Britain, France and Germany are respectively 68.5 per cent, 52.9 per cent and 39.2 per cent; OECD 1992: 159, table 4.3).

Inherent advantages of small firms

While the previous explanation referred to one alleged small-firm superiority – its greater flexibility – some 'small-firm' advocates attribute to it a host of other virtues. Some of the claims made by the Bolton Report can be seen as representative of this position, and more recently it has been espoused by economists, such as Bannock (1981, 1984), as well as by many politicians from both ends of the political spectrum. Let us examine these claims in the light of data on small-firm economic performance and social attributes from our three societies.

The first claim states that small firms are particularly innovative, in both process and product terms. This claim has caught the public imagination particularly strongly because the small owner of the high-tech firm seems to represent the core values of the enterprise culture. While such firms have undoubtedly increased in number from the late 1970s onwards (Oakey et al. 1988: 6; Saxenian 1989: 453; Grabher 1988; Walsh 1991b) and have made an important contribution in such sectors as electronics, scientific instruments, software and biotechnology, their share of all small firms is exceedingly small. A country's record of innovativeness still depends mainly on the R&D spending of large firms (Pavitt 1970). A German–British comparative study of the mid-1980s (Anglo-German Foundation 1988: 9) found that such small high-tech firms were more numerous in Britain and also more advanced in creating leading-edge technology and new market niches. The first factor is ascribed to the easier availability of venture capital in Britain, while the second is connected more speculatively with British individualism. Porter (1990: 377), too, connects the relatively low volume of new business formation in Germany with a poorly developed market for risk capital, as well as with a strong stigma attached to business failure and a high degree of risk-averseness in the population. Britain may thus have a critical edge in the founding of high-tech businesses, but it fares less well in sustaining and developing them. Thus a study of the Cambridge Phenomenon (Saxenian 1989) points out that the British business environment is not supportive of firms' longer-term needs and has prevented their growth and even longer-term survival (ibid.: 454; Alford and Garnsey 1994). Large firms have been too insular to encourage cross-fertilization of ideas and technology transfer, and any contact usually takes the form of acquisition (ibid.). Thus the few firms which have expanded successfully were promptly taken over by larger firms.

Small innovative firms in general are commended for generating more innovation in relation to R&D spending than large firms. They are often active in the early phase of the innovation process but usually have to hand over to large firms at the later, more costly stages. But a large proportion of small firms do not even aim to innovate, and function mainly as so-called 'extended work benches' to larger firms. National differences in process and product innovation were established by a comparative study on the use of microelectronics in production (Northcott et al. 1985). Although this technology is considered more suitable for small-scale production, the study found that, in firms with fewer than 200 employees, its introduction lagged behind that in larger firms. German small firms were found to be the most-frequent users in both product and process terms, French firms the least-frequent users, and British smaller firms occupied a middle position on both counts.

The French underdevelopment (relative to Germany) of high-technology small and medium-sized firms is also bemoaned by Stoffaes (1989: 121–2), who goes so far as to describe this sector as 'a technological desert'. The problems encountered by small innovative firms in France are described by Dubois and Linhart (1994: 77) in their review of 'technological districts'.

They are seen as highly reliant on large firms and state agencies outside these districts, impeding their growth and autonomy. In Germany, SMEs are widely seen as innovative problem-solvers for the large-firm sector (Löhn 1989: 96; Vitols 1994). A significant proportion of small industrial and craft firms are highly capital-intensive and use state-of-the-art equipment to produce for both national and international markets (Weimer 1992: 314; Kotthof and Reindl 1990). They can rely on more support from large firms, banks, sectorial institutions and government than can their British and French counterparts (Anglo-German Foundation 1988: 14; Bannock and Albach 1991: 10; Vitols 1994). This superiority of German SMEs in technical performance over their British and French counterparts is paralleled by superior export performance (*Economie et statistique*, 207 (1988): 18). Thus, to sum up, a significant proportion of SMEs have an important contribution to make in the field of innovation but it is largely complementary to that of large firms, and the magnitude of this contribution varies according to their national institutional environment.

The second claim for the superior performance of small firms is that in the 1980s they had a better record in net employment creation than large firms. This claim is confirmed for all three countries (Sengenberger and Loveman 1988: 18) but should not lead to exaggerated expectations. The biggest increase is recorded for the smallest firms, and the overall annual contribution to employment creation is very modest indeed, particularly if transfer of employment from larger firms is excluded. Storey (1982: 21) puts addition to gross stock of jobs annually over a decade at a mere 1.5 per cent, and Sengenberger et al. (1990) and Johnson (1991) point out that employment growth can mainly be attributed to a very small number of rapidly expanding firms, whereas the bulk of small firms grow very little or disappear completely after only a short period.

A third alleged advantage held by the small firm is that it offers a number of cost advantages, arising from both lower wage costs and from inferior social payments, as well as from less-stringent enforcement of regulations in such areas as health and safety. Data from our three countries confirm the lower wage costs, particularly for France and Britain, and to a much lesser degree for Germany. But this wage differential does not necessarily lead to greater savings because productivity is lower in small firms and thus does not lead to significantly lower unit wage costs (Sengenberger et al. 1990: 30–40). But there are also fundamental differences in the level of social benefits, where smaller firms lag behind in areas such as pension payments. But again, German SMEs are found to be somewhat exceptional, lagging behind large firms only in the payment of voluntary extra benefits (Kotthoff and Reindl 1990: 340). This overall moderate cost advantage of small firms may have played a small part in the shift to smaller units but, again, it offers only a small part of an explanation. First, this cost advantage is nothing new; second, the countries with the most pronounced growth of small firms do not have the largest differentials (Sengenberger et al. 1990: 45); third, the new production paradigm has moved away from pure considerations of cost to concerns with quality, versatility and innovativeness, which are difficult to achieve with a low-wage labour force.

What, then, can we conclude from the evidence on small-firm characteristics presented above? Does the SME possess inherent strengths which could turn this sector into the engine of economic regeneration? The above review has shown that, while SMEs have undoubtedly some positive contributions to make, these are often balanced by negative features. Furthermore, it is impossible to give one encompassing answer for all types of firms, and it is necessary to distinguish between subtypes: first, between independent firms producing for a market niche and firms acting as subcontractors for larger firms (in Britain, for example, 51.5 per cent of SME manufacturing firms undertake subcontracting; Small Business Research Centre 1992: 17); second, among the latter, between those entirely dependent on large firms and those innovative problem-solvers where there exists a degree of mutual dependency between buyers and suppliers. This variety of economic function is, in turn, linked to a wide range of social standards from sweatshops at one extreme to model employers at the other end of the continuum. The above type of explanation neglects this heterogeneity both within and between countries and focuses predominantly on the relatively small proportion of independent firms.

The 'flexible specialization' thesis

The explanation offered by Piore and Sabel (1984) and others following the flexible specialization paradigm is in a similar mould to the previous thesis, but sees the strength of smaller firms based more on collective, rather than on individual, capacities. Piore and Sabel do not focus merely on high-tech firms but also on more incremental innovation in fairly traditional industrial sectors, such as machine tools and textiles, and they outline the conditions under which innovativeness can develop. In contrast to the previous approach, Piore and Sabel do not make claims for the inherent strengths of small firms but see these as determined by the wider economic environment and by the social-institutional context in which firms are embedded. They connect the revival with a crisis in mass-production and in the large Fordist firm, due to intensified international competition, greater market volatility and the new opportunities for more flexible and decentralized production arrangements afforded by the new technology.

Their notion of industrial districts not only sketches out the institutional conditions necessary to sustain small-firm collaboration but also emphasizes the importance of a conjuncture between specialization and co-operation in regional agglomerations of such firms. It is well to remember that they do not see industrial districts present in all advanced societies but make it clear that innovative small firms and the formation of collaborative networks thrive better in some societies than in others. Their joint early work views small firms in isolation from large ones. It dwells on horizontal relations between small firms and puts forward a somewhat romantic notion of 'yeoman republics'. Sabel's later work (Sabel 1989 and 1990) also encompasses vertical relations between large buyer firms and their smaller suppliers, as well as seeing large-firm fragmentation strategies lead to smaller and more flexible units of production. But this work still focuses one-sidedly on the category of innovative problem-solvers.

Other writers adopt less restrictive definitions of industrial districts and dispense with the feature of innovativeness. Thus Dubois and Linhart (1994) stipulate simply a local base, a specific range of products, co-operation and a specific culture; while Zeitlin (1994), leaning on Alfred Marshall's original definition, retains the emphasis on specialization in distinct phases of a common industrial sector, but does not even assume a common cultural orientation. This ommission makes one wonder how co-operation comes about. Both also use alternative labels, such as local networks (Dubois and Linhart 1994) and productive system (Zeitlin 1994).

What, then, is the evidence from our three societies about the persistence or resurgence of industrial districts and other localized productive systems? France, according to Dubois and Linhart (1994), had numerous industrial districts earlier this century, but most were destroyed during the 1960s when government-initiated processes of corporate concentration and restructuring disrupted local networks. During the 1970s, new local networks began to emerge, and the authors distinguish between three different types: (a) old industrial districts, based on traditional products and specific local cultures which have experienced some renewal, such as the Cholotais; (b) networks of technological research and innovation, such as the Languedoc–Roussillon area; and (c) networks resulting from co-contracting between large firms and SMEs. But the authors' prognosis about these networks is, on the whole, pessimistic. While (a) is both economically and culturally autonomous it is not thriving, and (b) and (c) have remained too dependent on external economic and political agents. Political centralization has been too strong for too long a period to leave real autonomy to local institutions and networks, and 'the chances for the development of Industrial Districts in France are [considered] poor' (ibid.: 84).

Britain, the country with the largest increase in small-firm formation, also lends little support to the thesis about economic regeneration through industrial districts or even local productive systems (see the study by Penn 1992 of a Lancashire region for a vivid illustration of this claim). Like France, Britain once had thriving industrial districts. Indeed, as noted by Zeitlin (1994), areas like Lancashire cottons, Sheffield cutlery and South Wales tinplate led Alfred Marshall to coin the term 'industrial district' in the first place (Zeitlin 1994: 5). While some had already disappeared before the First World War, others became extinguished only during the 1960s, in the wake of the British wave of marked corporate concentration (ibid.: 5–6). But, given Zeitlin's denial of the necessity of a common cultural base of a religious, political or artisanal kind, it remains mysterious how extensive co-operation was generated and sustained, and one wonders whether, indeed, it was such a dominant feature of these local productive systems.

Both the demise of these systems and the complete failure to rekindle or create anew such local networks during the 1980s are plausibly explained by Zeitlin (1994) by reference to the following deficits in the British institutional 'small-firm' environment: the absence of close ties between firms and banks and the movement towards pronounced corporate concentration, facilitated by the financial system and supported by the state; and restrictive practices on the parts of unions, impeding timely innovation. More recently, re-emergence has been impeded by political centralization and the absence of an industrial public sphere, as well as by the weaknesses of trade and other business associations, preventing collective organization of firms. Here Zeitlin acknowledges that co-operation needs to be organized. But he stops short of recognizing that, in the absence of common traditional cultural orientations, trade associations could assume the role of developing common identifications, based on more formal associative ties, common interests and political values. Instead, he insists on a divorce between institutional structures and cultural orientations – a view shared by few institutionalists. He also fails to consider that British associations would need to fundamentally change their organizing principles and become more-encompassing organizations, able to develop and *implement* common policies.

The German state of Baden-Württemberg – the industrial district often quoted by Sabel – is not new but is primarily connected with the longer survival in Germany of remnants of the guild system and the craft culture developed on its foundations. In contrast to Italian industrial districts, German collaborative networks are not based on family, neighbourhood or political ties but are mediated by banks, Chambers, trade associations and often by regional and municipal states. Thus, for example, local businessmen, bankers and politicians may sit together on the supervisory board of the local savings bank to make sure that lending is orientated towards criteria favouring local economic development. Another example of such associative networking may concern R&D and involve firms, the relevant trade association and a local university. Although the literature has focused almost exclusively on

Baden-Württemberg, similar local networks focused on a particular industry can be found in other parts of Germany. Thus the furniture industry in Eastern Westphalia, tool-making in Remscheid, locksmith wares in Velbert/ Westphalia, medical products in Tuttlingen and optics in Wetzlar show comparable traits (Field notes 1993; Porter 1990: 373). It thus appears as if industrial districts depend on historically rooted cultural and institutional features which are extremely difficult to recreate through local political initiatives. They appear to be the exception rather than the rule.

What, if anything, can be rescued from the 'flexible specialisation' thesis? There is evidence from Britain (Small Business Research Centre 1992: 16) and from the various country studies reviewed by Sengenberger and Loveman (1988) that the scope for small innovative firms has significantly increased in recent years, both as independent niche producers and as suppliers with the characteristics of independent problem-solvers, and that such firms thrive particularly in conditions where institutional support structures for them are well developed. Amongst our three countries, this is particularly the case in Germany and, despite more than a decade of 'small-firm' government support, rarely in Britain, whereas France forms a somewhat ambiguous in-between case (see Lane 1991 for a systematic comparison).

When we turn to the consequences wrought by the move towards 'partnership' sourcing, Sabel's thesis of a process of dual convergence between large and smaller firms aptly describes some of the changes which have occurred in the last decade. The new and stringent demands now placed on small supplier firms will lead to a weeding-out process, resulting in an elimination of weak firms and a stabilization of the stronger small firms. This in turn will lead to an expansion of medium-sized firms and an overall reduction of the dependent small-firm sector during the 1990s. The surviving subcontractors will, in turn, be affected by their close collaboration with their large buyers. On the positive side, the high demands in terms of quality, design capacity and efficiency, coupled to some large-firm assistance to achieve higher standards, should raise performance levels in surviving small supplier firms. On the negative side, however, the increasingly closer organizational synchronization between large and small firms may come to undermine the very flexibility of small firms from which large firms set out to benefit in the new division of labour between firms. Last, the transformation of vertical relations between firms has been very uneven between industries and, given the different degree of embeddedness of SMEs reviewed above, between countries as well.

Fragmentation of large firms

Whereas the explanations for small-firm revival discussed so far ignore the often dependent status of SMEs, another approach, associated with the Regulation School and popularised by Shutt and Whittington (1987), goes to the other extreme. These authors attribute small-firm growth to a number of fragmentation strategies adopted by large firms in order to cope with the increasing demand and innovation risks, as well as with the ground lost to labour in the contest for control. In their account, then, the growth of the small-firm sector does not necessarily represent new and independent activity but constitutes a mere transfer. This may result in a net loss of employment and in a worsening of employment conditions and of opportunities for collective representation of labour. This theoretical approach thus regards small firms as largely unviable by themselves and thus dependent, and their negative features are given prime emphasis (see Rainnie 1993 for one example of this approach). The fragmentation thesis is, however, also promoted by some followers of the flexible specialization paradigm (for example, Sengenberger and Pyke 1990; Zeitlin 1994: 12), but is not accompanied by such indiscriminate negative stereotyping of small firms.

Statistics from all three societies, both on employment shifts from large to smaller units and on subcontracting and unbundling activities, confirm that a modest trend in this direction exists, although fragmentation is not evenly advanced in the three societies (for details, see Chapter 4). But the evidence is still sparse and ambiguous and consists mainly of data on employment transfer which is not generally accompanied by commensurate shifts in the volume of sales (see, for example, Bade 1987). Johnson's (1991) persuasive discussion of the situation in Britain – the country with perhaps the most pronounced corporate fragmentation in Europe – roundly discounts this process as having only very partial explanatory power. He concludes that it is the job-shedding policies of large firms rather than any fragmentation strategies which have played an important part in stimulating small-firm development (ibid.: 255). For France, however, strong links between 'small-firm' revival and fragmentation are claimed (Dubois and Linhart 1994: 75f), due to the greater emphasis by large firms on vertical disintegration and the adoption of co-contracting. But this claim is not supported by any data. It can thus be concluded that fragmentation trends are not uniformly strong in the three European countries and can, at best, offer only a partial explanation of the small-firm revival.

This explanatory approach also raises further questions. First, are small firms inevitably and invariably weak dependants of large firms? Second, if there has occurred some transfer in employment from large to smaller firms what does this transfer entail for employees in terms of employment conditions and working environment/work satisfaction.

The first question has already been addressed, and it is safe to conclude that Shutt and Whittington (1987) and other, mostly British, authors make too sweeping a claim. They completely ignore the independent strengths possessed by at least a significant minority of small firms, the efforts of some small firms to overcome their individual weaknesses through collective endeavour, as well as the changed market conditions working, at least partially, in favour of such firms. They also neglect the evidence from other countries, particularly Germany, that SMEs make considerable contributions to international competitive success (Porter 1990: 374) and should, indeed, be seen as an essential component of Germany's economic strength. This contribution is not a consequence of size alone but of the size-related private and family ownership and the craft culture so frequently found in this size category.

Whether or not fragmentation has been significant, a transfer of employment from large to smaller firms is now indisputable, and it is necessary to assess its consequences for labour. Is it possible to generalize on these consequences and, if so, how does the 'small firm' working environment compare to that offered by the large firm? To answer these questions we can examine such indicators as level of wages, fringe benefits, employment security, accident rates and degree of work satisfaction. It has already been established that in all three countries wages are lower and fringe benefits inferior in small firms (Sengenberger et al. 1990: 37; Vickery 1986: 30), although, due to the nature of the collective bargaining system, these differences are not pronounced in Germany (Vitols 1994). Employment security is lower, due to both greater instability and to a lesser degree of employment protection (Vickery 1986: 30, for France; Bosch 1988: 178, on German firms). Accident rates are higher, as a result of more-antiquated machinery, longer working hours, and due to less compliance with health and safety requirements. Thus, German statistics quoted by Wassermann (1992: 25) show that the fatal accident rate per 1,000 employees in the smallest size category of firms (1–19 employees) is double that reported for firms in the largest size category (over 1,000 employees). Lastly, the lack of bureaucratic hierarchy reduces promotion chances.

However, it may be argued that these inferior material conditions are amply compensated for by the greater work satisfaction gained in small firms and by the more personal work relations. While this claim is not sustainable for small firms in general, it does apply to a substantial proportion, particularly in the engineering industry and in high-tech firms. In such firms, workers are more likely to do a wide range of jobs and to gain opportunities to apply individual craftmanship (Sengenberger and Loveman 1988; Goss 1990) and hence to experience greater job satisfaction (Vickery 1986). A German survey on the content of work and the quality of work relations shows that SMEs tend to score better on autonomy and variability of work, on lower levels of shift work and noise, and on personal relations (Wassermann 1992: 26). Work satisfaction is particularly high in firms of the 'innovative problem-solver' type and also in high-tech firms (Scott and Roberts 1988: 13).

Such firms, unlike branch plants of large firms, provide the entire spectrum of employment functions and a high proportion of the manual jobs are skilled and semi-skilled (Mason 1987: 135; Sengenberger and Loveman 1988). The proportion of skilled workers is particularly high in Germany's craft firms which also train a discrepantly high proportion of apprentices. Sengenberger et al. (1990: 37) contrast proportions of 76 per cent of male manual skilled workers with 60 per cent for large firms. This high skill intensity is also confirmed by Kotthof and Reindl (1990: 15).

The next claim to be examined is that small firms generate less conflict than large ones. This claim of greater harmony in the employer–employee relation is based on the observation that both unionization and the incidence of strikes are much less pronounced. Thus, in Britain during the mid-1980s, a unionization rate of 29 per cent in very small (fewer than 25 employees) firms can be contrasted with one of 65 per cent in large firms (over 500 employees) (Gallie 1989: 11). Daniel and Millward (1983: 218), in their national survey, confirm the lower strike incidence for small firms. The pattern is similar in France (Amadieu 1990) and Germany. In the latter case, the low level of representation applies to both unions and works councils (Wassermann 1990: 220). A recent study of German SMEs claims that, independent of forms of representation, relations between owner-managers and employees are largely harmonious and that they work communally on the common project 'enterprise' (Kotthof and Reindl 1990: 14).

Opponents of this claim of greater harmony argue persuasively that the capitalist operating principle does not disappear in small firms and that, due to their greater exposure to market forces, exploitation of labour often has to be more intensive than in large firms. It therefore comes to undermine the demand for moral involvement of workers in the usually face-to-face relationship with employers. Low union density and strike incidence, it is further suggested, are due to a combination of employer reluctance to recognize unions (Gallie 1989: 11) and the difficulty unions face in organizing workers in dispersed units. Other indicators of the quality of the employer–employee relationship, such as labour turnover, unfair dismissal claims and evaluation of workers' preferences, show that in all three societies this relationship is far from uniformly harmonious (Mooser 1984: 47; Wassermann 1990).

Thus, to sum up this section, certain types of small firms do offer some advantages to their employees: they are particularly strong in opportunities for all-round skill utilization and the work satisfaction derived from a low division of labour and more holistic work tasks. But this advantage must be balanced against many disadvantages in material rewards, employment security and opportunities for collective organization.

CONCLUSIONS

None of the various explanatory approaches reviewed captures the diversity of small firms nor the complexity of the new division of labour between firms, both within societies and between them. The degree of small-firm dependence or complementarity depends on whether the firm functions as an innovative problem-solver or merely provides extra capacity; the incidence of either type of firm in a society is largely determined by the support systems made available to small firms. This applies with equal force to independent niche producers. Despite the many weaknesses in the notion of an 'industrial district', Piore and Sabel (1984) are best at appreciating this fundamental fact and in this way give important hints to 'small firm' policy-makers.

How, then, are we to evaluate the claims stated by both the political right and the soft left that the small firm is likely to point the way out of the present economic crisis and that it will lead to the regeneration of capitalist society? While it is unrealistic to assume that this mammoth task can be accomplished by small firms in isolation, it is not unreasonable to expect the small-firm sector to make a valuable contribution to this task. At the same time, it cannot be assumed that recent fragmentation tendencies and the resurgence of small firms point to the creation of a 'small-firm' economy and to a serious weakening of the large-firm sector. Many recent developments in capitalist society, such as competition based on constant technological innovation and associated globalization strategies, cannot be contemplated by independent SMEs. It is important to recognize, however, that large companies and SMEs have complementary strengths. A balanced size distribution, including also medium-sized enterprises, together with co-operation between large and small firms, is widely seen as a favourable condition of strong economic performance. Such a balanced composition and co-operative culture is most highly developed in Germany, and a significant part of the differential economic performance of the three societies is attributable to the pronounced differences in the SME sector highlighted in this chapter.

NOTE

1. Figures provided by Quack and Hildebrandt (1994: 15–16) show that the number of medium-sized companies with a turnover between FF50–500 million is almost twice as high in Germany as in France. Although we have no comparable figures for Britain, scattered evidence suggests that the British situation is closer to that of France than of Germany.

7. The transformation of industrial relations

One of the most striking transformations of the industrial scene during the last 15 years has occurred in the area of industrial relations: unions have lost influence both at the level of collective bargaining and in national politics, and there have occurred many shifts in the content and the level of bargaining. Managers have not only reasserted their right to manage but have also transformed industrial relations and labour management in significant ways. These transformations have had multiple causes, some of which suggest that we are dealing with more than a transitional phenomenon, although the new patterns have not yet acquired sufficient stability to warrant the label of post-Fordist. To appreciate the extent of recent changes in these areas and to grasp both the common and diverging experiences in different European societies it is first necessary to understand the state of industrial relations which was established during the earlier post-war decades, that is, during the Fordist period.

One of the central features of the Fordist period was the establishment of a class compromise between capital and labour. Mass-production, with its high concentration of workers in large establishments, led to high levels of unionization and the institutionalization of collective bargaining. Labour organizations were regarded as legitimate representative bodies of the working class and also gained a voice at the national level in more or less corporatist political bargaining. Economic expansion and rising productivity enabled capital to offer labour a trade-off for alienating forms of production organization and control in terms of high and rising wages and social benefits. Stable mass markets created the long-term predictability to grant employees employment security and to establish a standard employment relationship for the large majority of the labour force. In addition, in some countries labour's representative bodies also gained more or less formalized rights to participate in the allocation and utilization of labour in the production process.

But within this very general picture of industrial relations there existed a high degree of national variation: in the form and level of organization of both capital and labour; in the form and substance of bargaining; in the degree of class compromise attained; and in the consequences of all these features for economic performance. Britain, France and Germany each possessed very distinctive structures and styles of industrial relations, firmly grounded in historically evolved class relations and institutional structures, and leading to fundamentally different outcomes in terms of the balance of control between capital and labour.

ESTABLISHED NATIONAL PATTERNS

Germany

In Germany, industrial relations have been characterized by a dual structure: nationally co-ordinated unions that recruit and bargain at regional industry level are complemented by elected works councils and other forms of employee co-determination at the level of the enterprise and company boards; their functions, rights and obligations are clearly differentiated and regulated by law; formally, the unions have only an advisory role at the workplace, and works councils have no right to engage in collective bargaining or to strike, but have a peace obligation. But informally there has occurred a lot of mutual interpenetration between the two bodies in both functional and membership terms, and complementarity has been more prevalent than rivalry, contrary to the early fears of the unions (Thelen 1991). The wide range of information, consultation and co-determination rights possessed by works councils has endowed them with considerable leverage over managerial action in some areas, and managers need to secure the co-operation of their works councils. The 16 industrial unions are united in one union federation – the *Deutscher Gewerkschaftsbund* (DGB) – and, although there exist a few unions outside this federation, it has been the only one of general weight. The union movement, although only loosely co-ordinated by the DGB, nevertheless is cohesive, due to the small number of mostly large and industry-based unions and their centralized nature, and because the largest union – the giant IG Metall – assumes a trail-blazing role for the whole union movement. The state does not participate in collective bargaining but has shaped it through the provision of a comprehensive legal regulatory framework and its willingness to involve both unions and employer organizations in the social and employment aspects of national politics.

This orderly structure, the highly professional and efficient union organization, the moderately high level of membership and the legal guarantees of union and codetermination rights, have combined to create a strong labour movement. Although the unions are faced by an equally strong and united employers' association – the *Bundesvereinigung Deutscher Arbeitgeberverbände* (BDA), they have secured for the German working class high levels of wages and social benefits, as well as significant participation rights. The dual system has also served to defuse conflict and to resolve it via institutionalized means and has resulted in one of the lowest levels of industrial conflict in Europe. The mutually agreed substance of the class compromise has given rise to a co-operative style of industrial relations. Unions and works councils have not only asserted workers' rights but, in their moderate wage demands and avoidance of industrial action, have also been ready to assume joint responsibility for production and have been committed to keeping viable the German export-orientated production model. The weight of skilled workers in both unions and works councils has led to wage differentiation on the basis of skill, perpetuated the emphasis on training, and has also favoured the adoption of, and easy adaptability to, a technology-led production model. The co-determination rights of works councils have mainly centred on the social aspects of work and employment and have not approximated to the British pattern of joint regulation in labour deployment and allocation.

The good industrial relations record gained unions a high degree of political legitimacy and has secured their inclusion in many quasi-political decision-making bodies in a corporatist or quasi-corporatist manner, even after formal concertation came to an end in the late 1970s. The DGB – the umbrella organization – is politically close to the Social Democratic Party (SPD), but unions do not pay a political levy. It maintains its political independence and has taken care to retain a connection also with the labourist wing of the Conservative Christian Democratic Union (CDU). In sum, German industrial relations during the Fordist period serves as a textbook case of the establishment of a class compromise, serving both sides of industry well and contributing at the same time to the economic strength of the flex-Fordist model.

Despite considerable union adaptability and willingness to compromise, the system has created its own problems and has not been free from tensions. Industry-level bargaining has given insufficient manoeuvring space to enterprises and has weighed particularly heavily on SMEs. The strong juridification of the whole system and process of industrial relations has made for cumbersome, slow and costly decision-making processes in some areas and imposed very high costs, by world standards, on German employers. Wage and social costs are among the highest in the developed world and are increasingly viewed as an excessive burden by German industrialists, although high levels of productivity have, by and large, kept unit wage costs in line with those of major competitor countries (DIW 1994). A last problem, resulting from the relatively high degree of employment security of core workers achieved by the intervention of works councils, is the very closed nature of the employment system and the durable exclusion of weaker elements of the labour force from core jobs. Fears of a 'two-thirds' society, undermining social stability, are widely expressed (Turner 1991; Kern 1994).

France

In France, in contrast, the class compromise remained much more brittle and could only be sustained by the frequent substitution of state intervention for autonomous bargaining by the two sides of industry. There are a number of competing union federations, organized along political and religious lines. The two largest of them – the Communist *Confédération génerale du travail* (CGT) and the socialist-syndicalist *Confédération français démocratique du travail* (CFDT) – have traditionally regarded themselves more as class organizations locked into a battle for control than as negotiating bodies representing the interests of their members. Their militancy, lack of professional organization and relatively low level of membership have confirmed employers in their stance of avoidance or reluctant recognition. Elections to workplace representative organizations, however, have shown a much higher degree of informal union support.

Collective bargaining has occurred mainly between union federations and employers' associations at national inter-industry and industry level, and unions became negotiating partners without necessarily being representative of the workers for whom they bargain. Agreements were valid as long as one of the union federations signed. Unions rarely felt themselves bound by such agreements. Until 1969, bargaining rarely occurred at enterprise level, and bargaining between the two sides of industry has generally been considered poorly institutionalized. The state has often extended agreements to industries and regions which did not participate in the bargaining and hence also to non-unionized firms, thus reducing the incentive to join a union. There has been little legal regulation of strikes. Despite low levels of union membership, the level of conflict has been relatively high during the Fordist period. Periodic occurrences of mostly spontaneous and very short strikes have demonstrated a widely shared class antagonism. Union demands could not be ignored.

In addition to unions, there are other representative bodies at enterprise level: a health and safety committee; a system of works delegates who mediate between employees and employers on individual and collective grievances and who ensure that externally concluded agreements are implemented; a system of works committees, which are places for the exchange of information between employees' representatives and employers on conditions of employment and the economic situation of the firm (discussions on social and welfare issues were added in the early 1980s; Eyraud and Tschobanian 1985: 245). The works committee, which is chaired by a management representative, is not as strong as its German equivalent and dividing lines between the various bodies are not as clearly drawn. Hence management are often able to play them off against each other. The Auroux laws of the early

1980s added a further body: the innovative expression groups that involve all workers directly in discussions with management on issues relating to their work. They are in the nature of consultative groups, designed to bridge the wide communication gap between management and labour.

As indicated, the French state has played a very dominant role in industrial relations, intervening directly in collective bargaining and supplementing it by legal regulation. In addition, the exceptionally large public sector in the French economy has involved the state prominently as an employer, introducing exemplary practices and agreements. Lastly, the state's legal definition of the SMIC – *Salaire minimum interprofessionel de croissance*: the minimum wage – also represents a significant intervention in the bargaining process. But despite this prominent role in industrial relations to safeguard a class compromise, a genuinely corporatist political system with unions as partners in political decision-making processes has never developed.

Although there exists legal regulation of many aspects of French industrial relations it is not as dense and comprehensive as in Germany. The tenor of industrial relations has generally been antagonistic; distant and mistrustful relations between management and labour are said to have been widespread. At enterprise level French labour neither managed to achieve the high formal level of participation prevalent in Germany nor the widespread *de facto* joint regulation achieved in Britain. But the segmentation of the working class through competing unions has not prevented the establishment of a solidary wage policy and the institution of high levels of employment security and social benefits. The intervention of the state in these areas has presented French employers with highly regulated labour markets and considerable social costs.

The main concerns about industrial relations in France have been the lack of their institutionalization at enterprise level and the fact that class compromise was unstable and state-engineered rather than freely agreed upon by the two sides of industry. Among employers, the rigidity of the system of payment and of employment regulation have been prominent grievances, as have been the high social costs, exceeding those of all other European countries.

Britain

The British system of industrial relations has been characterized by a low level of formalization and the reliance, instead, on custom and practice and on voluntary and non-binding agreements. The large number of unions and the many diverse bases of recruitment have created a complex system, giving rise to a high level of friction. The unions are affiliated to a central Trades Union Congress (TUC), which is concerned with policy measures of national significance and has secured for unions a political voice at national level. The

TUC has been closely identified with the Labour Party through the political levy and the system of block votes. Unions are the only channel of industrial representation, and their long historical record and relatively high level of support have gained them a firm and widely accepted place in British industry. At the same time, however, the high level of conflict and the adversarial style of industrial relations, coupled with the impotence of the TUC to enforce any general policy, gradually began to diminish the social and political legitimacy of the British union movement.

Collective bargaining has a low level of formalization and could occur at a variety of levels. During the 1970s, however, a clear shift in negotiations from industry level to the work-place became discernable, and shop stewards became the most prominent negotiating agents. Although collective bargaining bodies and individual workers possessed few legal rights and obligations, customary rights in the areas of recruitment, training, work organization and labour utilization were far-reaching and strongly circumscribed the managerial prerogative and manoeuvring space in these areas. Demarcation practices by craft and other unions, that is the assertion of a monopoly right to certain work tasks and places, acquired particular notoriety. The notion of a worker's obligation to the employing firm and of the assumption of co-responsibility for its competitiveness has never been accepted. Although class compromise was firmly established in British politics, industrial relations were still adversarial in character. The system remained characterized by a high level of conflict, manifested both in the high incidence of strikes and of other less-organized industrial action. It has been widely regarded as contributing to Britain's undistinguished economic performance. The achievement of the British union movement for its members lay primarily in the comparatively high levels of workers' informal participation rights at shop-floor level. The level of wages, social benefits and employment rights, however, remained relatively low by European standards, although wage increases regularly exceeded increases in productivity.

The main tensions and rigidities in the British system of industrial relations thus differed from those in the other two countries. Employer and government grievances were focused primarily on the very low level of formalization and on the ambiguities and tensions created by this; the relatively high level of conflict and lack of employee involvement; and, last but by no means least, on the rigidities engendered by union control over many aspects of labour utilization. At the national political level, the lack of effectiveness of both the Confederation of British Industry (CBI) and the TUC in exerting influence over their membership led to disillusionment about the viability of corporatist modes of political decision-making.

Table 7.1 gives some indication of the comparative strength of the union movements in the three countries during the 1970s. An evaluation of these

Table 7.1   Union density among employed people, 1970–80 (%)

	1970	1975	1980
France	22.3	22.8	19.0
Germany	33.0	36.6	37.0
UK	48.8	48.3	50.7

Source: OECD, *Employment Outlook*, 1991: 101, table 4.1.

statistics must bear the following in mind: the level of membership is influenced not only by genuine strength of support but by technicalities, such as the British 'closed shop'; conversely, the German and French practice to generalize the applicability of collective bargaining agreements to non-unionized plants negatively affects the necessity to join. A similar effect flows from the informal influence of unions exerted through works councils/committees, particularly in Germany. In Britain, conversely, the absence of union representation in an enterprise translates into a complete lack of employee representation.

Table 7.2 illustrates the co-operative style of industrial relations in Germany, and the adversarial and antagonistic styles in Britain and France, respectively, as well as the different strike tactics.

Table 7.2   The pattern of strikes in comparative perspective, 1965–81

	Stoppages per 1,000 employees			Strike Days per 1000 employees		
	1965–9	1970–4	1975–81	1965–9	1970–4	1975–81
France	9.6[a]	17.7	18.5	126[a]	166	178
Germany	No information			6	49	22
UK	9.5	12.0	9.1	156	585	467

Note: [a] 1969 excluded from average.

Source: International Labour Office: *Yearbook of Labour Statistics*, various issues.

RECENT TRANSFORMATIONS

From the late 1970s and early 1980s onwards, these apparently stable national patterns of labour organization and industrial relations came under challenge from many sides. This led not only to reductions in union membership and influence of varying degrees but also to many transformations of industrial relations in both form and substance. The different tensions accumulated during the Fordist period, and the variable starting positions of the national union movements in organizational resources and legitimacy have inevitably come to shape the nature and extent of the transformations of the 1980s. Let us first examine the common reasons for these changes and then go on to review the particular ways in which they have been tackled in the national environments.

Four types of external influences have had a strong bearing on recent developments in industrial relations. First, conjunctural forces, leading to sluggish growth and high levels of unemployment, have made managements more cost-conscious and intent on deploying labour more efficiently or intensively while at the same time dealing with a docile labour force, weakened and cowed by unemployment. In addition, the drastic decline of once heavily unionized industries reduced the overall level of union membership.

Second, ideological shifts of a fundamental kind, which are only partly the result of recession, have undermined the principles of trade union organization. In the words of Grahl and Teague (1991), 'the crisis of socialism makes it difficult for unions to see themselves as the bearers of a universal project for social transformation'. The social philosophies which sustained working-class power have dissolved, and a new entrepreneurial ethos endows the managerial prerogative with new legitimacy. This loss of union ideological impetus and legitimacy is particularly apparent at the national political level and in party politics, and is the more pronounced the stronger the national political shift to market liberalism. A social-structural shift away from the working classes towards the expansion of white-collar jobs, particularly professional-managerial ones, has further contributed to the loss of ideological coherence.

A third factor is the sectoral shift from manufacturing to the service sector, giving greater numerical weight to traditionally weakly organized employees and to new precarious jobs. This has been accompanied by a shift within manufacturing away from the heavy industries where unionization has been particularly strong.

Fourth, the most complex and widely proliferating changes have resulted from the widespread adoption of a new production policy. This combines more-flexible organizational structures and technology with new forms of labour utilization and labour relations in the production of diversified quality products. The move to flexible production systems has often been accompanied by the creation of smaller production units, requiring speedier and more reliable responses from employees who in general deploy higher levels of skill and initiative in more highly integrated task profiles. This has brought a shift in the industrial labour force from highly unionized manual to less-unionized technical employees, and it has also necessitated the development of a closer and more co-operative relationship between management and labour. The new management quest for greater employee involvement has given rise to human resource management as a new paradigm of employee relations within the enterprise and has resulted in more direct and individualistic management–labour relations which carry the danger of marginalizing the collectivistic union practices and goals.

In addition to this strategy of achieving greater functional flexibility and commitment from core employees, there have also been efforts by both employers and the state to increase employment and payment flexibility with regard to peripheral employees, although this kind of polarization has been more prominent in the service than in the manufacturing sector. The move to differentiated products, to constant innovation in products and processes and towards faster responses to market demand has engendered a greater decentralization of collective bargaining and shifted its focus towards more qualitative goals and differentiated outcomes. This, in turn, has undermined the viability of centralized bargaining and generalizing, solidaristic union demands.

A consideration of these four external influences on industrial relations underlines the following points: (a) we are not merely dealing with temporary changes, due to recession; (b) the influences on industrial relations are on such a wide front that we can expect far-ranging changes; the external forces bearing on industrial relations differ in strength and character between our three societies, and, considering also their different *status quo ante*, we must therefore expect variable outcomes within common general tendencies. In addition to a review of these shared influences, there is a brief discussion of an external event that affects only the German system of industrial relations: reunification.

The impact of recession and political changes

Table 7.3 demonstrates that Britain was more seriously affected by unemployment than Germany and France, particularly in the first half of the 1980s, and Table 7.4 makes clear that recession and the growing loss of competitiveness in world markets had a particularly devastating effect on Britain's manufacturing sector. These economic influences became reflected in a strong decline in union membership: an overall decline between 1979 and 1990 of 23 per cent, and a decline in unions affiliated to the TUC of 30 per cent (Rose 1993: 292). This reflects both unemployment and the unions' growing inability to secure their members compensation for employment loss or job reassignment.

Table 7.3 *Standardized unemployment rates, 1979–92 (% of total labour force)*

	1979	1983	1985	1987	1992
France	5.9	8.3	11.3	10.9	8.9
Germany	3.2	8.0	10.2	10.6	9.7
UK	5.0	12.5	11.2	10.3	9.6

Source: OECD, *Employment Outlook*, 1988: 24, and 1991: 7.

Table 7.4 *Employment in industry, 1960–89 (% of civilian population)*

	1960	1979	1985	1989
France	37.6	36.3	32.0	30.1
Germany	47.0	44.2	40.9	39.8
UK	47.7	38.7	31.6	29.4

Source: Based on OECD 1991, quoted by Hyman and Ferner 1992: table A5.

Such decline in numerical strength also became expressed in a weakening of organizational strength, leaving a large minority of employees not covered by any bargaining arrangement. Thus, between 1984 and 1990 there occurred a fall in aggregate coverage by unions from 71 to 54 per cent (Millward et al. 1992: 93–4). The unions' loss of influence was further exacerbated by a loss of political legitimacy and the rise of right-wing ideology endeavouring to restrict union power and to marginalize unions at the work-place and in national politics. The most visible and dramatic expression of this was a spate of legislation which restricted union rights and legally defined union obligations. It is difficult to separate the effects of this turn to the right from conjunctural influences. The pattern of membership loss implicates economic forces more strongly than political ones, although the latter are by no means insignificant (Brown and Wadhwani (1990). Thus, decline in membership has been strongest in declining industrial sectors and started well before the laws took effect (Edwards et al. 1992: 32). But Millward et al. (1992: 71) also show that deliberate anti-union action by managers – withdrawal of union recognition – increased by 11 per cent between the 1980 and 1990 Workplace and Industrial Relations (WIR) surveys. It is, however, notable that, despite governmental efforts to weaken the role of unions in the labour market and despite severe recession, real wage rises stayed above increases in productivity during the first half of the 1980s. In France and Germany, in contrast, productivity growth outstripped that of real wages (Brown and Wadhani (1990: 64).

In France, unions have also suffered a drastic reduction of membership, the biggest decline being sustained by the radical left-wing unions, from around 25 per cent of the working population in 1975 to between 10 and 15 per cent in the mid-1980s (Bridgford 1990: 126) and to less than 8 per cent by the early 1990s (Dubois and Linhart 1994: 82). This serious decline is the expression of a high level of unemployment, particularly in previously highly unionized industries. In the context of strong anti-union feelings among French employers, this also deters young entrants to the labour force from joining, and thus foreshadows a longer-term decline (ibid.: 132). It should be noted that the degree of decline is serious, despite somewhat lower levels of unemployment and of decline in manufacturing than in Britain during the 1980s.

Changes in organizational representation and bargaining practices have been mediated more strongly by changes in legislation than by conjunctural factors. The predominance in government during much of the 1980s of a socialist party and the passing of pro-union legislation did nothing to halt the decline of union legitimacy in public opinion (Bridgford: 126). An important influence on union strength has come from a general political shift away from the extreme left, though not with the same strong lurch to the right and to anti-unionism as was experienced in Britain. Numerical and organizational decline, together with changes in management outlook, have been accompanied by a marked change in the tenor of labour relations. Whereas employers have ceased to regard workers as enemies or sources of problems, the unions, on their part, have largely abandoned the 'class struggle' rhetoric (Dubois and Linhart 1994: 81f).

In Germany, high unemployment in the later 1980s and employment reduction in many industries have had a much lesser impact on numerical and organizational strength. Thus, overall union density declined only moderately between 1980 and 1988 (see Table 7.5). Membership of unions affiliated to the DGB (the main industrial unions declined by only 2.8 per cent between 1980 and 1986, and among manual worker members there even occurred a

Table 7.5   Union density among employed people in the 1980s (%)

	1980	1985	1988
France	19.0	16.3	12.0
Germany	37.0	37.4	33.8
UK	50.7	45.5	41.5

Source: OECD (1991: 101, table 4.1).

slight increase (Jacobi and Müller-Jentsch 1990: 134). This pattern suggests membership growth in core industries that had been less adversely affected economically, and only a minimal impact of unemployment on skilled workers – the mainstay of German union support (ibid.: 128). Additionally, the unions' close links with works councils have helped them to retain their membership even in crisis industries and to gain new members in several industries.[1] The importance of union-dominated works councils during times of crisis in the negotiation of Social Plans, which compensate workers for both job loss and job reassignment, induce workers to keep or even seek union membership. Also new employees are often informally pressurized by works councils to join the union (Turner 1991: 196–7).

But this largely favourable outcome will probably not survive during the 1990s. The recession of the early 1990s, which affected hitherto untouched core industries and geographical regions, such as Baden-Württemberg, is predicted to have adverse effects on membership levels, and to put unions under increased employer pressure to reduce overall labour costs (Kern 1994: 33f). It is too early to predict the outcome of this new employer offensive.

The wider political climate became less favourable to unions in Germany during the 1980s. The Conservative/Liberal coalition government which came to power in 1982, adopted a neo-liberal marked ideology and committed itself to labour market deregulation. But rhetoric was much stronger than actual enactment of neo-liberal policies, and the social element in the ideology of the social market economy has never been repudiated. Existing law, regulating collective bargaining and, to a greater extent, enterprise- and company-level labour relations (the rights and obligations of successive Works Constitution Acts) was not touched. But the passing of a new law in 1986 – paragraph 116 of the Work Promotion Act – is designed to interfere considerably with the organization of strike activity, making large-scale and sustained strikes more costly (for details, see Jacobi et al. 1992: 240). This made relations between unions and the government temporarily more hostile, but no general collapse of union political legitimacy happened. Unions have retained their rightful place in the German political system and, together with the employers' organization – the BDA – are still represented in a consultative capacity on many political and quasi-political policy-making bodies. The following extract from a speech by Chancellor Kohl, made on the occasion of the centenary of the large metalworkers' union, IG Metall, in 1991, illustrates the vast gap between British and German politicians' attitudes towards unions: 'Free unions are supporting columns of the Social Market Economy and an important precondition for the stability of our democracy' (quoted by Crouch 1993: 233).

This greater legitimacy of the German union movement, together with the unions' capacity to participate in the resolution of crises and frequently to proceed proactively in resolving them (Turner 1991; Kern 1994), makes it likely that the union movement will retain, and perhaps even enlarge, its political role. Only a resolute shift to becoming a political organization, argues Kern (ibid.), can overcome the damaging impact of economic decentralization and fragmentation experienced during the last decade.

The different degree of severity in the impact of economic and political forces on the unions is illustrated by the comparative figures on union density and strike activity in Tables 7.5 and 7.6.

Table 7.6   Labour disputes: working days lost per 1,000 employees[a] in all industries and services (average[b])

	1983–7	1988–92	1983–92
France	60	40	50
Germany	50	20	30
UK	400	100	250

Notes:
[a]   Employees in employment; some figures have been estimated.
[b]   Annual averages for the years for which data are available, weighted by employment.

Source: *Employment Gazette*, Dec. 1993: 546, extract from Table 1.

The impact of sectorial and employment shifts

In all three societies there has occurred a shift in employment towards the service sector and white-collar occupations. This has brought with it two changes in employment structure, neither of which bodes well for unionization: the first is a growth of lower service occupations, characterized by feminization and an increase in various forms of non-standard employment (Bridgford 1990: 132). Such employees are both more resistant to unionization and much harder for unions to organize; the second is an increase in technical, professional and managerial employees who have generally had a more individualistic approach to the attainment of pay increases and employment rights or have favoured staff associations.

Britain has experienced the most pronounced sectorial shift of the three, as well as the biggest increase in female, part-time and self-employment, though not in temporary employment. An increase in employment from 1987 onwards, concentrated mainly in the service sector, brought no increase in unionization (*Employment Gazette*, 98 (5), (1990): 260). In addition, contracting-out of services from public- to private-sector employers has transferred many employees from relatively secure and standard forms of employment to more precarious employment in the private services. In Germany, both the shift to the service sector and privatization has been least pronounced, but the marked shift to temporary employment indicates increased deregulation. The continuing growth of white-collar employment heralds particularly large union problems for the future as their degree of unionization has been discrepantly low in international comparative terms. France occupies a middle position between the two in terms of a shift to the service sector and to more precarious forms of employment. Its considerable privati-

Table 7.7   Service sector employment as percentage of total employment in the 1980s

	1980	1987
France	56.5	63.0
Germany	51.3	55.2
UK	60.2	67.8

Source: Eurostat, *Employment and Unemployment*, 1989: 106.

Table 7.8   Increases in precarious employment, 1979–90

	1979	1983	1989
Part-time employment as percentage of total employment			
France	8.2	9.7	12.0[a]
Germany	11.4	12.6	13.2[a]
UK	16.4	19.4	21.8[a]
Temporary employment as percentage of total employment			
France	—	3.0	8.0
Germany	—	10.0	12.0
UK	—	6.0	5.8
Self-employment as percentage of total employment			
France	10.6	10.5	10.5
Germany	7.7	—	8.4
UK	6.6	8.6	11.5

Note: [a] Figures relate to 1990.

Source: Based on OECD, *Employment Outlook*, 1991: 46, 49, 52.

zation in the second half of the 1980s has probably not yet had a discernible effect. These facts will have been additional influences on the differential decline in union support. Table 7.7 illustrates the shift in employment towards the service sector, and Table 7.8 gives data on the growth of precarious employment.

The impact of the new production model

The move to a flexible production system and to diversified quality production has occurred in all three societies (Baglioni 1990; Amadieu 1992; Jacobi and Müller-Jentsch 1990). In Germany, the high degree of centralization of collective bargaining and the juridification of the industrial relations system at first sight appear totally incompatible with the flexible adjustment to change now aimed for. But the dual character of the system has made it reasonably adaptable to decentralization and differentiation, and German unions have shown themselves adept at exploiting their close connections with the still-influential works councils (Thelen 1991). Although pay bargaining still occurs at industry level, unions have adjusted to new, more differentiated employer demands in other areas by bargaining mainly for framework agreements. These are then amenable to adaptation at enterprise level and go some way towards satisfying employer demands for greater flexibility (ibid.; Keller and Henneberger 1991: 234). They have also taken the offensive in formulating qualitative demands in the areas of skill preservation and training, working time and influence over new technology. Unions have often been able to protect their members against the consequences of technological change and work reorganization and have gained concessions on the level of work intensity and on technological control (Turner 1991).

But as union influence over works councils is not uniformly assured there remains a real danger of a fragmentation of labour's strength and a loss of the basis for solidary demands. Although up to 80 per cent of works councillors are union members and union schooling and mobilizing activity among them is strong, clashes of interest arise. In such cases works councils are more likely to side with their enterprise policy than with that of the union (Schmidt and Trinczek 1991). Enterprise egotism is most likely to prevail over demands for more solidary solutions in the area of unemployment, giving rise to exclusionary tendencies which make it difficult to reintegrate the weaker segments of the labour force into employment (Turner 1991). Also the great flood of new and very demanding tasks which have engulfed works councillors as a consequence of decentralization are in danger of overtaxing their resources and capacities. Thus, to sum up, although unions have suffered a reduction in their homogenizing rule-setting function and assumed more support activities for works councils (Keller 1990: 386) they have by no means become emasculated but have remained a force to be reckoned with. Embryonic tendencies to assume a wider political role (Kern 1994), if further developed, would constitute an effective counterweight to such decentralization trends.

In Britain, during the 1970s, bargaining had already become decentralized, and structural features of union organization thus do not present the same handicap to enterprise-specific agreements as in Germany. But the trend towards decentralized bargaining has further intensified during the 1980s (Edwards et al. 1992: 22). Given the weakness of unions at the national level and their failure to formulate proactive policies, together with the customary lack of co-ordination of enterprise bargaining, there is a much greater danger than in Germany that enterprise egotism will become the norm and that employers will be able to impose solutions on ill-informed and isolated shop stewards. The most the latter can do in such circumstances is to engage in concession bargaining which has, indeed, been prominent in such areas as the surrender of demarcation practices.

In France, decentralization initiatives have come from the state and were initially opposed by employers, although they now see the use of localized negotiations to new production policies (Hoang-Ngoc and Lallement 1992: 2). Whereas before the passage of the Auroux laws an agreement at the highest bargaining level prevailed over those at lower levels, now firm-specific agreements can cancel out those concluded at a higher level. The flexibilization offensive has favoured the enterprise representative organs at the expense of the unions (Segrestin 1990: 110; Amadieu 1992: 70), even though the Auroux laws of the early 1980s have given unions a more securely institutionalized role at enterprise level (Eyraud and Tschobanian 1985: 242). But the French enterprise committees are much weaker than their German equivalents, and the numerically weak and fragmented unions have too few resources to guide and co-ordinate the conclusion of enterprise agreements. Although enterprise committees now have a wide range of consultation rights and some decision rights in matters of training and redundancy schemes, their largely unionized members still feel more at home with confrontation than participation (Amadieu 1992: 69). Thus, in France, unions are poorly placed to protect employees from the conclusion of disadvantageous enterprise agreements and even more, to promote a new micro-corporatism, and decentralization tendencies can only serve to further undermine the union movement.

But, in contrast to the situation in Britain, decentralization has been state-instigated, and it remains balanced by the 'centralized production of norms' by the state (Hoang-Ngoc and Lallement 1992) and by its continued intervention in collective bargaining. The majority of workers are still covered by central wage agreements (ibid.: 4), and the state continues to fix the SMIC.

Also, since the late 1980s, interindustry bargaining on some qualitative matters, such as technological change and working time, has taken place. Significantly, they have not got beyond declarations of intent, and some unions have refused to sign agreements (Amadieu 1992: 74f).

The newly created '*groupes d'expression*', which were designed to provide a base for the development of more direct management–labour relations, also fit in well with the flexibilization strategy. By the end of the 1980s, however, these initially promising groups had largely ceased to function (Amadieu 1992: 85; Wilson 1991: 448).

In all three societies, the new production policy requires greater initiative and responsibility from workers, and managements have striven to develop increased directness and co-operation with the shop floor. The aim of management to achieve greater employee involvement and commitment represents a complete break in both British and, particularly, French labour relations, being incompatible with the British adversarial 'them and us' style and the French class-based antagonistic style. The German co-operative style is more consonant with this recasting of management–labour relations. Although the changed circumstances have made both sides of industry more accommodative and realistic the historical legacies in Britain and France will make it difficult to achieve anything other than a superficial involvement. In Germany, in contrast, the participatory industrial culture will only need an intensification of established modes of co-operation.

In all three societies, managements have made more or less sustained efforts to develop elements of human resources management (HRM), which entails an integrated and systematic approach towards the selection, development and reward of employees, as well as efforts to improve communication and increase informal participation. In Britain, managements have been widely concerned to implement HRM, and 'have wrought a not inconsiderable measure of change' (Storey and Sisson 1990: 60). Managements have improved direct communication, experimented with Quality Circles (QCs) and Total Quality Management (TQM), introduced share ownership and declared their commitment towards training (ibid.; Edwards 1987; Marginson et al. 1988; Ramsey 1991). But at the same time, many of these schemes have been implemented in a haphazard and half-hearted way, the involvement and participation sought have been of a passive and reactive kind, and skill training and upgrading have remained dangerously underdeveloped (ibid.). Thus, a comparative survey on European HRM established that 41 per cent of HR specialists did not even know how much they had spent on training. Scarce labour would usually be attracted by extra financial incentives, rather than by the prospect of training for career advancement (Bournois 1991: 78–81). Most importantly, these schemes have been implemented against the background of much-increased employment insecurity and thus have had low resonance among employees (Marchington and Parker 1990). In addition, HRM has frequently implicitly or explicitly aimed at marginalizing unions through more direct and informal forms of employee involvement.

French managers, too, have greatly changed their attitudes towards employees and have been anxious to increase their involvement. Participative management has been in vogue, and a host of schemes to create a corporate culture and identity have been introduced (Dubois and Linhart 1994: 81–2). A greater rapprochement between management and employees came about in the 1980s through the formally instituted '*groupes d'expression*'. Although this form of direct contact and discussion between work groups and management representatives seemed initially promising it is now clear that they have not led to greater employee participation. They have, however, contributed to a lessening of mutual distrust and have improved communication. Building on Expression Groups, Quality Circles also enjoyed an unusual vogue in France (Wilson 1991). Employee share-ownership expanded greatly, and a notable increase in the training effort, based on government legislation but often going beyond its requirements, has also acted to increase employee integration.

But, on the negative side, changes in employment law during the 1980s removed some of the safeguards for employment security and reduced it overall. Also the continuing rise in unemployment and decreases in wages and social benefits in some cases are beginning to create a mood which threatens to undermine the as yet fragile consensus built during the decade (Dubois and Linhart 1994: 87).

Although the union federations, with the exception of the *Force Ouvrière* (FO), approved the introduction of the Expression Groups, old conflictual attitudes and poor resources meant that these management-initiated participation groups served to marginalize further French union influence at the enterprise level (Segestrin 1990: 105; Wilson 1991; Amadieu 1992). In general, the unions, particularly the CGT and the FO, maintain their suspicion against anything 'that smacks of joint management methods' (Amadieu 1992: 70). Thus, in the end, the French situation too has provided labour with few real gains and may have further strengthened management control.

In Germany, the notion of HRM gained less ground. Many of its basic tenets have long been established by law and have been well absorbed into management thinking. This manifests itself in a number of ways: the strong commitment to vocational training; the predication of the industrial relations system on social partnership and the existence of real participation rights through works councils and board membership in exchange for the assumption of co-responsibility for the competitive success of the enterprise; a cooperative style of labour relations; the existence of a craft community, founded on a homogeneous skill structure and high levels of skill throughout the

enterprise; and a strong productivist ethos, serving to integrate various levels
of the hierarchy around common tasks (see, on SMEs, Hildebrandt and Seltz
1989; Kotthoff and Reindl 1990). Additional integrating mechanisms are
provided by internal career paths and by a comparatively high degree of
employment stability (Bournois 1991: 81).

But the notion of employee involvement has had saliency also in Germany.
German managers' efforts to motivate and involve employees are seen as
flowing mainly from technological advance and systemic integration and, in
contrast to Britain, much less from financial belt-tightening in crisis situa-
tions. Thus Quality Circles and working groups have also been in vogue in
Germany (Pries et al. 1990; Beisheim et al. 1991; Turner 1991; and Turner
and Auer 1994). More recently, the notion of 'lean production' has captured
the minds of both managements and unions (HBS et al. 1992). Concerning
working groups, the metal workers' union IG Metall has, indeed, led the way
in developing a new concept that goes beyond Japanese ideas and, consequently, has had the upper hand in negotiation with management about their
introduction from the late 1980s onwards (Turner and Auer 1994). A bypass-
ing of unions and works councils is not feasible in the German context.
Whether or not real gains for labour result from the various participatory
schemes depends very much on the pre-existing strength of unions and works
councils in a given enterprise which tends to be reinforced by any new
scheme (Beisheim et al. 1991).

Another feature of the flexibilization strategy is the increasing fragmentation and dispersal of production structures, often entailing a move to smaller
units which are generally associated with lower union representation (for
details, see Chapter 4). These make it more difficult for unions to recruit and
to counter the new strategies of exclusion contained in the core–periphery
division of employees to achieve numerical flexibility. In France, the number
of enterprises with fewer than 50 employees has grown, and these firms are
exempt from the new Auroux law on obligatory firm-level bargaining
(Amadieu 1992: 74). In Germany, SMEs are also less unionized and more
vulnerable to employers' efforts to circumvent rights, but all except the
smallest enterprises do at least have works councils to defend them more or
less effectively. The strong reliance of SMEs on skilled labour also makes it
less likely that they will engage in the pursuit of numerical flexibility for a
peripheral labour force.

A fourth aspect connected to the flexibilization strategy is the increased
use of the new flexible technology. The introduction of flexible production
systems has been compatible with the German and French pattern of industrial unions. In contrast, the British principles of craft unions, multiple unions
and demarcation have made the implementation of new technology more
problematic for both managements and unions, despite the expression of

largely favourable attitudes towards new technology by shop stewards in the Workplace and Industrial Relations surveys. Such problems have become evident in inter-union rivalry over task division in programming computer numerical control (CNC) machines and, more prominently, in the slow phasing out of demarcation practices and the just moderate increase in multiskilling (Cross 1988). Some unions have been completely undermined by technological change, while others have been weakened by inter-union rivalry. Moreover, unions have generally been unable to influence the shape of work reorganization following technological change, which has resulted in further losses of legitimacy *vis-à-vis* their members (Turner 1991: 202f).

A last aspect of corporate strategy during the 1980s with a potentially undermining effect on unions is the marked increase in the internationalization of firms. This development will be particularly difficult to handle for the highly decentralized and lowly professionalized British and French unions. The former, moreover, are faced with a particularly high degree of corporate internationalization, while the latter have had to contend with large recent increases of outward FDI (for details on the latter, see Chapter 5). Although Japanese FDI in Britain is still small in proportional terms its impact on industrial relations has been dramatic in some industries. German unions, too, have reason to fear the increase in the internationalization of German business. There exists now a new willingness among firms of all sizes to locate production abroad, through both FDI and outsourcing of production. The marketization of Eastern Europe has become a strong 'pull' factor for this, and the high labour and social costs are presented as a 'push' factor of increasing importance.

German reunification

The economic and currency union in 1990 was followed by the wholesale transfer of the Western system of industrial relations to the Eastern states. As the Eastern unions were largely discredited through their close association with the ruling Communist Party the member unions of the then West German Union Federation, the DGB, were able to move in and organize Eastern workers with great ease. At the end of 1991, some 4.1 million new members had registered in the Eastern states (Fichter 1993: 34). The fusion has provided a significant boost to overall membership levels, as well as improving membership composition. Not only is there a higher union density in the East but the new membership also provides a welcome corrective to the previous imbalance between male and female, blue- and white-collar members (ibid.). (But the discrepantly high level of unemployment among women may mean that their comparatively high level of unionization will not be sustained.)

The absorption of Eastern union members has brought more problems than advantages. It has made the German union movement much more heterogeneous in terms of political experience and culture, as well as in terms of members' economic situation and industrial and political demands. This diversity is threatening to undermine union cohesiveness and has given employers opportunities to utilize divisions for their own ends. The worsening economic situation, due to only slow new investment in manufacturing industry and the accompanying increases in unemployment (over 15 per cent in the early 1990s) add to the unions' problems.

The developments causing particular concern are, first, that the dual structure cannot be relied upon to work as smoothly as in the Western states due to the economically more precarious situation and the lack of negotiating experience and of political sophistication of Eastern members and officers. The political values of state socialism, particularly the étatist mentality – the notion that it is up to the state to deal with any problems and that self-motivated action and individual responsibility are not called for – are still widely adhered to (Mahnkopf 1991: 272; Bialas and Ettl 1993: 72). 'In the short term, the new union members in the Eastern federal states are as little prepared for solidary action and for open engagement in conflict as they are for thinking in terms of legally determined rightful claims ... and obligations within the framework of a dual system of interest representation' (Mahnkopf 1991: 279). Although many top-level union officers are from the Western union bureaucracy, unions have to depend on local people at lower levels and on works councils.

For the dual system to work, unions are particularly dependent on the active representation of union goals in the enterprise. Economically weak firms have put pressure on their works councils to accept wage rates below those agreed by unions at industry level (Hoss and Wirth 1992; Bialas and Ettl 1993: 59), as well as terms and conditions or forms of labour utilization which undercut generally accepted Western standards. Works councils are persuaded by management arguments about a 'community of fate' in adversity or do not have the political resources to oppose managements (Mahnkopf 1991: 283). If such developments were to gain ground they would not only undermine unions' ability to achieve solidary agreements but the whole dual system. It would also favour a trend towards deregulation of labour contracts and towards segmentation of labour markets, already incipient in the West (Mahnkopf 1991: 283). A similar threat is posed by insistent suggestions that wage agreements should have opening clauses which would permit a flexible adjustment to varying economic performance levels in different regions and firms.

The second threat to a unified labour movement comes from the different needs and expectations of Western and Eastern workers and revolves around the DGB goal of wage parity for Eastern workers by the mid-1990s, despite their much lower levels of productivity. Wage rises far above productivity levels will increase unemployment, and the cost of paying for this will put further tests on the capacity for solidarity of Western workers. If employers accede to demands for wage rises from Western workers to compensate them for their growing tax and social insurance contributions, levied to pay for the costs of reunification, it will delay the achievement of wage parity for Eastern workers (Büchtemann and Schupp 1992: 90–106). It is, however, evident that a failure to aim for wage parity would initiate a mass exodus from the Eastern to the Western states and would lead to severe labour market competition and a downward pressure on wages. Alternatively, it could lead to dualism and price competition between Eastern and Western firms. Wage settlements during 1994 in the West below inflation levels (Silvia 1994) raise hopes that unions have persuaded their members that a solidary solution, although costly in the short term, is the right solution in the longer term.

It is not a foregone conclusion that the government and employers will utilize intra-union divisions to undermine the whole system of industrial relations. Both industry-based wage bargaining and the division of functions between unions and works councils has worked extremely well for large sections of capital and for the state. It has ensured greater transparency and predictability in economic policy, as well as a low level of industrial conflict and generally co-operative labour relations.

It is also notable that employers are not united on the issue of wage parity. The employers' federation, the BDA, which exerted a lot of influence on this matter in 1990, declared itself in favour of working towards parity to prevent the development of 'cheap labour' competition from Eastern firms (Bialas and Ettl 1993: 60). Eastern firms have been divided in their responses to the 'wage parity' demand: for a large proportion of firms the *Treuhandanstalt* (TA), the government-run privatizing agency holding Eastern publicly owned firms in trust, is still the employer in the first half of the 1990s and has not been taking a hard line on wage parity; another group of firms has been taken over by Western capital and expect to raise productivity to Western standards in the near future; only the third group of firms – smaller firms bought out or started by individual or groups of Eastern managers – find the prospect of wage settlement above productivity levels threatening to their economic survival.

The third threat to the unity of the all-German union movement flows from the different expectations and demands of Western and Eastern members in more general terms. While employees in the ex-GDR are primarily interested in bread-and-butter issues, such as pay and employment security, the old Western unions had, prior to reunification, began to assume a wider political role and to voice demands of a broader socio-political and cultural nature, as discussed above. It will be difficult to mobilize Eastern members in support of such demands. Conditions in the ex-GDR will probably force union leaders to reallocate material and intellectual resources towards the resolution of these basic industrial issues and delay the political modernization process (Mahnkopf 1991).

But even on this issue of common goals and political resources of the unions in the two formerly separate parts of Germany the prognosis need not be completely pessimistic. The description by Kern (1994) of two recent political interventions on the part of IG Metall in both a Western and an Eastern state has shown that the two not only share the important common goal of economic regeneration and employment creation, but the Eastern union – in Saxony – has shown itself to be as politically adept as the Western union at proactive intervention to pursue this goal. Contrary to the fears of Kädtler and Kottwitz (1994) about the absence of a supporting institutional network in the ex-GDR, the Saxon IG Metall have networked very skilfully with their regional state government and have managed to influence the politico-economic agenda (Kern 194).

Thus, to conclude, although reunification has created new divisions and tensions in German industrial relations it is by no means clear that these will undermine a basically sound system, valued by both sides of industry and by the main political parties. The final outcome will, of course, depend on the pace of economic restructuring in the ex-GDR and on the continued ability to pay for this process on the part of the Western federal states.

CONCLUSIONS

It has become evident that in all three countries unions have been on the retreat in the 1980s and that industrial relations have undergone many changes. But numerical decline has been uneven and does not convey the whole picture on union influence. In Britain, for example, despite strong decline in membership and political legitimacy, as well as extensive procedural change, collective bargaining practices have changed much less and are still recognized as a legitimate part of industrial life. In France, where unionization has reached a dangerously low level, employers have not used this circumstance to launch a fundamental attack on the trade union movement, and the state has even stepped in to strengthen it.

At the same time, however, it is becoming more evident that the foundations of the labour movement, the existence of a large and united working class, have been seriously undermined. This is most striking in Britain where a traditionally segmented and competitive union movement has been faced with both serious numerical decline of blue-collar workers and an exceptionally high degree of labour market segmentation into core and periphery. It is slightly less pronounced in France where union federations still aim for a united class approach. It has been least advanced in Germany where the working class has been least decimated and where industry-based bargaining is still extant. But in all three societies, in the words of Baglioni (1990: 9), 'segmentation, differentiation and the diversification of occupational statuses complicate the formation and management of representative structures and make the goal of generalized defence of the interests and rights of working people harder to achieve'. At the same time, employers have adopted methods of personnel management which, in terms of intent and procedure, have sometimes served to bypass the unions.

In all three societies there has occurred an increase in decentralized bargaining. In Britain it was an intensification of existing trends, while in Germany and France it was a new development. So far decentralization has not ousted industry-wide bargaining in the latter two societies, and one can only speak of a loosening of centralized systems (Jacobi and Müller-Jentsch 1990: 146; Segrestin 1990: 119). But such decentralization is a further step in the direction of reducing labour solidarity, disguising conflict of interests between capital and labour. It is conducive to participation and negotiation rather than risking conflict by posing demands. Further intensification would thus bode ill for unions.

It should, however, be noted that the flexibilization strategy and the attendant new approach to labour deployment does not play solely into the hands of management and damage labour's claims to participation in production organization. The increasingly integrated high-tech production systems make management dependent on responsible worker initiative and involvement, and these cannot be attained by mere social engineering and pseudo-participation schemes. Management is obliged to offer core workers opportunities for real participation, as well as good employment conditions and career opportunities. It is up to the unions and other representative bodies to make use of this new opening.

In conclusion, it is clear that many features of the industrial relations of the Fordist period have disappeared and that a new order is in the process of emerging. The system is still characterized by accommodation between management and labour, but the balance of power has shifted perceptibly in favour of management. At enterprise level, a new compromise is being worked towards, but so far there are only vague indications of how this could be translated to the national political level. Due to the growing inability of the unions to act as class organizations, the class character of management–labour relations is becoming submerged. The full contours of any new post-Fordist system of industrial relations are yet to emerge.

NOTE

1. The German Union for Textiles and Clothing, for example, has increased union density from 22 to 40 per cent between 1971 and 1983, despite catastrophic reductions in employment during that period (Turner 1991: 194).

8. Changing patterns of production organization: towards neo- or post-Fordism?[1]

There is now widespread agreement that, during the last 15 years, or so, there have occurred substantial changes in production organization, manifested in new ways of utilizing both fixed capital and labour. But there is still disagreement about the extent and nature of such transformations and their theoretical interpretations. Recent influential conceptualizations of such transformations discuss them in ideal-typical terms as either neo- or post-Fordist. Although such a simple dichotomous categorization cannot encompass the rich diversity of patterns uncovered by empirical work, the notion of a continuum between Fordist and either neo-Fordist or post-Fordist types overcomes some of the objections and also allows for the notion of a developmental path which is not yet completed. Whereas the concept of post-Fordism is connected mainly with the flexible specialization thesis and its refinement by writers such as Badham and Matthews (1989) and Sorge and Streeck (1987), neo-Fordism is more often associated with regulation theory, although this is not a hard and fast distinction. The German literature on work organization speaks of 'new production concepts' (Kern and Schumann 1984), on the one side, and 'systemic rationalization' (Altmann et al. 1986 and 1992), on the other. (For a lucid discussion of the two approaches, see Lutz 1992). Figure 8.1 shows how the latter relate to the concepts of neo- and post-Fordism.

This chapter will concentrate on transformations in production organization affecting the use of labour, and will explore new trends in the following areas: management's production policy; aspects of work organization, such as division of labour, skill development, work intensity and control; and the extent of polarization along one or more of these dimensions of work organization. Such a review will highlight similarities and divergencies between the societies and explain them in terms of institutional arrangements, impingeing on production organization. Finally, these national patterns will be situated on the continuum between Fordism and neo- or post-Fordism. Such generalizations can only be tentative, due to the diversity of patterns between different industries and types of firm. This diversity is particularly pronounced in

Post-Fordism   **New production concepts**

Significant increase in product innovation and process
variability

Widespread enhancement of skill and discretion

Work intensification
Danger of polarization

Neo-Fordism   **Systemic rationalization**

Increase in product   Increase in product
variability (modified   innovation and
mass-production)   process variability

Increase in management   Changed form and increase
control   of management control

Work intensification and polarization

Figure 8.1   Work organization strategies

Britain where, due to a weak general regulatory system, industrial organization is particularly decentralized and fragmented.

Although patterns of production organization during the early post-war
decades had Fordist features in all three societies, it is now widely agreed
that such a general label obscures important differences between them, and
these different starting positions must be borne in mind when evaluating
more recent transformations.

THE HISTORICAL LEGACY

Although some elements of Fordist mass-production methods entered European firms between the two World Wars, widespread implementation came
only from the 1950s onwards, in the wake of mass consumption. The main
features of the Fordist regime were the production of standardized goods in
large runs, combining dedicated machinery with the use of semi-skilled
labour. A high division of labour and a separation of production planning and

control from the shop floor made for low-skilled, repetitive and machine-paced work tasks. The institutionalization of collective bargaining secured for workers a reasonable share of profits, and rising wages were linked to increases in productivity. Together with receipts from the newly established welfare systems, they provided the means for rising levels of consumption. In none of the three societies, however, were all the characteristics fully realized.

In Britain, large corporations did not always rationalize newly acquired plants, and the conditions for large-scale production were often not fulfilled. Productivity did not increase to the same extent as in other countries, and, according to Jessop (1989), mass consumption was financed through demand management and the social wage, in addition to productivity rises. Although mass-production methods became widely established, craft labour and craft methods continued to occupy an important place in British manufacturing industry. Rigidities in the use of labour were paralleled by organizational compartmentalization and problems of communication at all levels. Low-cost production usually took precedence over considerations of quality. Some of these features were maintained by the disorderly but influential collective bargaining system, whereas others were caused by the constraints on management's, emanating from the financial system. Boyer (1988) coined the label 'flawed Fordism' for the British case.

Germany, in contrast, Boyer associates with 'flex-Fordism', due to the fact that highly skilled labour and small-batch and customized production stayed dominant in some important core industries. In these sectors, the division of labour remained less advanced, and hierarchical control was balanced by craft autonomy of the skilled work-group. Considerations of quality were as important as those of cost. Fordism did not come to Germany until the mid-1960s when it was grafted on to craft production (Mahon 1987: 35). The post-war settlement came only from the early 1950s onwards, and post-war expansion of German industry came through export-orientated production of capital goods rather than through a focus of consumer goods and domestic demand. In collective bargaining, strong unions were faced by equally well-organized employers. From the beginning, a co-operative system of wage bargaining took account of conjunctural factors so that wage increases rarely surpassed productivity rises and often stayed below their level. But the new and highly effective pin-point strategy for industrial action, developed by the metal-workers' union IG Metall in the 1960s, created a Fordist wage dynamic (Mahon 1987: 38). Recruitment of foreign workers (*Gastarbeiter*) cushioned the effect of increased semi-skilled work for German workers. Organizational boundaries within firms were more fluid than in the other two societies (Maurice et al. 1980) and created fewer problems of co-ordination and communication between functional departments, but a highly centralized management created its own rigidities. Although large firms in many sectors attained sufficient scale to make Fordist production methods viable, the industrially highly significant sector of SMEs never conformed to the Fordist pattern.

In France, Fordist production organization had its own national characteristics. An elaborate and rigid division of labour characterized not only the shop floor but the whole organizational structure, and the separation of conception in staff departments from execution on the shop floor was particularly marked (Linhart et al. 1989: 152). This dominant feature makes it appropriate to talk about Fayol-Fordism – an allusion to the French author of *Principles of Modern Management*, who outlined a distinctively French hierarchical system of management control. (Boyer 1992a prefers the term 'state Fordism'). Mass-production methods with the use of semi-skilled labour were widespread. The early post-war expansion of manufacturing was accomplished mainly with low-skilled female and former agricultural labour. A national system of vocational education developed slowly from the late 1950s onwards, and training remained predominantly firm-specific and, until the 1970s, of a limited nature. Workers were strictly controlled, and a mutual distrust between management and labour characterized labour relations. Although industrial relations were highly conflictual, the weakness of the unions kept wage demands in reasonable balance with increases in productivity. But, as in Britain, many large firms never created sufficiently large production units to get the necessary economies of scale for a fully developed Fordist system. Furthermore, the long predominance of SMEs in the French economy posed further barriers to a generalization of mass-production methods. Finally, Fordism was not boosted initially by mass consumption but by state policy on public procurement (Boyer 1992b: 95).

It should be clear from the preceding discussion that these national differences in the extent and nature of Fordist production organization influenced the nature of the industrial crisis each country began to face from the 1970s onwards and the manner of transition to the adoption and implementation of

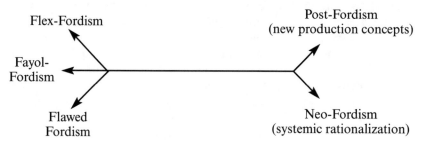

Figure 8.2   A trajectory of change in patterns of work organization

a new production paradigm. Figure 8.2 summarizes the theoretical assumptions, guiding the analysis of such changes.

PRODUCTION POLICY

In recent years, changed market demands, greatly intensified competition and the availability of automated production technology have exerted pressures for a changed production strategy towards diversified quality production (Sorge and Streeck 1987) and towards associated reorganization in process terms. Management effort to raise productivity and lower costs is no longer directed solely towards labour utilization but is equally concerned with the efficient use of fixed capital and knowledge, as well as with the reduction of wastage. These pressures have been experienced by managements in all three societies, but the adoption and implementation of a new production paradigm have been mediated in important ways both by the historical legacy and by institutional constraints and opportunities. Among the latter, the following have been significant: the financial system; management education and style; the national engineering culture; the system of vocational training; industrial relations structures and the quality of labour relations.

Britain

The depth and breadth of the British industrial crisis made managements concerned to move away from established patterns of production organization; and the slack labour market, together with a tough national political line on the employment and utilization of labour, created new openings for change. Thus a move towards a more flexible regime of accumulation has been high on management agendas. This has been expressed in the commitment to new product strategies (see, for example, Rubery et al. 1987; Walsh 1991a), the search for greater functional flexibility (Atkinson and Meager 1986; Whittaker 1990: 142), new organizational forms and new working practices, as well as in the pursuit of changed labour relations (Marginson et al. 1988; Elger 1991; Marsden and Thompson 1990). A dramatic reduction in overmanning, together with the gradual elimination of other restrictive practices, has led to remarkable increases in productivity during the 1980s (Mahoney et al. 1994: 49). Finally, there has occurred a gradual shift away from market-orientated employment relations towards the organization-orientated type, as conceptualized by Dore (Whittaker 1990: 48). Thus, while the pursuit of increases in quality and versatility has involved both upgrading/flexibilization of labour and the use of more automated processes, British managements have not put a strong emphasis on either of these two factors and no very clear production strategy is discernible. Frequently, crisis management and the search for cost reduction have come to overshadow the pursuit of diversified quality production.

Survey and case-study data show that automation has advanced unevenly in different industries and sizes of firms (Daniel 1987; Marginson et al. 1988; Martin 1988) and has often been applied only to discrete operations rather than being of a systemic nature (Senker and Simmonds 1991). Where technologically sophisticated machinery has been acquired it has often been under- or poorly utilized (ibid.; New and Myers 1986). Change in production arrangements has been often of an organizational rather than of a technical kind (Daniel 1987). Interfirm systemic integration has remained confined mainly to foreign-dominated industries, such as automobiles and electronics (Morris and Imrie 1991). This hesitant and uneven process automation has often translated into lagging product innovation, variability and quality, although moves away from low-cost low-quality products have occurred in some industries and firms. The lag in skill development is expressed in the fact that, during the 1980s, the proportion of skilled workers in the labour force did not increase (Millward et al. 1992: 15f). During 1987–9, the proportion of the total workforce holding an intermediate qualification was only 27 per cent, compared with 40 per cent in France and 63 per cent in Germany (Mason et al. 1992, quoted in Mason et al. 1993: 24). The drastic decline in apprenticeship training will permit no improvement of this trend in the 1990s although many firms have stepped up their on-the-job training.

The absence of widespread, radical and consistent change in production policy is ascribed to a number of factors: short-term investment horizons and low technical competence in key managerial and supervisory positions (Rothwell 1987; Nolan 1989; Senker and Simmonds 1991; Storey and Sisson 1990; Mason et al. 1993: 28). Additional influences have been the shortage and insufficiency of functional flexibility of skilled labour (Lane 1990; Marsden and Ryan 1991; Mason et al. 1993: 29, 33) and the persistence of low-trust/ low-responsibility labour relations. Finally, a fragmented and demoralized union movement has not produced any proactive policies which would promote change towards diversified quality production and harness it to the interests of members in higher levels of skill and more-challenging work tasks.

France

In France, competitive pressures and slack labour markets have influenced managements to adopt product and process innovation, to step up training efforts and to develop new labour relations, as well as seeking greater flexibility in the deployment of labour (Amadieu 1992). Large firms have been greatly concerned to change from Fordist to Japanese-style firms and have aimed for greater organizational and operational flexibility (Dubois and Linhart 1994: 82). All the major car manufacturers, for example, have sought to change work organization in their most highly automated subsections in a post-Fordist direction. Thus, several innovative and far-reaching company agreements were concluded in the late 1980s (ibid.: 79). Generally, there has been a strong emphasis on automation as a means to gain greater mastery of the production process and to control the work activity or ordinary production workers (Coriat 1992). What then have been the opportunities for, and impediments to, the implementation of diversified quality production?

One of the main impediments to a generalization of such a production policy still lies in the dualistic structure of French industry and the technological lag of many traditional industries and of a large proportion of SMEs (Stoffaes 1989: 122). Within the large industrial groups, in contrast, neither investment behaviour nor managerial technological expertise pose the barriers identified in Britain. Impediments are more often encountered in rigid organizational structures and excessive centralization which militate against quick adjustment to market demand and the achievement of product versatility (Boyer 1992a: 8, table 2). Flexible utilization of labour is still hindered by rigid job classification schemes and associated payment methods (Eyraud et al. 1988). Although skill resources on the shop-floor have greatly increased during recent decades their full utilization is still prevented by the persistent low-trust culture and rigid vertical division of labour between technical departments and shop-floor, and the raising of quality standards has only been imperfectly achieved (ibid.).

Germany

While Germany has also felt the stiff winds of global competition, in most industries managements have been more concerned to hold on to and improve attained positions (Müller-Jentsch et al. 1992: 93). Although the objective of cost-cutting has become increasingly important, it has not overshadowed the goals implied by diversified quality production in the way experienced in Britain. The strategy of diversified quality production is pursued consistently throughout manufacturing industry, ranging from biscuits to machine tool production. An industrial strategy for the 1980s according to principles of flexible specialization was formulated by the quasi-governmental Council of Economic Advisors, the *Sachverständigenrat*, in 1981:

> The improvement of competitiveness must be achieved through the introduction of new products, i.e. those whose production requires special technical knowledge available only to a few suppliers. Such products are competitive not because they

> are particularly cheap, but because of their utility to those who use them; in short, because they are particularly expensive. In other words, in a dynamic economy, competitiveness is the ability to develop new speciality products ... (Quoted in Jacobi et al. 1992: 221).

Also the lesser degree of crisis, together with the greater degree of employment protection of industrial workers, has so far not jeopardized the co-operative tenor of labour relations.

Automation of the production process has advanced to a considerable degree in Germany and has become an important pillar of competitive strategy. Although advanced forms of systemic integration, such as Computer-integrated manufacture (CIM), are still at an early stage, lesser forms of integration of both material flows and of information are now widespread in most industries (Altmann and Duell 1990; Pries et al. 1990; Schutz-Wild 1992). In contrast to the situation in France and Britain, this trend has also engulfed most SMEs (Hildebrandt and Seltz 1989; Kotthoff and Reindl 1990). The German move towards a new production paradigm is thus very much premissed on, and driven by, advanced technology to be mastered and fully exploited by a highly skilled labour force.

Extensive process innovation has been accompanied by constant product innovation and diversification. In industries where small-batch production of quality goods has always been prominent, such as in machine tools, there has occurred a notable increase in product variability and customized solutions (Hildebrandt and Seltz 1989; Pries et al. 1990; Manske 1991). In the former standardized mass-production industries, such as the car, electrical, steel, furniture and chemical industries, module production has greatly enhanced product variability and has led to customer-orientated batch production. Product innovation, such as new materials and chemical treatment of surfaces in textiles, has also been on the increase (Pries et al. 1990).

This more radical and consistent introduction of product and process innovation has been facilitated both by pre-existing reservoirs of flexibility and by more auspicious institutional environments than in either Britain or France. It has required merely an intensification and generalization of old practices rather than demanding radical ruptures in established structures and relations. Factors favouring this adjustment process have been long investment horizons (due to the underdevelopment of the stock market), an 'engineering' bias among managers, and the existence of a highly skilled and functionally flexible labour force (Lane 1990). Germany's highly professionalized union movement has been an active participant in this transformation process: its recent skill offensive is one example of this (Müller-Jentsch et al. 1992; Cressey and diMartino 1991). But it would be unwise to overstate the ease of change as organizational conservatism and hierarchical rigidities have constituted barriers to enterprise modernization (Boyer 1992b; Kern 1994).

WORK ORGANIZATION

Britain

Despite unfavourable preconditions for a change in production policy, change has nevertheless been widespread and has occurred on many fronts. But attempts to translate new production policy into changes in work organization have been for the most part piecemeal: they have either become overwhelmed by institutional impediments or been displaced by other more pressing goals dictated by crisis.

Although the immense diversity in patterns of work organization, due to variation in contextual features, makes an identification of national patterns difficult, some generalizations can be ventured. There is now extensive evidence, both from case studies (Martin 1988; Penn 1990; Hendry 1990; Senker and Simmonds 1991) and from survey evidence (Batstone and Gourlay 1986; Daniel 1987; Gallie 1991) that the introduction of new technology has usually led to moderate positive changes in work organization: to the reversal of a rigid horizontal division of labour; more task integration; to moderate upskilling or to changes from manual to conceptual skills. (The definition of skill employed is almost invariably task skill.) Employment statistics focusing on individual skill levels show a moderate shift away from unskilled manuals towards the category of 'craft and skilled' (Brown 1990: 312). There is, however, still debate about the direction of task integration – job enlargement or job enrichment – and whether the pursuit of functional flexibility has affected more than a small craft elite (Pollert 1991). Changes in working practices have been widespread, with operatives taking on routine maintenance and quality control tasks and maintenance workers accepting additional areas of competence. But at the same time, increases in functional flexibility have been limited by insufficient training backup (Batstone and Gourlay 1986: 229; Rothwell 1987: 67; Crewe 1991: 49).

Investigations of dual- and multiskilling of craftsmen across old demarcation lines, covering a large variety of firms and industries, have found only very limited change in this field (Daniel 1987; Cross 1988; Marsden and Thompson 1990). Both of the latter accounts emphasize the tremendous obstacles to be overcome in this endeavour: it requires complex negotiations with the various entrenched crafts and their unions, and involves high costs from training and increased wages and relatively long pay-back periods. Marsden and Thompson (1990: 97) also draw attention to the fact that upgrading of semi-skilled workers is a highly sensitive union issue and thus occurs rarely. Jürgens's (1991: 208) comparative study of the car industry describes the gulf between craft and other workers as extraordinarily wide, precluding the formation of work groups with task rotation. An investigation of skill profiles of workers on flexible manufacturing systems finds a middle path: there is neither full polyvalence and vertical job enlargement, nor is there a high division of labour and responsibility between workers and engineers (Jones 1988: 465).

Increases in task integration, multi-skilling and expansion of responsibility, it is widely concluded, have led to notable increases in work intensity and occasionally to loss of control over the pace of work (Elger 1991; Delbridge et al. 1992). But a rise in work intensity is not necessarily associated with increased stress or exploitation. Often such increased intensity has resulted from reduced waiting times rather than from increases in the pace of work, and frequently it coincides with upskilling and upgrading (Batstone and Gourlay 1986; Edwards 1987: 147; Cross 1988; Walsh 1991a).

Thus, to conclude, changes in British work organization have brought moderate gains for workers on several fronts. But the low incidence of measures to train workers and to create new forms of group work and participation makes it inadvisable to speak about clear and consistent moves in the direction of a post-Fordist pattern.

France

As in Britain, the new production policy has led to many changes in work organization, but the strong entrenchment of hierarchical structures and Fordist approaches to labour utilization have prevented a reorganization of work in a post-Fordist direction (Eyraud et al. 1988: 76; Dubois and Linhart 1994: 83). Vertical rigidities have been mitigated, but not eliminated. Although a dialogue between management and labour is now more common than in the past (Wilson 1991), old suspicions about management motives and new fears about more precarious employment protection have prevented the development of trust relations.

The 'competence' model, aiming explicitly at the use of constant training to increase numerical (of core employees) and functional worker flexibility, has been introduced in a very patchy manner by only a small number of large firms (Dubois and Linhart 1994: 83). Despite extensive skill upgrading since the 1970s, there is still insufficient use of shop-floor expertise, due to both lack of trust and vertical rigidities. In the car industry, for example, engineers have been loath to relinquish control over maintenance work (Amadieu 1992: 62f); and in the machine-tool industry, setters and technicians are said to monopolize programming activities for CNC machines (Eyraud et al. 1988; Cavestro 1989) and leave machine operators to play only a secondary role. But, according to Cavestro (ibid.: 231), operators play a decisive role in programme correction, in 70 per cent of the cases surveyed. The same author also notes a shift towards the assumption of routine maintenance and quality control tasks on the part of operators and generally holds a less pessimistic view than most French sociologists about a move away from Fordist principles. Workers themselves have sometimes opposed increases in skill and autonomy, due to an ingrained distrust of management motives. Thus, there has occurred opposition from workers to multi-skilling and to team work (Amadieu 1992: 62).

Germany

The German literature on changes in work organization is agreed on the fact that Taylorist–Fordist approaches to labour utilization are no longer accepted orthodoxy among managements (Schumann et al. 1990: 25), and recent discussions on 'lean production' have further increased the unanimity about the necessity to move further from Taylorist towards more human-centred approaches to innovation in production organization (Schumann et al. 1994: 33). But interpretations of skill development still diverge between the two schools of industrial sociology outlined above. The balance of evidence shows that the trend has been more strongly in the direction of upskilling and upgrading than in the opposite direction. But so far post-Fordist forms of work organization have affected only a large minority of workers (Hildebrandt and Seltz 1989; Schumann et al. 1990; Manske 1991; Vosskamp and Wittke 1992; Schultz-Wild 1992; Schumann et al. 1994) although many firms are now experimenting with innovative work patterns (Köhler and Schmierl 1992 on the capital goods industry). All this applies not only to the former small-batch producers in the core sectors but also to former mass-producers and more traditional industries. In low-tech processes and assembly-line work, however, Tayloristic practices and undemanding work remain prevalent (Schumann et al. 1994: 30).

Post-Fordist changes in work organization have been paralleled by widespread upgrading of formerly semi-skilled workers and by the introduction of apprenticeship programmes in former mass-production industries (Schumann et al. 1990; Vosskamp and Wittke 1992), as well as by changes in existing training courses aiming at broader skill profiles and the fostering of group autonomy (Casey 1991). Moreover, a pattern of skill creation and labour utilization, approximating more closely to the post-Fordist type, is evident in a whole number of cross-national comparisons with British, American and French practices (Sorge et al. 1983; Jürgens 1991; Hirsch-Kreinsen 1989; Lutz and Veltz 1989; Boyer 1992).

The consensus between managements and unions on skill preservation and enhancement, backed by a very efficient training system, has been the cornerstone of work reorganization. The predominance of skilled workers in industry has made it both possible and necessary to combine a full utilization of shop-floor human competence with high levels of automation. Examples are the widely accepted practice of permitting the programming of CNC machines by operating personnel (in 70 per cent of machine-tool firms, according to Schultz-Wild 1988, quoted by Müller-Jentsch et al. 1992: 96) and the existence of co-operative rather than hierarchical relations between operators and the CNC bureau (Hirsch-Kreinsen and Wolf 1987: 185). This is in stark contrast to French and, to a lesser extent, the British practice. A history of flexible deployment largely has eliminated the vertical and horizontal barriers found in France and Britain respectively. The British debate on new working practices would sound very strange to German ears.

In Germany, too, greater task integration, product variability and continuous processes have notably increased work intensity (Pries et al. 1990), although unions have been more able than in Britain and France to mitigate this process (Turner 1991). This is seen as the fly in the ointment of otherwise rewarding work structures. Whether this constitutes a transitional phenomenon, due to outmoded payment systems, or a permanent part of the new work organization is not clear.

Thus, to sum up so far, the German picture of new forms of work organization shows a more consistent and integrated move in the direction of post-Fordism than is found in the other two societies, although the transition is as yet not assured.

CONTROL

What has been the impact of new production policy and new technology on the exercise of management control? To what extent has the revolutionary control potential of new technology been utilized by managements in the three societies and how has it been integrated with other management objectives, such as increased worker initiative and creativity? Control – that is, the ability to keep a check on and increase to its highest possible degree the effort expended by employees – remains a vague concept which needs clear specification before any changes can be assessed. Pries et al. (1990) distinguish between four different types of control which are, however, only analytically distinct:

1. active organizational control where an electronically controlled production planning and control system (PPCS) prestructures the whole production process and determines at what level decisions about work operations are taken. Thus, control can be highly centralized and prescribe every detail of the labour process or may be in the form of framework control which leaves scope for decentralized worker discretion. Each

form also has implications for the permitted degree of communication and co-operation between workers;

2. passive, person-orientated control or surveillance which utilizes information about work behaviour and effort, fed back to the centre by the computerized production system, making work operations transparent to management. It has obvious potential for performance checks and for more precise specification of the effort bargain;

3. control in the sense of supervision, which ranges from control over individual effort through machine pacing to control of collective effort in PPCSs;

4. psychological control through various social techniques, such as Quality Circles and participation schemes. This has already been discussed in Chapter 7.

Britain

The first aspect of control – active organizational control – receives little attention in the British literature, probably due to the lesser degree of systemic automation. Authors who do consider this aspect (Child 1987: 123; Jones 1988: 481) see technological integration with centralized control as the British pattern. Autonomous work groups, often associated with flexible manufacturing systems, are uncommon in Britain (Jones 1988: 469). In the motor industry, efforts to build such teams have been opposed by the unions (Willman and Winch 1985; Jürgens 1991). Most observations on control relations cover the second and third aspects of control: surveillance and supervision. Whereas Daniel (1987) detects a slight increase in management control, Batstone and Gourlay (1986) find an increase in worker discretion more typical. Concerning surveillance through technology, most studies report that managements do not bother to exploit their new powers fully, because it would be either too costly or counterproductive (Martin 1988: 119; Jones 1988: 470). Thus, the data on control are somewhat inconclusive, and it seems unlikely that radical changes have occurred. A notable exception is the recent study of JIT/TQM in Japanese-owned companies by Delbridge et al. (1992) which detects large management gains in both active and passive control, resulting in a total loss of worker control.

France

French analyses of changes in management control are fairly unanimous in their conclusions: technology is used to control workers, and workers are not permitted to utilize their knowledge to exploit technology to its fullest potential (Boyer 1992a: 10). Lack of management trust in workers has served to preserve the old Fordist vertical division of labour between conception and execution (ibid.; Coriat 1992: 10). Control in highly automated systems is exercised almost invariably in a centralized and prescriptive manner. Thus a French–German comparison of the implementation of flexible manufacturing systems in the mid-1980s found that all were operated with a central computer whereas this was the case for only half the systems in Germany (Lutz and Veltz 1989: 235). Another cross-national comparison of production control systems in the clothing and electronics industries found the prescriptive (tell-and-do) logic more prevalent in France than in Germany. This was attributed to manufacturing management having less say in the matter in France and to the greater professional, social and even spatial distance between production control and production areas (Dubois 1993: 152–4; Heidenreich 1993: 252).

Germany

German studies are very preoccupied with the changed control relationship resulting from systemic integration. Systemic control is most advanced in the steel and chemical industries; a middle position in this respect is reached by the car, electrical, furniture and textile industries; whereas the machine-building industry is still in the process of coming to grips with it (Pries et al. 1990: 51f). Evaluations of these trends vary greatly. Some authors posit predominantly centralized system control which severely circumscribes the space for autonomous decision-making by even highly skilled workers (Altmann et al. 1986; Pries et al. 1990). But more studies either see a turning away from this centralized control or view the decentralization strategy as more prevalent (Fischer and Minnsen 1987: 204; Hildebrandt and Seltz 1989: 414f; Manske 1991; Jürgens 1991: 202; Heidenreich 1993: 249). The latter points out that such decentralization has won out because the voice of the production foreman in favour of such a strategy still carries a lot of weight in Germany. Homogeneity in qualifications and experience between production control and shop floor staff also works in this direction (ibid.). In the circumstances it is safest to assume, as do Bechtle and Lutz (1989) that, concerning active control, the situation rests between a neo- and a post-Fordist scenario. This conclusion also receives support from the fact that German designers of production planning and control (PPC) concepts have come up with alternative and more flexible concepts which are better suited to the needs of SMEs (Schultz-Wild 1992: 136f).

Passive transparency control, it is generally concluded, is not being exploited to its full potential (Hildebrandt and Seltz 1989; Pries et al. 1990; Schumann et al. 1994: 30), or even that largely collective activity in automated systems renders such control nonsensical (Schumann et al. 1990). Some accounts, however, point out how captured information has been fed back into and sharpened active control, particularly in the area of time specifications for individual jobs. As such a practice crucially undermines workers' discretion it has been fiercely contested by them, and managements have had to make concessions (Manske 1991: 138f). The latter are well aware that rigid neo-Fordist methods of control would undermine worker initiative and motivation. Furthermore, many locally negotiated agreements limit such monitoring, and legally binding clauses of the Works Constitution Act proscribe person-orientated effort control (Hildebrandt and Seltz 1989: 415f; Fischer and Minssen 1987: 207; Manske 1991: 167; Turner 1991).

Lastly, semi-autonomous work groups, showing the relaxation of management control and giving teams responsibility for a complete task or project, appear to be more common in Germany than in either Britain or France, particularly in the car industry of the early 1990s (Turner and Auer 1994). Their introduction, sparked off by proactive union development of a new concept of group work and its zealous propagation among works councils in the industry, together with a management response to the Japanese example, promise a systematic and relatively smooth establishment of egalitarian group work throughout the industry in the near future (ibid.; Turner 1991).

In sum, the German evidence suggests that systemic automation has brought about greatly expanded potential for management control. Even if it is not fully utilized, it exerts significant influence over the wage relation, and it is advisable to speak of controlled autonomy (Manske 1991). How this control potential is actually used depends strongly on the pre-existing balance of power between management and labour and on the quality of labour relations. In comparative perspective, this would lead one to expect more decentralized forms of control in Germany than in either Britain or France.

POLARIZATION

Many interpretations of changes in production and labour utilization strategies claim that any move towards functional flexibility and upskilling has only benefited a small elite and that it has been accompanied by a growing polarization of the labour force in terms of work organization and employment conditions. This claim is prominent in neo-Fordist accounts (see, for example, Elger 1991) but is also advanced by analysts tending towards post-Fordist interpretations (such as Kern and Schumann 1984; Gallie 1991).

The term polarization is used in a very cavalier way in the literature and is often confused with segmentation. Polarization should be understood in either of the following ways: in its classical Marxist definition, it implies the elimination of occupational groups in the middle of the skill hierarchy, making contrasts between high- and low-skill groups more glaring; alternatively, it can signal the widening of a gulf between groups in relation to one or more valued attributes, such as skill or employment security, and the deterioration of one group's position is seen as directly connected with the improvement of the other. British work on the 'flexible firm' (Atkinson and Meager 1986) posits that polarization in skill development has been reinforced by polarization in employment terms. A functionally flexible core of employees with favourable employment conditions is contrasted with a periphery of employees who provide numerical flexibility and enjoy neither upskilling nor employment security.

Britain

There are no accounts providing evidence of widespread and systematic polarization in either skill development or employment security. There is, however, evidence of some limited trends in this direction. The first is given by polarization along gender lines in industries where women are employed in significant numbers, such as textiles. Here men have been able to make gains in terms of both skill and pay at the expense of women workers, and women have experienced a greater deterioration in their conditions of employment and have been more prone to technological unemployment (Walsh 1991a: 131f; Crewe 1991: 50f). A second emerging trend is discernible in highly automated production systems where skilled tasks are moved away from manual and craft workers and even from technicians towards graduate engineers (Batstone and Gourlay 1986: 222; Campbell and Warner 1991: 154f; Jones 1988: 462). Although this upward shift in competence is a general feature of occupational change it is seen to be much more pronounced in Britain than in Germany (Campbell and Warner 1991; Mason et al. 1993). It is attributed to severe skill shortages at the skilled manual level but also to a reluctance to invest responsibility in manual workers, due to a lack of trust (ibid.: 155; Batstone and Gourlay 1986: 220). This development would fit the second definition of polarization, while the widespread elimination of unskilled manual grades contradicts the first definition. A last significant feature of British labour utilization strategies that suggests growing segmentation is the almost total exclusion of semi-skilled workers from programmes for upskilling and upgrading (Marsden and Ryan 1991; Jürgens 1991). Although the notion of continuous training is now more widely accepted it mainly benefits skilled workers (with an apprenticeship certificate) and technical staff, and excludes other workers (Whittaker 1990: 64).

Concerning polarization in employment terms, there is no conclusive evidence about such a trend in manufacturing industry. Although there have been notable increases in some forms of numerical flexibility at the aggregate level – particularly in part-time employment and in insecure self-employment – this development is mainly concentrated in the service sector. It has been relatively insignificant in manufacturing (Millward and Stevens 1986; Batstone and Gourlay 1986), and empirical studies have also found no confirmation that firms systematically divide their labour forces into core and peripheral sections (Marginson et al. 1988: 95; Rubery 1989: 70–1).

France

In France, skills have been significantly upgraded since the mid-1970s, widening the gap with Britain and bringing France nearer to the German position (Steedman 1990). At the same time, low-skill jobs have rapidly declined, as have manual jobs in general, particularly in the high-tech industries (Amadieu 1992: 62). This suggests not so much polarization as a growing tendency towards segmentation. In France segmentation tendencies appear to be stronger than in either Britain or Germany. The strong hierarchical tradition and the entrenched division between conception and execution has not been superseded in new production strategies but has merely appeared in a new form (Eyraud et al. 1988; Coriat 1992).

Social distance between manual and mental labour has endured and is often reinforced by a spatial distancing of mental labour (production control) at headquarters, away from production sites (Heidenreich 1993: 256). Skilled technical tasks are rarely assigned to operatives, even in enterprises where their level of skill would warrant this (see, for example, Eyraud et al. 1988; Lutz and Veltz 1989: 258). To bridge the gap between the technical departments and the shop floor, managements recruit a small elite of young technical workers with diplomas straight from college – the so-called production technicians (*techniciens d'atelier*) who deal with programming and other skilled tasks (Eyraud et al. 1988: 73). This small elite receives permanent training, good wages and career prospects, whereas the majority of shop-floor workers remain low-skilled and low-paid (Coriat 1992: 10).

Thus, lack of trust in manual workers seems to be a primary reason for this elitist strategy, although blocking strategies from technical workers and management efforts to achieve cost savings on training and pay also enter the equation. But even in industries where managements are now committed to a broader upskilling strategy, such as in the car industry, entrenched divisions between technical cadres and workers are hard to overcome. Thus, engineers are reported to be reluctant to relinquish any maintenance tasks to manual workers (Amadieu 1992: 64). In contrast to the situation in Germany, there are now few career paths leading from manual to technical or engineering status, so that lines of segmentation also become career barriers. The strongly scientifically orientated training of French engineers also creates social distance between production and technical departments and prevents the easy interchange of knowledge which has become crucial in the new production paradigm.

Polarization in employment terms has experienced an increase during the last decade, particularly through the rising incidence of fixed-term contracts for young workers (Lane 1989). But, as in Britain, it cannot be said that this development has divided industrial labour forces into core and periphery, nor is it clear that women have been worse affected by numerical flexibility. Thus, in the late 1980s, the male and female share of temporary workers of all employed in industry stood at 4.1 per cent for both groups (OECD 1989: 176–7, table 5.6). Women are, of course, predominant among part-timers, but in France this category of work cannot necessarily be equated with precarious work (Lane 1993).

Germany

The situation concerning skill and employment polarization is complex and highly ambiguous. In some senses, polarization is far less pronounced than in the other two societies, but, given the generally very high level of skill and the significant advance towards post-Fordist work organization, the gap between winners and losers in the transformation process sometimes appears starker than in Britain or France. The following lines of segmentation and polarization are causing concern. An upward shift in competence towards technical workers is also occurring in Germany in the most highly automated sectors (Pries et al. 1990: 84, 95), but it is mitigated by several countertrends. First, there has occurred an increase in the 'skilled and highly skilled manuals' category and these workers are utilized in functions which in Britain and France would be handled by technical staff. Second, the line of segmentation is much less rigid as co-operation between technical staff and manual workers is the norm, and promotion paths towards technical status still usually start from the shop floor (Lutz and Veltz 1989).

Advancing automation, however, has created new processes of segmentation *within* the working class between highly skilled system regulators and the shrinking proportion of semi-skilled workers who perform low-skill residual jobs and are cut off from paths of upward mobility (Schumann et al. 1990: 26). Even in the early 1990s, the move towards new production concepts had still not touched large segments of semi-skilled workers in assembly and less highly technicized work processes (Schumann et al. 1994). But this trend is counterbalanced by the opposite trend of upskilling and upgrading formerly semi-skilled workers in several of the former Fordist mass-production industries (Kern and Schumann 1984). Also, in contrast to the situation in Britain, skilled and semi-skilled employees work together in groups more often, sharing certain work activities (Pries et al. 1990: 95; Turner 1991).

Sociologists who favour the theoretical perspective of systemic rationalization (such as Sauer et al. 1992; Deiss 1992) go beyond claims on intrafirm skill polarization to pose the notion of interfirm polarization in the new subcontracting relationship. Powerful buyer firms, they argue, impose on dependent supplier firms strict control and harsh conditions, which the latter then pass on to their work-forces. But so far this claim has not been backed up by relevant data on several industries.

There are indications that skill segmentation along gender lines is also a considerable problem in Germany (Bechtle and Duell 1992: 244), but details are not provided in the literature. Here it is noteworthy that the influential metal workers union IG Metall has launched a new policy initiative on skill training for traditionally disadvantaged groups, such as women, but, despite the conclusion of one regional agreement with employers, acceptance of this demand has been low (Mahnkopf 1992). A modest increase in numerical flexibility has taken place, particularly in fixed-term contracts as a screening device before permanent employment (Lane 1989), but this cannot be unambiguously translated into a division of the industrial labour force into core and periphery. A more worrying trend is the strong exclusionary tendency, encouraged by aspects of the German system of industrial relations, which makes re-entry into the labour force by low-skilled unemployed and vulnerable groups almost impossible. Although this group is comparatively small, its exclusion is much more durable than in other advanced societies (Esping-Anderson 1993).

In sum, although the new production policy has led to the creation of new lines of segmentation and a marked polarization between those inside and outside employment there has been no pronounced polarization in terms of either skill or numerical flexibility. Moreover, the German experience shows a more pronounced trend towards skill enhancement and towards the blurring of skill divisions than under Fordism. But polarization between employed and unemployed is clearly an issue which unions and works councils need to keep on their agendas.

CONCLUSIONS

In all three countries, manufacturing industry has undergone substantial changes in production organization leading to transformations in patterns of work organization and control, as well as to shifts in labour relations. But the similarity in the overall direction of change hides important differences in where the main accents have been placed, in the degree of transformation achieved and, most importantly, in the coherence and stability of the emerging new patterns of production organization. Although a great deal of the impetus for change has come from global economic developments the forces of globalization have not overridden national distinctiveness shaped by long-standing institutional influences. The latter, although not immutable, have acted very much as the prism through which global influences have been refracted.

The German pattern of change is very consistent and presents an intensification and a development of prior tendencies rather than an abrupt rupture with previous traditions. Pre-existing differences between mass- and small-batch production industries and between large firms and SMEs have been eroded to a significant degree. Production policy is overwhelmingly in the mould of diversified quality production, and the main instrument of change is automation. The implementation of the new process technology occurs particularly in the framework of a strong pre-existing commitment to utilize and develop human resources and on the whole well-functioning institutional structures for conflict resolution and employee participation.

The process of change has, however, not been without its tensions. The first arises from the emergence of a much enlarged management control potential on the one side, and the necessity, on the other side, to utilize the initiative and creativity of the labour force, arising from both claims for autonomy of a highly skilled labour force and the demands posed by the use of complex forms of systemic integration. At the present time, the evidence points more strongly towards the adoption of compromise solutions than towards the fact that this tension will come to undermine the whole production paradigm. Second, there is the incipient danger that the expensive and cumbersome human-resources strategy will remain confined to one section of the working class only and that unions and works councils, dominated by skilled workers, will be unable to resist such a strategy. It remains to be seen whether existing lines of skill segmentation will diminish or increase as the new production model moves towards a more mature stage. Third, the 1990s have brought high labour costs to the forefront of management concerns. German goods are seen to be no longer able to compete simply on the criterion of high quality, and managements increasingly strive to combine high quality with stable labour and social costs. It remains to be seen whether unions will make this management concern their own, or whether the latter will further increase relocation of production to lower-wage countries in Eastern Europe and thus put into jeopardy the whole German production model.

For French enterprises, the move towards a new production policy has imposed far-reaching adjustments in labour utilization and organizational patterns, and Fordist inertia has often undermined these adjustment efforts or channelled them in a neo-Fordist direction. In the words of Boyer (1992: 9), 'the weight of hierarchical controls, the reliance on science and technology instead of a more pragmatic approach and finally quite adversarial industrial relations explain the persistence of mass production principles'.

Due to the entrenched hierarchical structure and the ensuing absence of trust between manual workers and cadres, the strong division between conception and execution has been maintained. Although the skill levels in production have risen and efforts have been made to reduce the organizational barrier between production and technical departments the solution adopted has been very elitist and has maintained old lines of segmentation between manual workers and technical staff. This continuation of Fordist practices is also due to the French tradition in engineering where a scientific and highly theoretical approach has always militated against the utilization of production experience (Lutz and Veltz 1989). Whereas in Germany workers' knowledge and commitment are deployed to get optimal use of equipment, in France technology is utilized to maintain control over workers (Boyer 1992: 10).

It is doubtful whether this approach will achieve the flexibility demanded by the new production paradigm and whether new labour relations of a co-operative nature can be built on such foundations. This new high-tech production strategy is, of course, mainly confined to large enterprises, and the gap between them and SMEs has remained larger than in the German case. Thus, the French pattern of production organization has neither fully overcome old Fordist rigidities nor has it removed the old tensions between management and labour, although the highly antagonistic tenor of labour relations has been muted to some extent.

For British manufacturing enterprises the move away from the Fordist production paradigm has also demanded deep ruptures with past practices. The pursuit of diversified quality production has necessitated fundamental reorientations in the fields of product strategy, investment behaviour, training, working practices and industrial and labour relations. Moreover, these have had to be accomplished in the context of a deep recession and a more unfavourable political climate than in the other two countries. In addition, management strategy for a transformation of production organization has been less consistent than in either France or Germany, and change has occurred in a more piecemeal manner.

Although diversified quality production is now the declared goal in many industries the actual routes adopted show neither a strong emphasis on highly automated production systems nor on the development of a highly skilled labour force to exploit the new technology to its full potential. Differences between industries and types of firm remain considerable in both respects. The most notable changes have probably been of an organizational kind, such as the development of more flexible organizational structures and working practices. Considerable management efforts have also been made in the field of labour relations in the direction of gaining greater employee involvement and trust. But these efforts have only infrequently been accompanied by practices that ensure labour gains in the fields of employment security, skill enhancement or active participation in work design. It must, therefore, remain doubtful whether mutual trust and a focus on common goals have been significantly enhanced. A neo-Fordist emphasis on technical or psychological control is the probable outcome.

Thus, in conclusion, whereas in Germany a coherent strategy for change has led to transformations in production organization which point more strongly in the direction of post-Fordism than neo-Fordism, in France an equally consistent strategy is widely perceived to have strong neo-Fordist tendencies. In Britain a highly diverse and not always consistent pattern of industrial change is more difficult to label, but it would be fair to say that, overall, the points have been shifted more strongly in the direction of neo- than of post-Fordism, although of a less rigid kind than in France.

NOTE

1. 'Germany' in this chapter refers to the former Federal Republic. Although evidence is now emerging about patterns of production organization in the former GDR, there is insufficient detail and the new developments are, as yet, insufficiently settled to make a general evaluation. But a few general points to indicate developmental trends in the East can nevertheless be made. Given the very small share of Eastern industrial production of total industrial production – 3–4 per cent in the early 1990s (Kern 1994) – the impact of emerging Eastern patterns on the whole German model is bound to be slight. This slight impact is all the more likely, given the wholesale transfer of Western institutions to the East. In addition, the decision to aim for wage parity and the rejection of a dual economy (see figures by Schmierl and Schutz-Wild 1994), condemning the Eastern states to low-wage and low-skill production, will also introduce a trend towards homogeneity.

   But the institutional and cultural legacy of the command economy will nevertheless retain a lingering effect. Mahnkopf (1991: 272) conjures up the following pessimistic scenario. Production relocated from the West to the East, she suggests, will predominately have a 'low-technology' component and will be organized along undemanding 'mass-production' lines. Labour utilization will tend towards rigid Taylorist forms of work organization and control rather than towards a strategy that utilizes human resources. While this negative picture may apply during the transition period it is by no means clear that Mahnkopf's scenario will be valid in the longer run. The large reservoir of skilled labour, the move to wage parity and the installation of the most modern technology in many large firms established by Western capital (such as the Opel car plant in Eisenach and the new Mercedes plant) make it likely that a convergence in patterns of production and work organization will evolve by the end of this century. Furthermore, a recent large survey in the capital goods industry (Schmierl and Schutz-Wild 1994) shows that the movement away from a Taylorist production policy has already started and that the majority of enterprises favour decentralization of operations and decision-making, a reduction in the division of labour and of hierarchy and the introduction of skilled group work (ibid.).

9. Industrial change and the state: disengagement or re-engagement?

Previous chapters have shown that the last 15 years or so have witnessed significant transformations in all aspects of industrial organization, as well as a growing internationalization of economic activity. This general turbulence in the industrial arena has been accompanied by, and is reflected in, a growing uncertainty about the role which the state can and should play in guiding or shaping industrial development. During the early post-war decades, up to the mid-1970s, there existed a widespread political consensus that the state has a considerable role to play, and strong expansion of state involvement in this sphere was largely condoned and, in many cases, applauded. But subsequent years have seen many doubts about the wisdom of extensive state involvement in industrial development, particularly, though by no means exclusively, by academics and politicians on the political right. It has become almost a political commonplace that the state should be rolled back and that more scope should be given to market forces. While this call for a disengagement of the state and a strengthening of the market has been particularly insistent and strident in Britain it has also assumed political significance in the two continental societies. At the same time, it has been claimed by authors from all parts of the political spectrum that, due to growing economic globalization and European economic integration, the nation state is becoming increasingly unable to influence national economic development. Proponents of a radical globalization thesis would thus further contend that national state intervention in the economy has become futile.

The activities of the state impinge on industrial development in a multitude of ways, and any discussion of the role of the state in this respect has to define the latter in a way which renders the task manageable in the space available and also assists in understanding recent developments. Among the narrowly economic functions of the state we can distinguish that of macro-economic management (monetary and fiscal policy) from industrial policy itself where the state intervenes directly in the affairs of individual firms, industries or regions, with a view to stimulating industrial activity according to a more or less clearly conceived plan. Alternatively, the state may merely provide a regulatory framework to guarantee the working of the market or to correct and adapt its working. A fourth way in which the state impinges on

167

industrial adjustment lies in its role as a provider of a physical and social infrastructure, more or less supportive to a favourable development and combination of the factors of production. A last and more intangible way in which the state affects national competitiveness has been highlighted in the work of New Institutionalists (see, for example, Hall 1984 and 1986) and received further interesting development by followers and interpreters of flexible specialization theory, such as Hirst and Zeitlin (1992) and Hirst and Thompson (1992). In this work, the institutional structure of the state and the values and attitudes engendered by it become regarded almost as an additional factor of production.[1] A focus on this institutionalist interpretation of the role of the state in the economy is highly illuminating in understanding the different patterns of economic development of the three European societies before the 'industrial divide' of the 1970s. It also assists interpretation of the different patterns and styles of economic policy-making during the period of alleged state disengagement and loss of role, due to growing globalization.

The scope and nature of state activity in relation to industry depends not only on how the role of the state is defined in dominant societal ideologies and current governmental political stance. Institutionalists emphasize that it is also crucially determined by the structure of the state itself – particularly by the extent of integration and cohesion between different elements of the state and the degree of their relative autonomy from pressure groups and established elites, as well as by the degree of its centralization (Whitley 1992: 27). Further variability between societies in the role of the state *vis-à-vis* industry stems from the degree of inclusion into, or exclusion from, the policy-making community of the organizations of capital and labour (Hall 1984). Intermediary organizations, such as banks, trade associations, development agencies, Chambers and union federations, are able not only to assume many regulatory and quasi-political functions but also contribute crucially to the consensual formulation and effective implementation of state policy. Adoption of this institutionalist approach implicitly rejects state-centric theory in favour of state-structural theory (Hall 1993), even for societies like France, where the state has traditionally played a strong central role in industrial policy.

Hirst and Thompson (1992: 373f) further define the last crucial role of the state mentioned above: they designate it an 'orchestrator of economic consensus' which is played with greater or lesser success, depending on state structural characteristics. This role, in turn, entails three key functions: (a) the state constructs 'a distributional coalition', that is, it wins the acceptance of key organized social interests for a pattern of distribution of national income which, amongst other things, promotes industrial competitiveness; (b) it creates a collaborative political culture in which there occurs consensual bargaining over economic goals between key economic actors and their organizations, their lasting and consistent implementation and, lastly, membership compliance with bargains struck; (c) the state achieves an adequate balance in the distribution of resources and regulatory activity between different territorial interests at national, regional and municipal political level. This is not only a matter of distributional justice but also one of organizational effectiveness in terms of transaction costs.

This chapter is structured in the following way: first is a brief summary of the current debate on the role of the state and the market in economic life and of the arguments put forward by those favouring a rolling back of the state; the second part applies the institutionalist approach outlined above to an analysis of the structure of the state in our three European societies and shows how structure has shaped actual policies. Here I first outline how the resulting state capacities have in each case interacted with the structure of national economic problems and opportunities during the earlier post-war decades. This is followed by an analysis of changes in industrially relevant social and economic policies of our three societies during recent decades. These reviews of both past and current state policy will be mindful of the various roles of the state in the economy detailed above. A concluding section assesses whether and to what extent disengagement or loss of economic role on the part of the state has in fact occurred in each case.

FROM STATE TO MARKET

Economists and politicians on the political Right have argued that many of the economic difficulties which beset the advanced economies from the 1970s onwards were caused by an over-extended role of the state in the economy which syphoned off too much capital from the productive private sector and seriously impaired its working. Although the shift from the market to the state has been occurring during the last 100 years it became particularly pronounced after the Second World War, as a consequence of the post-war settlement and the establishment of welfare-state capitalism or the Keynesian welfare state. This involved a number of policy innovations. The first was state management of the economy to create full employment, thorough an injection of money into the economy in order to increase demand which, in turn, would stimulate employment. This was achieved through increases in public-sector borrowing and budget deficits and through fiscal policy. In addition to the assumption of this general economic management function, the state also increased more specific economic intervention to both restructure firms and whole sectors, as well as shore up firms and industries in crisis which were deemed important in terms of either employment or national

prestige, or simply in terms of political expediency. The second innovation
was the introduction of an extended system of social security, covering virtu-
ally the whole population and including also the extension of health and
education systems. The tremendous cost of these innovations does not need
emphasizing. A third feature of welfare capitalism was the inclusion of
labour in economic progress by translating increases in productivity into
wage increases and thus creating the basis for mass consumption. Following
from this was the final characteristic, the institutionalization of class conflict
and the establishment of a class compromise between capital and labour. This
was not only evident at the level of the enterprise but also in more or less
continuous and successful tripartite bargaining at the political level. These
four features then are seen to constitute the social structure of accumulation
in the early post-war decades (Berger 1990).

For a long time these policies seemed to be highly successful, creating
economic growth, prosperity, full employment and greater distributional justice, although it remains arguable to what degree Keynesianism had actually
contributed to these achievements and how much was due to the contribution
of accidental and external factors (ibid.). When the economies of advanced
capitalist societies began to falter from the mid-1970s onwards this became
blamed on these four features of welfare capitalism. The simultaneous occurrence of unemployment and inflation contradicted a basic Keynesian tenet. It
was alleged that the welfare state had created a governmental overload,
hindering the working of the market. Full employment and social cushioning
of those not in employment, it has further been argued, have eliminated an
industrial reserve army and downward pressure on wages and have thus
finally led to a squeeze on profits in all advanced economies.

While it is indisputable that indicators of economic failure, such as a slow-
down in productivity, a fiscal crisis of the state, unemployment and inflation,
became much more prominent from this time onwards, it has remained difficult
and controversial to prove the suggested causation. Also different countries
displayed different combinations of indicators of failure, as well as different
levels of malfunctioning, and some countries with highly developed welfare
states and interventionist governments did not experience high unemployment.
Because of this uncertainty about causation it remains controversial to introduce political remedies which are designed to scrap all the elements of the
post-war settlement. While it is now widely accepted by economists and politicians from all parts of the political spectrum that, due to extensive changes in
the economic environment, traditional Keynesian demand management is no
longer the answer to economic problems (Hall 1993: 285; Berger 1990), there
remains disagreement about the economic implications of the other elements of
welfare capitalism. Current debate thus remains focused on what might be the
right balance between state and market and on what role is left for the state in

the governance of the economy. Here it is notable that greatly increased internationalization of economic activity, particularly of capital markets, and the resultant volatility of markets have made it much more problematic for national states to engage in macroeconomic management; it also makes them wary of adopting and implementing an industrial policy which implies a government blueprint for industrial development. The main issue thus becomes whether or not such insights should lead to a rolling-back of the state or merely to a reorientation of the state's role in industry. In what follows, most attention will be given to economically relevant policy, as issues relating to the political inclusion of labour have already been discussed in Chapter 7.

INSTITUTIONALIST ANALYSIS OF THE STATE: VARIATION IN STATE STRUCTURE AND POLICIES BETWEEN EUROPEAN SOCIETIES

New Institutionalists, such as Weir and Skocpol (1985) and Hall (1984 and 1986), see the state as an autonomous actor with more or less pronounced capacities for action. The latter, in each case, are due both to historical legacies and to state structure or, for Hall, state organization. State structures affect not only the goals that policy-makers adopt but also the constraints on, and opportunities for, the decision-making they experience. National differences in such structures lead to fundamentally different policy outcomes, regardless of the common economic framework and comparable economic problems confronted. Such institutionalist analysis throws light on the processes of both policy-making and its implementation. This analysis need not be confined to agencies formally designated as part of the state but should also encompass intermediary institutions between state and firms which fulfil quasi-political functions. Among these, according to Hall (1984), the organizations of capital and labour and their relation to the state are a particularly important object of study. The latter are not only important in the implementation process. Knowledge of their organizational capacities also contributes to an understanding of the distribution of power among the key social groups and of the interests which can be expressed through given organizational structures. Let us apply this theoretical framework to economic policy-making and implementation, first, during the period of welfare capitalism, and second, during the period of market capitalism.

Germany

The German state was created anew after the military defeat of the Second World War. Some of its elements revived older German traditions (federal structure, industrial self-administration); others were genuinely new inventions, and the old and the new do not always pull in the same direction. Great care was taken to avoid the dominance the German state had asserted over the economy at earlier periods of history. The institutional structure expressed both the new liberal-democratic political ideology and the new economic philosophy of Ordo-Liberalism and the notion of the social market economy founded on it. The latter extols the idea of a free market with a strict competition regime and confines the role of the state to devising the framework conditions which safeguard the functioning of the market.

But Ordo-Liberalism is also an expression of a compromise between capital and labour, inspired by the paternalism of the social Catholic wing of the Christian Democratic Union (CDU), the then ruling party, which wants to see labour compensated for damage suffered as the result of market rule. Lessons of history had taught conservative politicians like Adenauer that an economic system must provide opportunity for all social groups in order to avoid the political extremism of excluded and frustrated social groups. Thus the state's role as an orchestrator of social consensus became uneasily combined with that of a mere regulator of the economy. This syncretist ideology has informed the economic policies to a greater or lesser extent throughout the post-war period and has led to the pursuit of a German-style liberal supply-side policy (Streeck 1992: 186), although there was a relatively brief interlude when Keynesian policy curtailed the influence of liberal ideology. In Germany, the role of the state in the economy has remained a constant topic for discussion, and restrictions on the level of state intervention have been given strong emphasis in theory, if not always in practice.

This ambiguity in political ideology is also reflected in institutional structures and economic policies. On the one side, structural arrangements limit the scope of state intervention in the economy, but on the other, there exist a variety of political mechanisms to restrain the influence of the market. It is notable that German economic governance is both vertically and horizontally divided. The federal political structure divides economic resources (tax revenue) between the central and the regional states and also cedes to the latter extensive powers of local economic development. A horizontal division of governance refers to the division of macroeconomic management between government ministries, particularly that of Economic Affairs, the independent Bundesbank and the (less independent) Monopolies Commission (*Bundeskartellamt*). The independence of the Federal Bank is guaranteed by the Constitution but is limited by the obligation to support the general economic policy of the government. This does create conflicts of interest but, on the whole, the mechanisms to safeguard the Bundesbank's independence make it an influential actor in the political economy and have generally proved to be highly effective. Thus both monetary and competition policy have largely been taken out of central government control, and many other economic functions usually executed by central states had to be shared with the local states (Allen 1987: 84, 97). These multiple divisions of power have had many highly beneficial consequences, such as the removal of monetary policy from parliamentary political pressure and an effective control of inflation, relatively low levels of regional economic imbalance and, lastly, industrial policies well attuned to local industrial needs. But such divisions also created immobility and impotence in central government and explain the short duration of Keynesian demand management in the German case.

Central power has been further curtailed by the German tradition of giving extensive powers of self-government to strong and well organized economic interest associations, such as trade associations, chambers of craft and industry, employers' associations and unions. (For details on their functions and organizational strength, see Smyser 1991: 55f). The large universal banks, although not formally given such quasi-political functions, nevertheless frequently act on behalf of both individual capitals and industrial capital as a whole and have assumed many self-government functions in the running of industries (see Chapter 3). German capital thus shows an unusually high degree of self-organization, as well as a high degree of unity between financial and industrial capital. Whereas the trade associations and their powerful peak organization, the BDI, speak on behalf of large capital, the Chambers effectively promote the interests of the *Mittelstand vis-à-vis* the state. The highly centralized and unified employers' association, the BDA, faces a moderately centralized but well-co-ordinated peak organization of labour, the DGB. On the one side, these arrangements have been very conducive to 'the orchestration of economic and social consensus.' On the other side, the existence of influential interest associations introduces much collusion into economic policy-making and is thus in conflict with the 'free market' protestations of the official ideology. The power of these associations also turns them into influential lobbies and, paradoxically, often compels the state to remain involved when it would like to withdraw.

All these horizontal and vertical divisions of power thus weaken the German central state in crucial ways, conveying a picture of 'a Goliath tied down by powerful checks and balances [and by] highly organised and centralised societal interests' (Schmidt 1992: 2). It would be wrong, however, to view the central state as completely enfeebled and the concept of 'the enabling state' more appropriately describes its role. Capacities for direct industrial intervention still remain in some areas, and central government agencies, such as the Ministry of Technology, have played an important role in stimulating industrial innovation. Furthermore, the federal state has played a central role in the establishment of framework conditions which have been influential in setting general norms, providing effective regulatory mecha-

nisms and, last but by no means least, a social infrastructure highly supportive of industry. Here the social component of the social market economy has
been both strengthened and redefined over time, partly through the influential
union movement. Within the social framework, the system of education and
training at all levels and the facilities to create scientific and technical knowledge and make it relevant and available to industry are particularly noteworthy (for further details, see Lane 1989, 1990 and 1992). Lastly, it is worth
noting that these policy-making organizations have shown an unusually high
degree of stability over the post-war period. While some commentators see
this stability combined with enough internal flexibility to initiate incremental
change in response to new economic challenges, others associate this consensual model with increasing tardiness, if not paralysis, in the face of such
challenges.

How has this complex institutional structure of the economic and industrial policy-making community affected actual policy during the early post-
war decades up to the late 1970s? How have different elements contributed
to, or diminished, the crisis of the state outlined in general terms in the
introductory section of this chapter?

In the area of macroeconomic management, the German pattern was for a
long time notable for a seriously undervalued currency which provided a
subsidy to industry and contributed to the export boom but imposed costs on
consumers – features supported by both industrial and financial capital and
condoned by the Bundesbank and hence highly resistant to popular criticism
and political effort to revalue. In the area of fiscal policy, the government
behaved in a distinctly non-Keynesian way and tended to run a budgetary
surplus, although policy changed somewhat from 1967 onwards. The
Bundesbank always kept a close watch on public expenditure and reacted to
increases by tightening monetary policy, even to the point of creating mini-
recessions. Prevention of inflation has always been its top priority. After the
1966–7 recession, however, the central government was empowered to assume a stronger part in stabilization policy through medium-term financial
planning and budgetary policy and the issuing of longer-term financial orientation data that provided signals to capital and labour. But this new optimism
in financial planning turned out to be short-lived.

The ability to maintain consistently low levels of inflation was considerably enhanced by the maintenance of what Hall (1984) calls a 'tacit tripartism',
that is, an incomes policy resting more on a mutual understanding between
capital and labour than on an explicit bargain between the three most important political actors. The reasons why for the most part it worked well have to
be sought in the high degree of disciplined co-ordination between levels of
the union hierarchy: a structural feature which sets the German union movement clearly apart from those in Britain and France. Workers could be sure

that wage restraint would be generally observed and that a pay-off in terms of low inflation would therefore be assured. Other pay-offs, such as greater participation rights and generous social benefits, also gradually increased over this period. The lack of influence over monetary policy by government ministries, however, made a guarantee of full employment impossible and explains why, since the mid-1970s, unemployment has risen to high levels, given the relatively healthy state of the German economy in comparative terms.

In the sphere of industrial policy, different approaches prevailed during the early and later post-war decades. Early German governments, inspired by the economic liberalism of the social market economy, claimed not to have an industrial policy; a systematic approach, under the heading of *Strukturpolitik*, was developed only from the mid-1960s onwards. German governments have consistently eschewed direct intervention and have preferred to leave indus-trial reorganization of firms and sectors to the banks, although often with the help of considerable government subsidies. The most important influence of both federal and *Länder* governments probably lies in factor creation (Porter 1990: 378): in the provision of a very effective infrastructure for the creation of general and vocational education, science and technology and their trans-fer to industry.

Another feature of this liberal stance has been the low importance of the nationalized sector in governmental industrial policy. All the state-owned firms were inherited from the pre-war period, and no expansion has occurred since then. Furthermore, such firms have been expected to function in the same way as privately owned ones (Esser 1988). But the publicly owned banks (owned by the municipalities, the *Länder* and by the federal govern-ment) have played an extremely important role in regional industrial policy and in the support of the *Mittelstand*.

A non-interventionist policy, however, has not been pursued with total consistency, and intervention also increased from the late 1960s onwards. The central government has persistently given direct subsidies to some indus-tries, such as coal and aerospace, and more intermittently to others, for example, ship building and steel. Also some local states have shown them-selves willing to provide direct support for industry. Often the 'social' com-ponent in the economic ideology obliged governments to intervene where the 'free market' component would have urged standing aside. This slightly incongruous mixture of liberal economic and neo-corporatist social policy, however, has been seen more often as a strength than as a weakness of the German system (see, for example, Streeck 1992: 188).

Further contradictions exist in the area of competition policy. On the one hand, the creation of the Monopolies Commission and its prevention of a return to pre-war cartellization of industry are in tune with the liberal market policy. On the other, the high degree of concentration and interconnectedness in industry, the power of organized capital and the occasional overruling of the Commission's decisions by the government, strongly contradict liberal competition policy. Another apparently contradictory feature of the German social system of production associated with its economic success is the coexistence of sharp competition in the areas of product innovation and market share with a collectivity-orientated acceptance of common framework regulations and a readiness to conform to general standards and co-ordination efforts (Allen 1987: 88; Smyser 1992: 41). Although the consensual style has many strengths, it also entails a very slow and cumbersome decision-making process which is becoming increasingly unresponsive to the dictates of continual innovation and other demands connected with the regime of flexible accumulation.

In sum, the German version of the capitalist welfare state was never pure, but mixed statist intervention with an emphasis on moderate market liberalism in a distinctive way. Keynesian demand management was never very important. Although the industrial policy function of the state, narrowly defined, has not been highly developed, industrial competitiveness has nevertheless been boosted by the way other economic roles have been executed: particular importance must be attributed to the orchestration of economic consensus and, partially overlapping with this role, the provision of a social infrastructure highly favourable to industry.

The crisis which developed from the mid-1970s onwards was not characterized by the same degree of profit squeeze and inflation as in Britain, nor was the crisis ever as deep as in the other two countries. But German economists are showing increasing alarm about what they perceive as a failure to keep pace with global industrial innovation. They charge that industrial policy has been too defensive and has invested too much in the modernization of traditional sectors, while 'leading-edge' industries, such as microelectronics, are badly lagging behind American and Japanese competitors (Smyser 1992: 105f). Lack of innovatory spirit is also seen to be evident in the failure to provide sufficient venture capital for new small high-tech firms (ibid.: 107). A final problem which might threaten future economic strength is Germany's relative lack of success in attracting inward FDI, due to high labour and energy costs, high environmental burdens and high corporate taxes (Dierkes and Zimmermann 1989).

France

The French state did not experience the fundamental political reconstitution of the German state after the Second World War, but it nevertheless engaged in far-reaching institutional restructuring to deal with the tremendous problems faced by France at that time. They consisted not only of material devastation, dented national pride and low popular morale but also of relative economic backwardness, expressed in a large and backward agricultural sector, a traditional industrial structure and a preponderance of firms largely sheltered from, and unsuitable for, international trade and economic competition with other advanced countries. In this context, economic modernization could only be accomplished under strong state direction. This led to the revitalization of an old French ideology: *Colbertisme* or state *dirigisme*, and the creation of an activist and developmental state. State intervention in the economy became a prime means to achieve not only economic development but also political grandeur and national independence. As in Britain, France's aspiration to remain a major military power strongly determined the pattern of its industrial policy. Conversely, *dirigisme* entailed an under-emphasis on the market and a sheltering of firms from its effects.

This *dirigiste* stance was largely incompatible with orchestration of economic consensus, which entails some political delegation. Although the distribution of the fruits of new-found prosperity was to include labour, the labour organizations were never seen as active participants in this restructuring process. Capital, although better organized than labour, was nevertheless too fragmented in the early post-war years to become an equal partner in the economic policy-making process. Consequently, economic governance in France was highly centralized. There was neither any power-sharing with political structures at lower geographical levels nor any other horizontal sharing with quasi-political bodies, such as an independent central bank. Within the state, economic power and influence was concentrated in the executive, particularly in the Ministry of Finance and, given the frequent turnover in ministerial staff, in the permanent administrative staff, guiding politicians of the day. The exceptional degree of power vested in the civil service, particularly in its so-called *Grands Corps*, is expressed in the term 'the administered state'.

The administrative elite, willing and able to take on this gargantuan task of economic modernization, was created by an institution deeply embedded in the French state: the *Ecole Nationale d'Administration* (ENA). This *grande école*, especially founded for the purpose, was even more elitist academically than the already very elitist system of *grandes écoles* generally. It provided the stream of highly educated and self-confident technocrats who devoted themselves to the re-establishment of French economic power and, through it, political glory. Thus, the absence of vertical integration of the organizations of capital and labour was at least partially compensated for by a high degree of elite cohesion.

But expertise and blueprints for economic development, as contained in French economic plans, were not a sufficient basis for the extraordinary concentration of economic power. They had to be married to control over investment finance. In France, as in Germany, large firms have obtained their investment capital mainly through bank credit, and the stock market remained unimportant. Due to their very high debt–equity ratios, French firms depended on long-term loans and on the state to secure for them access to such loans. Although the ties between financial and industrial capital are not as close as in Germany (Boyer 1991a), the high degree of reliance by French firms on long-term debt nevertheless creates dependence on banks.

In the post-war years, investment finance from the French banking system came under various kinds of state control. At that time, the state set up various financial institutions for, on the one hand, the collection of savings and on the other, institutions specializing in lending to different branches of the economy (Hall 1984). The state's control over these funds then gave the government influence over the rest of the banking sector and over the terms and conditions under which capital was made available to private industry. Nationalization of some banks further strengthened this influence. In addition, the government had considerable influence over the Bank of France and thus over monetary policy. Consequently, monetary, fiscal and industrial policy have been conducted mainly by one government ministry: the Ministry of Finance and particularly the *Trésor* within it, and these various policies could be formulated in a mutually reinforcing manner.

The second important institution during the early decades was the General Planning Commission which devised the overall strategy for the development of industry. All these factors together gave the French state and its functionaries a strong capacity to influence the development of industry in a relatively coherent manner which was lacking in both Germany and Britain. The insulation of economic policy-making from day-to-day political pressure – the French parliament is much less influential than the British – ensured a high degree of continuity in policy-making bodies, if not always in economic policy.

What then has been the influence of this state structure and of the organization of capital and labour on French economic, industrial and social welfare policy? The overriding goal of economic policy during the early post-war decades was to stimulate industrial investment. This was accomplished through the development of an almost continuous public-sector deficit and stimulation of demand; and, to an even greater degree, through the provision of large quantities of cheap credit to industry (Hall 1984: 30–1). The ensuing high level of inflation was handled through frequent devaluations of the franc. In contrast to the situation in Britain, there was no independent financial capital to oppose such a policy, and macroeconomic management was thus consistently organized in the interest of industry. Although the French economy became much more integrated into the international economy from the late

1950s onwards, belief in national political independence, articulated by de Gaulle, made the state resistant to inward FDI, which at this stage came mainly from the USA.

Industrial policy was carried out mainly by the Ministry of Finance which, in contrast to the British Treasury, totally accepted this responsibility (Hall 1984: 32). Policy was strongly interventionist, particularly in the 1945–58 period. Industry was modernized and restructured according to state plans, and industrial sectors and firms were reshaped accordingly. Control over investment finance constituted the means to accomplish this ambitious goal. The Planning Commission and the *Trésor* selected six industrial sectors as worthy of fast development and encouraged mergers of industrial firms. An additional important instrument of restructuring was the nationalization of a number of banks and industrial firms, making the French state-owned sector the largest of our three countries.

After 1958, the importance of the Planning Commission and of comprehensive state planning declined, and interventionism assumed a more selective character: major industrial and technological projects and incentives for merger in the major sectors (Stoffaes 1989: 108–9). These *grands projets*, linked to either national defence or to the secure supply of basic materials, encompassed both public research institutes and private firms. Merger policy was highly motivated by the belief that only firms of sufficient scale – the so-called national champions – would be able to compete in international markets, become MNCs and develop the necessary research capacity. Industrial capital largely welcomed this policy. By the end of the 1960s such firms had been created in most sectors (Stoffaes 1989: 110). As in Britain, industrial policy thus mainly supported large firms and, despite political rhetoric to the contrary, the large sector of SMEs often suffered from the 'sometimes artificial and hasty manner' in which concentration was accomplished (ibid.: 123; Dubois and Linhart 1994).

Given the fragmentation and weakness of the organization of labour, there was never any attempt to engage it in either implicit or explicit tripartite bargaining and to introduce an incomes policy. Maintenance of price controls disciplined employers to keep wage rises in line with productivity, and periodic devaluation of the currency also contributed to the suppression of wage inflation. The turning-point came in 1968 with the increases in wages and social benefits granted in the Grenelle Accords after the strikes and general unrest of that year. From this period onwards, more attention was given to the social needs created by industrial restructuring, and budgets for welfare and for the development of the infrastructure were greatly increased (Stoffaes 1989: 108).

These early post-war decades, now known as the *Trentes glorieuses*, thus saw a fundamental transformation of French industry, bringing above-average growth rates and a steep increase in all-round prosperity, as well as a growing integration into the world economy. (The share of exports in the GNP doubled between 1958 and 1973; Stoffaes 1989: 107.) The state's central role in this process endowed its interventionist style with legitimacy. But towards the end of this period, from the early 1970s onwards, negative effects of *dirigiste* industrial policy became apparent: many of the national champions prospered mainly because of their close association with the state as both investor and secure main purchaser, such as in the field of military hardware. Firms were ill-adapted to trading in free markets, particularly as the latter became increasingly internationalized. Increasing economic integration into the then EEC also made some industrial policy measures problematic. French firms were heavily indebted and this, at the macro level, aggravated the degree of inflation.

Thus, to sum up, the French developmental state concentrated heavily on the two roles of economic management and on the execution of highly selective interventionist policy measures. Provision of social infrastructure received only moderately strong emphasis – particularly before 1968 – and orchestration of economic consensus relatively low consideration. Both the nature and the causes of the industrial crisis which developed in France from the mid-1970s onwards differed in many respects from that in Germany and Britain: it was connected to a greater degree with the lack of industrial and political integration of labour and the conflicts engendered by it. It cannot be connected with an encumbrance of economic decision-making by too much collusion between organized interests, as in Germany. Many of the increasingly evident weaknesses of French manufacturing industry became attributed to the highly dominant role of the state. What was once the success of the state gradually became regarded as its failure.

Britain

The British state, van Waarden (1993: 8) points out, at first sight presents something of a paradox. On the one hand, it is, in principle, a very powerful state: state power is highly concentrated, activated through the majority party in Parliament and its leader in the executive; there is no judicial review and no constitutional safeguards for the autonomy of regions and local authorities; and the executive can call on a 'career' civil service with high public status. On the other hand, however, this potential state power is not often applied to the affairs of industry or else is used inconsistently and to generally poor effect. This feature of the British state, it will be argued, is due to reasons which are partly ideological – a liberalism with a strong emphasis on voluntarism – and partly to various structural features of the state and the wider policy-making community. Consequently, the British state of the early post-war decades has been characterized by a continually oscillating economic policy and by an underdeveloped and unsystematic industrial policy.

The structures of the British state have never been as decentralized as in Germany, nor has economic policy-making been as highly centralized and co-ordinated as in France. Although there has always been some devolution of power to the regions, particularly those outside England, an appropriate institutional framework for devolved economic and industrial policy-making was never established. At the level of central government, responsibility for monetary and fiscal policy has been divided between the Bank of England and the Treasury. Although Bank decisions were formally subordinated to the Treasury after the Second World War, the Bank in fact has enjoyed considerable independence in its decision-making (Hall 1984: 34). It has been the principal manager of monetary policy and the representative within Whitehall for the financial markets (ibid.). In contrast to the situation in Germany, however, the Bank of England has usually decided in favour of financial capital, and its persistent refusal to contemplate deflation has been very damaging to industry. The Treasury, for much of this early period, was mainly charged with the control of public expenditure, and it had no department or specially trained staff explicitly concerned with the affairs of industry, nor was there any capacity to assess the impact of fiscal and monetary policy on industry (ibid.).

The institutional preconditions for developing an industrial policy were not created until the late 1960s when the Ministry of Technology was founded. Even then, the institutional structures for industrial policy-making were subjected to continual change and never acquired sufficient continuity and influence to resist the less-than-benign influence of the Treasury. The general lack of consideration on the part of the state of industry's needs has also been evident in broader policy areas, such as the development of a social infrastructure favouring industry.

The lack of an appropriate institutional base for industrial policy-making at the level of the state has not been compensated for by the intervention of strong intermediary organizations representing the collective interest of capital and labour. In contrast to the situation in France and Germany, the interests of industrial and financial capital are strictly divided, due to the historical prominence in the financial system of the City and the lack of long-term involvement with industrial firms on the part of the clearing banks (for details, see Chapter 3). Although the peak organizations of both capital and labour have been regularly consulted over issues of economic and industrial policy, neither has been sufficiently well organized to give direction to it. Organizations of industrial capital, such as the Confederation of British Industry (CBI), have never been powerful enough either to redress the unfavourable balance of power between industrial and financial capital, or to make the state adopt a coherent industrial strategy. Nor have the organizations of industrial capital ever been sufficiently united and strong to take on tasks of industrial restructuring themselves. Small and medium-sized capital had no collective voice to influence governments until the late 1970s. The labour organization, the Trades Union Congress, has been equally unable to exert an active influence in industrial policy-making; but it has nevertheless exerted strong indirect influence, due to relatively high levels of union membership, coupled with considerable militancy and, under Labour governments, due to political ties between the Party and the union movement. Such influence has been asserted both through veto power and through its inability to unite its membership behind commitments made by leaders in tripartite negotiations with the government and the CBI. Thus, to conclude this section, although the British state did not repudiate the role of 'orchestrator of economic consensus' during this period, both economic ideology and state structures have militated against success, in both territorial and social terms.

The above pattern of institutional instability and incapacity to influence industrial change positively has been clearly reflected in actual economic and industrial policy during the early post-war decades. The first notable feature, relating to macro-economic management, has been the continual stop–go cycle where expansion of monetary supply was followed by a policy of deflation in order to reduce the level of imports and stop the outflow of foreign reserves. In contrast to their French counterparts, British governments, influenced by the interests of financial capital in a high exchange rate and advised by the Bank of England to support this interest, refused to devalue. In contrast to the situation in Germany, the currency was for a long time overvalued and thus impaired the chances of British exporters, relative to their competitors. In addition, increasingly severe deflation discouraged industrialists from making investments (Hall 1984: 36). Neither deflation nor the incomes policies of the 1960s and 1970s succeeded in bringing wage increases into line with rises in productivity and thus seriously impaired the usefulness of governmental deflation policy.

A number of other enduring characteristics relate to industrial policy. Industrial restructuring out of declining and into growing industries and the elimination of overcapacity were not contemplated until the 1960s. Even when plans for restructuring were devised, policy instruments and staff were not attuned to the sustained intervention needed for sectorial restructuring. Although ministries with special responsibility for industry were created during the 1960s the Treasury's enduring control over all expenditure impaired their effectiveness. Most of the time intervention occurred in response to crisis rather than on the basis of any long-term strategy. Organizations of capital have been unable to compensate for government inactivity. Hence attempts at industrial restructuring remained unsystematic and intermittent, and the results of direct intervention – in terms of consolidation of firms and support for new technology – have generally been considered disastrous (see, for example, Porter 1990: 505). Due to considerations of regional policy, government subsidies often went towards declining rather than growing sectors (Hall 1984: 37). Rather than tying government subsidies to compulsory measures of restructuring, as occurred in France and Germany, deeply ingrained British voluntarism relied only on persuading firms, and thus mostly achieved suboptimal solutions.

In sum, the British state intermittently performed all the roles associated with support to industry. But both economic ideology and state structures, as well as the weaknesses of wider policy-making networks, ensured that these roles were played in an unsystematic and amateurish way of more harm than benefit to the competitiveness of the manufacturing sector. Britain during the first three post-war decades approximated most closely to the model of the Keynesian welfare state, although attempts to move away from this model had already been made towards the end of that period. The crisis which had developed by the mid-1970s combined the following features: low rates of profit; industrial stagnation and the threat of de-industrialization; high levels of inflation and growing unemployment; strong regional imbalances; and, by comparison to its European neighbours, a persistently poor social infrastructure for industry.

THE CHANGING ROLE OF THE STATE

Cumulative pressure from the oil crises, the abolition of internationally fixed exchange rates, greatly intensified competition and instability on world markets and the growing trend towards internationalization, if not globalization, all interacted to create changes in the political climate, changes in government parties and new approaches to economic management and industrial policy. These policy shifts have been described in very general terms in the second section of this chapter. The third section concluded with an outline of both the common elements in the experience of crisis in the three societies and the differential impact shaped in large measure by structural characteristics of the economic policy-making community in the three economies. It is thus not surprising that state responses during the 1980s and 1990s have also had their distinctive national characteristics, although there were no simple continuities from the traditional patterns outlined.

Germany

In Germany, espousal of economic liberalism signalled a return to an early post-war tradition rather than a radical departure from it, as it did in different ways in Britain and France. Although a return to a liberal economic philosophy had already been evident in the late 1970s, under the Social Democrat–Free Democrat coalition government, philosophy became general economic policy only with the change of government in late 1982. But even then the *Wende* was more pronounced at the level of rhetoric than in concrete measures, and market liberalism was embraced with much greater moderation than in Britain. It retained its social elements in stronger measure, and remained tempered by the surviving German traditions of industrial self-administration and the capacity to resolve matters in a consensual manner.

The conservative–liberal government's determination to reduce its involvement in industrial policy has also been put into question by German reunification. The necessity of complete industrial reorganization in Eastern Germany, without endangering social peace and political consensus, calls for extensive and detailed state involvement and cannot be left to market forces.[2] Reunification has also had important consequences of a structural kind. (The following brief account is based on an excellent overview of such changes by Schmidt 1992). It has increased the number of *Länder* by five and made highly uneven the composition in terms of level of economic prosperity. These two facts will slow down processes of policy formation in the Upper House (*Bundesrat*) and greatly increase the chances of conflict and stalemate. Due to the material and administrative weakness of the new federal states, the role of the central state has been strengthened. Greater centralization has also developed out of economic policy in the Eastern states, administered by the highly centralized Trust Fund (*Treuhandanstalt*) responsible for the privatization programme.

The political programme of 1982 shows a striking similarity to the Thatcherite equivalent: promotion of private initiative and competition and de-emphasis of state regulation; cutting back public expenditure both on social measures and on subsidies to industry; industrial policy in support of innovative industries through temporary subsidies, without presuming to select 'industrial champions'; and restoring profits and weakening the bargaining position of labour, as well as generally widening income differentials (Stille 1990: 91).

When we examine how much of this programme has actually been accomplished and how strongly the government has been prepared to push it, both the more moderate German objectives and the less confrontationist style become evident. Deregulation in both social and labour law occurred to strengthen the hand of management. Thus the passing of the 1985 Employment Promotion Act, increasing labour market flexibility, did marginally weaken labour, but it was accompanied by some reregulation, for example, in the area of part-time work. Social spending was not as dramatically curtailed as in Britain, and spending on education and training remained high throughout this period. A new regulation, abolishing social security payments for labour locked out during industrial disputes, temporarily soured relations between the unions and the state. In comparison with the situation in Britain, deregulation was not serious and confrontation was largely avoided (Keller 1990: 390). But high levels of unemployment have weakened the bargaining power of labour. The 1980s were a period of wage moderation, with the annual growth in unit labour costs staying well below those of France and even further below those of Britain (OECD, *Employment Outlook* 1991). This brought about a shift from incomes to profit, and profit levels improved considerably.

The privatization programme, devised to give market forces more rein, resulted in the full-scale privatization of only one company by the end of the decade: VEBA, a conglomerate in the energy industry. Other companies considered suitable for privatization were either only partially sold off to leave the government a controlling share, or privatization was completely rejected in the interest of either industrial or regional policy. Neo-liberal economists advocating privatization had clearly not appreciated that various political interests would oppose a radical privatization strategy (Esser 1988: 68–72), and further privatizations were postponed until the mid-1990s. Subsidies (cash flows and tax allowances) increased rather than decreased during the 1980s, despite a strong commitment to their reduction. Part of the explanation for this is that only a minority of total subsidies is under the control of central government (Smyser 1992: 115); but another important problem has been the strength of industrial lobbies to prevent change. However, the lion's share of subsidies goes to housing, agriculture and transport rather than to industry, and the level of German subsidies in manufacturing is no higher than that in Britain (OECD, quoted by *The Economist*, 23 November 1993, *France* Survey: 15). Of the subsidies to industry, however, a large proportion has continued to go to the traditional sectors of coal, iron and steel, and shipbuilding. Altogether, there has not occurred a strong enough shift away from defensive subsidies towards more offensive ones (Stille 1990: 97).

But there has also occurred an increase in subsidies to industries which are export- and RD-intensive, as well as to the SME sector which is believed to strengthen industrial competition (ibid.: 96). These subsidies were part of an activist innovation policy which, in contrast to the situation in Britain and France, was targeted at RD-intensive firms in all industries, rather than just at new industries. The excellent German infrastructure for R&D activity and technological innovation (co-operation between research institutes, trade associations and firms) ensured for governmental innovation policy greater success than has been the case in France and Britain (van Tulder and Junne 1988). An emphasis on maintaining and improving the social infrastructure for industry has remained prominent in the policy arsenal, as have efforts to achieve an equitable distribution of regional industrial assets.

Although the German economy has been formally open to FDI, many of its features have deterred investors and the level of such investment stagnated in the 1980s. In the face of significant increases in outward FDI, economic policy analysts are becoming concerned about Germany's lack of attractiveness as an investment site. But as the latter is intimately connected with German industrial culture, policy-makers will find it difficult to ameliorate the situation.

The relatively moderate neo-liberal policy of the German state and employers has brought about some shift in the balance of power between capital and labour but no fundamental transformations in the relation between state and industry. It eased the problems of management by affording them greater internal flexibility in the deployment of labour and by raising profitability and investment funds. The consensual manner of solving problems of industrial adjustment has been strained but not jeopardized, and patterns of industrial organization are well set for the transition to a new accumulation regime. A strong emphasis on the human aspect of manufacturing – skill, scientific knowledge, *Technik*, as well as co-operative problem solving in relations between both capital and labour and various capitals – continues to confer competitive advantage. But, at the same time, this moderate and cautious liberalization policy was unable to resolve the deeper institutional problems of German industry: its inability to shift resources to new industries and new innovative firms, thus curtailing fast responses to innovative challenges encountered from Germany's major competitors, Japan and the USA. Although there have been slight shifts in the way the state influences industrial development – away from macroeconomic management and industrial restructuring through direct intervention – the general style has changed remarkably little.

In addition to the 'old problems' of the Western part of Germany, the reunified Germany also has to solve the massive problems of output collapse and mass unemployment in the Eastern states. The success of this monumental task depends crucially on the continuing transfer of resources from West to East and hence on the continued ability of Germany to retain its place among the economically most advanced countries. The latter, in turn, will decide whether the old and proven model of consensual economic policy-making will endure into the next century.

France

The move to the market occurred somewhat later in France than in Britain and Germany, due to the renewed experiments in statist economic intervention and redistributive Keynesianism by the Socialist government between 1981 and 1983. But measures taken by the Barre government in the late

1970s and again by the Socialists from 1983 onwards already foreshadowed some recognition of the growing impotence of the developmental state and a turning away from *dirigiste* principles (Stoffaes 1989; Hall 1990; Boucek 1993). Given the strongly entrenched and all-pervasive neo-Colbertist tradition in France, the open and more systematic move to the market after 1986 and the introduction of sweeping changes in a short time constitute a radical change, not dissimilar to the Thatcher programme, albeit with an enduring Gallic flavour. But there remain divisions within the French state between those holding *Colbertiste* views and those intent on giving the market more emphasis (Cerny 1989: 146). Of the latter, there are further disagreements between those who admire the Anglo-American model of capitalism and those who wish to emulate the more muted German model (Albert 1991; *The Economist*, 23 November 1991).

Macroeconomic management had already changed in the late 1970s when French monetary policy was aligned to that of Germany. Entry into the Exchange Rate Mechanism (ERM) further curtailed independent monetary policy. The 1987 Single European Act, which outlaws any non-tariff barriers to trade, undermines an independent industrial policy with a strong penchant for state protection of industries and firms and for state tutelage. Whereas previous governments had concentrated on industrial restructuring to create capital concentration and large, internationally orientated firms, the new industrial policy was concerned to make existing firms more efficient and profitable (Boucek 1993). The 1986–8 conservative coalition government adopted a radical liberalization programme, and the socialist minority government after 1988 did not reverse marketization. The new centre-right coalition government, which came to power in 1993, has made strong pledges about further privatization. In sum, the last decade or so has seen consistent moves away from the long-established *dirigiste* model, although the strong legacy of state intervention has made the liberalization process less radical and wholehearted than in Britain (ibid.).

The hallmarks of the 1986–8 period have been a continuation of budgetary rigour, corporate tax reduction to increase profitability and investment, and privatization and deregulation on a very broad front (Stoffaes 1989: 116–17; Hall 1990: 178f; Boucek 1993). Among the latter measures, deregulation of the financial system, begun under the socialists, was continued and had important consequences: the creation of many new financial services created new sources of finance for French firms, and it has begun to free them from the tutelage of the state in their investment activities. (Subsidized credits fell from 43 per cent of total credits in 1980 to 21 per cent in 1988; *The Economist* 19 May 1990). But, given the absence of large institutional investors, capital shortage remains a problem (Boucek 1993: 76). As in Britain, deregulation of capital markets was part of the state's international competitive strategy (Cerny 1989: 143). Deregulation of prices was another important measure, and a new emphasis on competition was exemplified in the creation of a Competition Commission (Boucek 1993: 81) – an institution established much earlier in the other two European countries. Budgetary rigour dictated a significant scaling-down of public subsidies to industry, as well as a dismantling of the many committees which had previously channelled funds to industry. The French economy has become open to market competition in other ways as well, increasing its share of both outward and inward FDI, and making progress in reducing protectionism in the face of international competition. However, subsidies to manufacturing industry remain higher than in both Britain and Germany (*The Economist*, 23 November 1991) and government involvement in the restructuring of industry more pronounced. The example of consumer electronics shows that, while the British state stood by and saw the complete collapse of national capability in this industry, the French state systematically intervened to build up a globally viable national champion (Cawson 1994). Government involvement in the promotion of R&D and modern industries has increased rather than diminished, as have efforts to provide appropriate infrastructure.

Privatization occurred on a grand scale, reversing not only socialist but also Gaullist nationalizations (Bauer 1988). Sweeping reversal of earlier policy was, however, accomplished in a typically French *dirigiste* manner, granting little scope to market forces (ibid.). But Bauer's sharp criticism of the autocratic and self-seeking manner in which the Ministry of Finance handled privatization – it appointed its own technocrats to head the privatized companies – should not detract from the dramatic nature of this change and from the fact that it will cancel out any future *dirigiste* large-scale industrial restructuring. By enacting both financial deregulation and privatization, the state has deliberately deprived itself of the chief instruments to continue neo-Colbertist industrial policy.

Another indicator of the state's determination to scale down its directing role is the continuation of the policy of decentralization of economic decision-making to the regions and localities, begun by Mitterand in the early 1980s (Hall 1990: 182; Ashford 1990). Regions like Languedoc-Roussillon and St Etienne-Lyon have adopted their own local development plans and enterprise zones, forcing central state agencies such as the *Délégation à l'aménagement du territoire et à l'action regionale* (DATAR) to decentralize their operations. The decentralization of economic resources which this entails disperses elite power (Boucek 1993: 69).

Labour market deregulation has been another prominent plank of state policy. It gave employers more manoeuvring space in their hiring and firing activities and significantly reduced the employment security of employees (Lane 1989). Wage rises remained very moderate during the second half of the 1980s (*The Economist*, 19 May 1990). In contrast to the situation in Britain, however, the labour market is still highly regulated, and its deregulation was not accompanied by any attacks on unions. Also it was flanked by a much more active labour market policy than in Britain and than had been common in France in the 1970s (Hall 1990: 183). State effort to withdraw from the sphere of industrial relations by increasing the institutionalization of collective bargaining has had only partial success (see Chapter 8). There has been some chipping away at welfare benefits, but the fundamental principle of the welfare state has so far not been relinquished. The Rocard government quietly continued most of these policies after 1988.

In general, there has been a strong attempt to achieve a shift in the state's role in industry. As economic management and selective industrial intervention have become less important, efforts to create a more skilled and more co-operative industrial community have gained greater prominence. A more active labour market policy, the Auroux laws and a greater involvement of regional and municipal governments in economic decision-making all point in this direction.

These measures have all brought some results but they did not deal fully with the problem of transition to a new accumulation regime, securing for French firms improved competitiveness in international markets and reducing the level of unemployment. Thus, in the late 1980s inflation declined, output grew, profit levels and private investment improved significantly, and firms gained more flexibility to react quickly to market opportunities (Stoffaes 1989: 117; *The Economist*, 19 May 1990). But, at the same time, problems of low-skill production in some sectors and low innovation and low international competitiveness in other sectors have remained (Stoffaes 1989: 120; Hall 1990: 184; *Blick durch die Wirtschaft*, 28 July 1994), while over-investment in some ailing sectors delayed their adjustment. The proportion of employed people on the payroll of central government is still high in comparison with other industrialized countries (*The Economist*, 23 November 1993). Labour relations have improved but are still far from co-operative, and skill upgrading has not been sufficiently targeted towards operatives.

Britain

Britain was not only the trail-blazer on the route from state to market but also pursued its neo-liberal policies in a much more aggressive manner than its two European competitors. Deregulation was introduced on a very wide front. On the one hand, this entailed a partial withdrawal of the state where it had never been solidly established in the first place – for example, in industrial policy. On the other hand, this policy of freeing the markets brought about government intervention on a scale never before experienced, as in the field of labour market deregulation. More specifically, the new policies involved a decisive move away from demand management in macroeconomic policy, a determination to bring down inflation by curtailing government spending and a repudiation of government intervention in industry. Industrial capital was to be strengthened by changes in taxation policy, by deregulation and by weakening the position of labour in collective bargaining and in the labour market more generally. Large-scale privatization was conceived to contribute to the achievement of several of these goals (Heald 1988).

One of the central pillars of Thatcherite economic policy was to strengthen the financial sector and to ensure that it became the centre of international finance in the changed circumstances of the 1980s. Deregulation was the main instrument to achieve this goal. By the end of the 1980s, according to Coakley and Harris (1992), it looked as if that goal had not been accomplished. Moreover, this strategy had done nothing to address and alleviate the problems of industry, but had contributed to its worsening performance: 'financial deregulation fuelled both a credit boom and an increase in international finance that, between them, created a high level of company indebtedness without a change in the markets' and banks' short-termism and lack of interest in production development' (ibid.).

If there was any policy towards industry, it was the assertion that state intervention in industrial restructuring was harmful and that the state must withdraw from it. The only way to assist competitiveness, it has been held, is to give markets free rein, to ease regulation constricting enterprise and to encourage enterprise by stimulating the development of new innovative firms. Although subsidies to industry were not discontinued, they were significantly reduced and applied very selectively in keeping with this philosophy. R&D activities and technological innovation were specifically targeted while aid to 'lame duck' firms and traditional industries was ruled out. The same philosophy was applied to regional policy (Gibbs 1989; Martin and Tyler 1992). Regional imbalances were no longer viewed as being due to unfavourable industrial structure, to be corrected by restructuring and investment subsidies, but to supply-side failures which would only be righted by overcoming market rigidities (ibid.). A last important component of both industrial and regional policy has been the active encouragement of foreign direct investment through direct and indirect subsidies to investing companies.

Although privatization was not a vital component of economic policy at the beginning of Conservative rule, it gained greatly in importance during the 1980s and 1990s. It involved not only the denationalization of industrial firms and of utilities but also the injection of market mechanisms into many public bureaucracies. Despite the governments' strong emphasis on stimulating enterprise through competition in other contexts, privatization was not accompanied by the break-up of monopolies. Privatization also necessitated new forms of state involvement in affected firms.

Deregulation of labour markets and the weakening of labour was another central concern of Thatcherite economic policy, due to a switch to, first, monetarism and then to supply-side policies. It included both the erosion of employment rights and the weakening of unions through a series of legislative measures which terminated the long British tradition of voluntarism in the conduct of industrial relations in a new uncompromising style. Britain became practically the only Western European country which failed to provide basic minimum rights to terms and conditions (Deakin 1992: 176).

To what extent has Conservative economic policy since 1979 achieved the goals it set itself, and how has the attainment of some of the goals affected British industrial performance? Among the achievements of the Thatcher years were a strong reduction in the long-standing budget deficit and a significant decrease in the level of inflation, albeit at the cost of a reduction in social spending and an increase in unemployment. Although labour market deregulation and weakening of the unions achieved some of the goals the government had set itself, overall it was only partially successful. The main achievement was a strong increase in labour productivity, but this was only very partially due to the measures outlined above (Hirst 1989: 117; Glynn 1992: 77f). Little progress was made in linking pay increases to productivity. Real wage increases in the private manufacturing sector were high by international standards (Deakin 1992; Glynn 1992) and outstripped both increases in productivity and levels of inflation (Brown and Wadhwani 1990). Legislation had not changed union structure (multi-unionism and decentralized bargaining), nor had it greatly weakened the practice of collective bargaining. Functional flexibility of the core labour force in manufacturing was only moderately improved (Cross 1988) and hardly in terms of internal temporal flexibility – annualization of hours and flexible shift-working (Deakin 1992). The reliance on relatively cheap, insufficiently trained and lowly committed labour has not been tackled in a general way.

The severe restraint on public investment had particularly negative effects on education, health and public infrastructure (Rowthorn 1992: 271) – all areas with strong indirect long-term effects on industrial performance, as well as individual well-being. (In education real per capita spending for the 1980–8 period showed both a decline on British spending in the 1970s and a significantly lower spending than France and, in particular, Germany; data quoted by Rowthorn 1992: 274). In contrast to the French and German states, British governments have openly eschewed the role of 'orchestrator of economic consensus'. Deregulation bore particularly heavily on labour, and the co-operation of the Trades Union Congress is no longer sought. Centralization of economic decision-making was increased, and regional imbalances between the North and the South have not been corrected (Martin and Tyler 1992). All these developments seriously jeopardize the transition to a new production paradigm.

But perhaps Conservative governments have made important gains in other areas. How do we assess their claims that British industry is greatly improved in terms of international competitiveness? It is certainly true that the big shake-outs of less-efficient firms in the early 1980s and again in the early 1990s have rendered British manufacturing leaner and in some respects moderately fitter, but the claim about greatly improved competitiveness receives scant support from the facts of industrial change. Improved profit margins have not been translated into increased investment and output. Manufacturing investment at the end of the 1980s barely exceeded its 1979 peak (Glynn 1992: 87). Due to the nature of the British financial system and the growing likelihood of hostile takeovers during the 1980s, increased profits resulted in increased dividends for shareholders and rising share prices (ibid.: 81). The high interest rates during most of this period further discouraged investment. The so-called 'small-firm' boom has failed to make the expected contribution to innovativeness and competition. Both public and private investment in R&D has continued to lag behind that of other advanced countries (Porter 1990: 498; *The Independent*, 10 June 1991: 20), and a disproportionate share of public investment has gone into defence-related industries, with insufficient spin-off effect for other industries (van Tulder and Junne 1988: 186–7; Porter 1990).

Although Conservative governments have devised and financed programmes for the production and diffusion of automated technology throughout the 1980s (van Tulder and Junne 1988: 156f), an unstable institutional structure and an underdeveloped infrastructure have curtailed their effectiveness. Britain now holds only weak positions in the new industries, and technologically advanced firms are weakly represented in most manufacturing sectors. During the 1978–85 period, far more competitive industries lost export share than gained it. Net losses involve many of the sophisticated industries (Porter 1990: 494). 'The market forces unleashed by the Thatcher government, and the rationalisation of industry which resulted, most blatantly failed to provide a durable basis for future growth' (Glynn 1992: 87–8). One of the few areas in which Britain has outperformed her continental neighbours is in attracting FDI. It remains to be seen, however, whether the short-term economic boost derived from it will benefit manufacturing industry in the longer run.

CONCLUSIONS

These accounts of transformations in economic and industrial policy during the last 15 years or so have illustrated a number of points. First, although all three states have made substantial reorientations in their policies, the British and French states have gone much further than the German. In Germany changes have been modest in all areas, and actual policy has stayed far behind liberal rhetoric. Despite much emphasis on the freeing of the market, the old quasi-corporatist way of policy-making, interfering considerably with the market mechanisms, has not been touched at all. As the central state never had a strong role in industrial policy narrowly defined, a rolling-back of the state has been unnecessary. Supply-side policies have always had a central place in the German arsenal of state policies, and indirect support for industry through the provision of a favourable infrastructure and a stable economic environment have retained their importance. The distributional coalition between capital and labour, although weakened, is still in place, and social and regional consensus have remained high priorities, sometimes at the expense of short-term flexibility and efficiency. Germany's curious mixture of economic liberalism and corporatist self-government is set to continue into the next century.

Although Britain has been the most strident advocate of neo-liberal reform, actual change has been less dramatic than it appears at first sight. In many ways, policies have just served to intensify prior deeply entrenched patterns of voluntarism and *laissez-faire*, and privatization has merely brought greater internal consistency to this broad industrial orientation. Old policy stances, such as giving the financial sector priority over industry, have been continued and been advanced to a higher stage. Also efforts at deregulation of labour markets and privatization have not finally eliminated state intervention but merely changed its form. But it would be wrong, in the British context, to claim that there have been no fundamental changes. The termination of consensual policy-making and the exclusion of labour from the policy-making community is a new and radical development. Labour market deregulation and the weakening of unions have crucially changed the balance of power, and the state has progressively taken on more powers and become more centralized. But few of these changes have significantly affected the British institutional mould which forms the basis of the decline of manufacturing industry. Despite much political interference in the labour market, no stable distributional coalition has been established, and the operation of capital markets has sharpened, rather than lessened, competitive conflicts. In sum, social consensus has been weakened rather than strengthened.

French moves from the state to the market started much later than in the other two societies and, due to a greater consensus on the necessity for basic change, have appeared as less dramatic than those in Britain. But if we view these liberalization measures against the background of previous *dirigiste* policy and the leading role of the state in industrial change they must be considered as striking. These policies do not merely herald an intensification of an old policy stance but signal a fundamental transformation in the role of the state. The times of the developmental state appear to have passed, but the state has found it difficult to withdraw entirely. Not only are its functionaries trained to take an active role, but in the absence of structures of self-administration of industry on the German pattern, such withdrawal would leave too much of a vacuum. Cerny's (1989) identification of a replacement of strategic *dirigisme* by tactical *dirigisme* appears pertinent. Efforts to build a more collaborative political culture have been made, but seem to be difficult to reconcile with the legacy of *dirigisme*. It is, however, too early to judge their outcome.

Thus, in none of these European countries has the national state lost its role as promoter of economic growth and prosperity and as co-ordinator of the various actors which share some interests in this promotion and expect a fair share of the wealth generated (Hirst and Thompson 1992: 21). Distribution of the latter remains strictly a national matter. Increasing interconnectedness and openness of markets have made it more difficult and complex to play this role in a meaningful manner. Independent monetary policy has been almost totally undermined, and national industrial policy has been curtailed in many ways by European economic harmonization, following the establishment of the single market.

At the same time, ensuing intensification of competition on world markets and industrial transformation away from the old Fordist pattern have made it more imperative to adapt national manufacturing sectors to the resulting new demands. Although advanced societies are becoming increasingly dependent on inward FDI, national states retain some influence over it and are in no way totally at the mercy of transnational companies. In any case, France and Germany are not yet dominated by foreign MNCs in a range of key industries, as is becoming the case in Britain. It is clear that claims such as Ohmae's (1990), that large global corporations have totally eclipsed the state's contribution to, and control over, national economic performance, accord poorly with actual developments. The nation state still has at its disposal a number of instruments to influence the internationalization of capital: it can influence trade through the introduction of tariffs, import quota and technical standards; it adopts policies for inward investment and the transfer of technology; and it tries to strengthen national MNCs through R&D support and procurement policy – although many of these policies have become obsolete *vis-à-vis* other countries. Whether the role of the national state has now become more important than in the past, as claimed by Porter (1990), is, however, also contentious.

It would be more correct to highlight a shift in the state's role. In the words of Hirst and Thompson (1992: 371), 'governmental policies to sustain national economic performance retain much of their relevance, even if their nature, level and function have changed'. It is true that self-contained national economic management has become undermined by economic globalization and that industrial policy has become much less selective and defensive and orientated rather towards securing certain supply-side outcomes. Despite much deregulationist activity in labour and capital markets, re-regulation or alternative forms of state regulation have often occurred and the regulatory function of the state remains very important, particularly in the absence or slow evolution of new international regulatory bodies. At the same time, governments' roles as providers of social infrastructure and 'as facilitators of private economic actors' (ibid.) and orchestrators of economic consensus have increased their importance. In conclusion, the national state has neither disengaged nor lost its economic role. As this review of recent state policies in the three largest European countries has shown, the state is at present searching more or less systematically for new ways of playing this role and is developing more or less coherent and appropriate responses to industrial reorganization and globalization. New modes of response remain strongly determined by pre-existing forms of state organization.

NOTES

1. Piore and Sabel (1984) themselves and proponents of the regulation approach (see Jessop 1990: 196f), reacting against Marxist determinism, left the role of the state theoretically underdeveloped. (A recent work – Demirovic et al. 1992 – has remedied this omission to some extent.)
2. There has been an annual flow to the Eastern Länder of about DM150 billion (£60 billion) in public funds; this is scheduled to continue until at least the end of the century and represents an historically unprecedented transfer of wealth.

Conclusion

The preceding chapters have systematically studied patterns of industrial organization and change in the three largest European societies. They have been viewed in both their national social-institutional context and their wider European political and economic environment, as well as being considered in terms of their growing international economic interconnectedness. The focus on industrial organization has placed the individual firm in a web of relationships with other firms and with organizations supplying the factors of production and/or safeguarding their timely and efficient co-ordination. This emphasis on the constant interaction between firms and markets, on the one side, and social institutions, on the other, has been conceptualized in terms of national industrial order. It has entailed an holistic perspective on all aspects of industrial organization, involving not only a stronger focus on capital than previous studies of industrial organization but constantly showing the interaction between capitals, as well as between the latter, labour and the state. Additionally, the analysis of industrial organization has aimed to link the micro level of the firm with meso- (regional and sectorial) and macro-level (national and international) structures and processes, although attention has centred on the national rather than the regional level. The strong concern with the social embeddedness of economic structures and processes has necessarily led to an emphasis on national distinctiveness of industrial orders and on their historical shaping and reproduction.

At the same time, the writing of this book is very much founded on the awareness that the 1980s and 1990s have been a period of widespread and far-reaching industrial change, involving and affecting all three main actors and ushering in dramatic shifts in power relations and strategies/policies. Change has flowed from a number of different sources. First, world-wide recession and sluggish growth, leading to high levels of unemployment, a dampening of labour militancy and searches for new union and employer agendas. Second, the emergence of new competitors on world markets and the ensuing intensification of competition, as well as shifts in the international division of labour between highly and newly developed industrial societies. This has put pressures on managements to cut costs by deploying both capital and labour in new ways, while at the same time keeping their place in the competitive race through constant innovation in organizational,

196

product and process terms. Third, this compulsion towards innovativeness has been further fuelled by the simultaneous emergence of several new core technologies impacting on products and processes in a large range of industries. It has necessitated new approaches towards human resource management and R&D, challenging both managements and governments to harness resources towards the cultivation of competitive advantage. Fourth, the growing internationalization, if not globalization, of both financial and industrial capital has led to growing interconnectedness of firms across national boundaries, as well as to their common exposure to homogenizing global influences. Fifth, integration into larger economic units and collaboration on a supranational level has been hastened by political and legal mechanisms in the European Community. Lastly, the collapse of the state socialist regimes in Eastern Europe and the former Soviet Union has lent further impetus and greater legitimacy to processes of marketization, as well as opening up new markets and creating further low-wage competitor countries. This development has had a particularly strong impact on Germany. It has ushered in reunification, with all the attendant problems of institutional transfer and reproduction. It has also restored Germany to its old pre-war role as the nation which bridges Eastern and Western Europe and is bound to benefit most in the longer run from the opening up of new markets.

The combined influence of these multiple external forces has had a strong dislocating impact on both societal institutions and firms and markets. The ensuing predominance of industrial transformation and flux has thrown up a number of pressing research questions, as well as giving a new edge to the old sociological preoccupation with convergence or divergence of advanced industrial societies. The first question is how this change is best conceptualized and how far existing theories serve to illuminate the nature and outcomes of change. Both flexible specialization and regulation theory are good at capturing the fundamental nature of this change and the decisive break with past patterns of industrial organization. Although transformation in each separate area, for example, in corporate structure or in globalization strategy, is still hesitant and peacemeal and it remains difficult to discern the overall direction of change, the ubiquity and interconnectedness of change, engulfing all aspects of industrial organization, leaves little doubt that we are experiencing a conjunctural break. Flexible specialization, if anything, even underestimates the holistic nature of change, focusing mainly on production organization and neglecting transformations in the nexus between financial and industrial capital.

Recognition of such a fundamental break does not, however, commit us to the acceptance of a 'stages' model of industrial development nor to Piore and Sabel's espousal of strategic choice. Adaptation to external pressures and the pursuit of new opportunities by managements and governments is neither a matter of strategic choice between an infinite number of alternative options, nor does adaptation occur in the manner of 'lucky finds', as envisaged by regulation theory. Structure is more determinant of strategy than strategy of structure. Adaptation to change has happened in a different manner in each of the three societies studied in this book, and, although responses of management, labour and the state are not totally predetermined by established industrial orders, existing institutional arrangements nevertheless channel the efforts of individual industrial and political actors. By determining the scope for and speed of change in different areas of industrial organization, as well as the manner in which it can be accomplished, they influence the broad direction of change. This insight is fully grasped only by analysts working within the theoretical perspective of New Institutionalism, which views social relationships and actions within organizations as based on shared cognitions with a 'taken-for-granted' quality which define what actions are possible (Powell and DiMaggio 1991). Institutional rules even define how roles are understood and what power relations are legitimate or illegitimate.

This diversity in national modes of adaptation to current environmental pressures also makes it clear why it is so difficult to typify and label the overall direction of change, let alone a new stage of industrial development. Although part of the difficulty lies in the fact that we are still in the midst of change and thus find it difficult to discern clear contours, the main impediment to such all-encompassing labelling is persistent national diversity in trajectories of change. While this diversity has always been recognized by regulation theory, with its emphasis on nationally distinctive modes of regulation, emphasis on diversity has uneasily coexisted with the identification of one overarching global regime of accumulation. Recent work in the regulation paradigm, however, such as that of Boyer (1991a, 1991b), shows a distinct shift of emphasis from convergent to divergent developmental trends and emerging models. Such championing of divergent models of capitalist societies is also found among some institutionalists within political economy (for example, Hall 1994) and economic sociologists with an holistic 'systems' approach to industrial organization (Whitley 1994; Hollingsworth et al. 1994). It is with these two latter approaches that the theoretical orientation and empirical findings of this book agree most closely, and the different labels of 'varieties of capitalism', 'business systems', 'political economies' and 'industrial orders' are indicative of only minor differences of emphasis.

This insistence on the continued importance of the 'divergence' approach, even in the face of strong multiple forces towards increasing homogenization, obviously rejects any one-sided approach from 'convergence', be it of the Marxist 'laws of capitalism' kind or the technological determinism of 'industrial society' theory. But this book has not ignored the fact that pressures towards uniformity have become greater during the last two decades, that national actors have lost some of their independence, and that diverse social and economic goals have become more difficult to pursue. These pressures have been of a formal legal kind, such as the narrowing of national choice in industrial policy in the face of EC competition policy, and of a more informal kind, resulting from the growing homogenization of markets (emphasis on diversified quality products across a wide range of industries), the greater deregulation and integration of financial markets, or the growth among corporations of internationalization and of cross-national mergers and strategic hegemonic alliances. In addition, the emergence of the new economic hegemonic power of Japan has, indeed, often conveyed the impression that there is 'one best way', and that only Japanization of production organization can prevent economic decline.

However, empirical investigations have shown that managerial practice lags far behind declared strategy and that widespread hype about the Japanization of organizational structures and employment policies grossly overstates the degree of convergence. All these caveats are, however, not to deny the incidence of some convergence in goals and even in the broad strategies/policies to achieve them. But this book has insisted on the fact that national institutional heritage strongly structures the means chosen to pursue given economic goals, the capacity for adaptation in various fields and the manner in which change is being accomplished. This results not only from different capacities for strategic action among capital, labour and the state in different societies but also from the way they have historically interacted with each other. Although a shift in power from labour to capital is discernible in all advanced societies the resulting new patterns of interaction still retain distinctive national features. Inevitably, these different modes of adaptation to change partially affect the outcomes, making transformation more dramatic, speedy and consistent in some cases than in others.

What, then, to summarize the arguments of the various chapters, have been the main characteristics of the three national modes of adaptation and to what extent can they be seen as varieties of capitalism? Industrial change has probably been most radical in Britain, affecting a large number of aspects of industrial organization, as well as the manner in which it has been accomplished. While right-wing advocates of transformation would probably point to the dynamic and flexible nature of the new British industrial order, those viewing the changes more sceptically would speak of a climate of continued turbulence, partial institutional crisis and widespread individual insecurity and disillusionment. Importantly, however, the only fixed point in this period of institutional and organizational flux has been the financial system: the institutional complex at the very core of British industrial order, with immense shaping influence on organizational structure and strategy.

Pervasiveness of change does not necessarily equate with consistent and thorough implementation, and many of the newly created structures and

modes of interaction have a piecemeal, makeshift and even unstable character. Whereas in the past change has generally been accomplished consen-
sually, even if only through the use of veto power by organized capital or
labour, in recent decades the government executive has introduced even quite
sweeping changes without always involving industrial capital and with complete disregard for organized labour. The capacity of the organizations of
capital and labour to shape the nature of adaptation, let alone resist it, has
been weak, due to low degrees of national solidarity, emphasis on voluntarism
and the absence of established channels and legal procedures to intervene in
policy-making. Such one-sided, government-driven change begs obvious questions about the stability of new institutional arrangements.

While British industrial order has always been less institutionally regulated and more market-orientated than its German and French counterparts,
the last two decades have seen a further intensification of these features and a
much wider reach of market mechanisms. The low degree of regulation and
co-ordination of economic actors has left more scope for individual large
firms to do 'their own thing' and has created greater diversity within the
British industrial order than is found on the continent. The resulting flexibility of structures and adaptability of actors, at first sight, would make British
manufacturing industry ideally suited to implement the 'flexible specialization' paradigm. This comparative lack of structural constraints on industrial
actors is said to be conducive to innovation and to the development of
industrial sectors and new firms which depend on quick reaction to market
demand and on product innovation, such as the software industry, some
sections of entertainment electronics and biotechnology (Ebster-Grosz 1994),
as well as new high-tech companies more generally (Anglo-German Foundation 1988). But this initial advantage of relative freedom from structural
constraint is all too often lost at a later stage when new firms and industries
need a supportive institutional environment to consolidate and grow. Thus
the long-term time horizons necessary for R&D, capital investment and skill
development, which are a vital precondition for sustained adoption of the
'flexible specialization' model, remain absent in the British industrial order.
Although the liberal market model is high on flexibility in terms of quick
response and creative adaptation, it lacks several of its other vital ingredients.

Of the three industrial orders, the German has been by far the slowest to
change, and where transformation has occurred it has been more incremental
and has displayed greater continuity in the manner in which adaptation is
being accomplished. The historically high degree of co-ordination in the
German economy (Lash and Urry 1987) and the co-operative manner of
problem solution has endured into the 1990s. Despite the shift in power
towards capital and the conflicts which have inevitably accompanied the
enormous problems following reunification, (particularly over the threat of

de-industrialization and demands for wage parity in the Eastern states), consultation and co-operation between the two sides of industry, with or without
state participation, have been far more dominant than the occasional confrontation (Silvia 1994). Stability has been sustained by the pronounced interlocking between the various component elements of the industrial order, held
together by a distinctive set of norms and values. Commitment to long-
termism, technological perfectionism, clear and binding rules to reduce risk
and a limited communitarianism, expressed in associational networking, have
all been diffused throughout the industrial order. As pointed out by Hall
(1994: 21), these features serve German managers and policy-makers wishing to implement the kind of initiatives which demand sector-wide co-ordination and long time horizons.

Although these features of the industrial order are still serving German
manufacturing industry well, this very stability is increasingly being likened
to staidness and inflexibility in the face of new demands from a swiftly
changing environment (Kern and Sabel 1994). But it is extremely difficult to
pinpoint the exact institutional or organizational sources of lack of innovativeness and cumbersome processes of reaction. Rather than the malfunctioning
of any one institution, it is the very high degree of co-ordination, the considerable power of highly organized producer groups and the slow decision-
making processes resulting from it which are the cause of what is seen as lack
of industrial dynamism. Industries and firms which thrive on speculative
venture and fast responses to market demands have, therefore, not flourished
in Germany. Until the 1980s, German firms placed high reliance on the
German industrial order and sourced and invested mainly in their own country. But cost competition from lower-wage countries has put this degree of
embeddedness increasingly into question and in recent years firms in many
industries have started to shift production to low-wage countries (*Manager
Magazin*, 7, 1993: 94–113). While this trend is bound to continue, the German emphasis on high-quality products with a high technology content will
put definite limits to this movement. Whether German solidity, quality and
reliability will continue to sell well enough to finance a high-cost economy
and society, or whether other countries will increasingly be able to imitate
Germany at lower cost levels is a matter of growing concern to German
industrialists and policy-makers.

In French industry change has also been very radical, particularly if one
bears in mind the starting point of a highly structured and centrally directed
industrial order. The French mode of adaptation to change, however, has
shown more continuity than the British, in that the state has remained the
main agent of change. Thus, paradoxically, deregulation and the shift from a
highly co-ordinated economy to a more market-orientated one has been accomplished by a *dirigiste* state which increasingly uses its power in a tactical

rather than a strategic manner. The French industrial order shares some of the German and some of the British features and combines them in a loose amalgam of elements. With Germany it shares a closer coupling between financial and industrial capital and a commitment to long-termism in investment in both fixed and human capital, although human capital development does not occur in close collaboration with industry as in Germany. Communitarian leanings in France have always been state-mediated and have never expressed themselves in associational networking as in Germany. With the state's partial withdrawal from co-ordination and in the absence of any new dominant actors, this limited communitarianism is bound to wither, although radical individualism of the British free-market kind will meet more resistance in France.

French firms also share with German ones a relatively high degree of structural rigidity which is not mitigated, as in the German case, by impulses towards integration and (functional) flexibility coming from the system of vocational education and training. With Britain, the French industrial order shares the weakness of organized capital and labour, their low capacity for initiating strategic change either singly or in a concerted manner. The greater emphasis on the market in recent years has, however, given more scope to individual firms to escape from state tutelage and to adapt independently to their rapidly changing environment. But the French industrial economy remains highly polarized in terms of types of firms. A relatively small number of very large and competitive industrial groups face a large number of SMEs which have insufficiently benefited from government intervention and are ill prepared for the growing intensification of global competition. Increasing autonomy is also facilitated by the growing weakness of unions and their impotence in the face of employer initiatives. It is difficult to deduce from this hybrid model of French industrial organization where its industrial strengths lie and how it will influence adaptation to new market demands. Perhaps there is no single clear pattern of competitive strengths and weaknesses as in the other two cases, but instead the emergence of individual large industrial groups showing competitiveness in an unpredictable manner.

These very rough sketches of the different national modes of adaptation to their changing international environment have also tried to highlight the fact that an institutionalist approach needs to move away from dwelling exclusively on the shaping influence of institutions and to consider the role that different actors play in the recasting of institutional and organizational structures. Here attention has been drawn to the different degrees to which actors co-operate in the pursuit of strategic change and to what extent they can bring about lasting change independently. While this approach in no way endorses the centrality accorded to strategic choice by Anglo-Saxon proponents of the flexible specialization approach, it has pointed to the different space accorded managerial choice in the three societies. The institutionalist analysis of change focuses on changing power relations (Knight 1992; Hall 1994) but sees even the latter influenced by institutions. Generally, the role of actors in the initiation of non-incremental institutional change still remains insufficiently understood among theorists of industrial change of *all* theoretical persuasions, and it is in this area that future research effort should be concentrated.

Such a focus on actors within industrial orders also raises questions about policy initiatives towards institutional reform or transformation: what is the scope, if any, for the reshaping of industrial orders, where should political reshaping start, and which actors are most likely to undertake it? Previous analysis has made it clear that the elements of industrial order are interrelated but also that interlocking is much tighter in Germany than in Britain and France. Consequently, one precondition for change – loose coupling – is most developed in Britain and least developed in Germany. At the same time, policy initiatives cannot transform all elements simultaneously but have to aim for change in areas particularly critical to the whole order. It has been suggested that the financial system is at the very core of industrial order and that far-reaching change cannot be accomplished without institutional reform in this area. This fact is also recognized by the current British leaders of the Labour Party, and it remains to be seen whether, if they form the next government, they will be able to overcome the likely resistance from leading actors within the financial system.

While the financial system is also central to German and French industrial order, other considerations about the agents of change also enter the picture. In France, the problem is that the state is both the most likely agent of change and the target of institutional transformation, and the question remains whether continuing self-transformation can be sustained. In Germany, the state occupies a less-central role in many respects than in the other two countries, and change is usually effected in a concerted manner in co-operation with organized producer groups and representatives of financial capital. This associational networking, it has been pointed out, represents both the long-time strengths of German industrial order and an emerging impediment to the accomplishment of swift and radical transformation. The identity between agent and object of change and the multiplicity of actors involved poses even greater challenges for the transformation or even adaptation of German industrial order than it does for France. If, however, this monumental task is accomplished in Germany, the resulting institutional change will be a good deal more stable than any British or French institutional reform.

Bibliography

ACAS (1988) *Labour Flexibility in Britain. The 1987 ACAS Survey*, Occasional Paper 41, London: ACAS.

Aglietta, M. (1979) *A Theory of Capitalist Regulation*, London: New Left Books.

Albert, M. (1991) *Capitalisme contre capitalisme*, Paris: Seuil.

Alford, H. and Garnsey, E. (1994) 'Flexibility and specialisation in supplier relations among new technology based firms', Research Papers in Management Studies, Judge Institute of Management Studies, University of Cambridge.

Allen, C.S. (1987) 'Germany': competing communitarianisms', in G. Lodge and E. Vogel (eds), *Ideology and National Competitiveness: An Analysis of Nine Countries*, Boston, Mass.: Harvard Business School Press.

Allen, J. and Massey, D. (eds) (1988) *The Economy in Question*, London: Sage, with Open University Press.

Alt, J.E. and Crystal, K.A. (1983) *Political Economics*, Brighton, Sussex: Wheatsheaf.

Altmann, N. and Duell, K. (1990) 'Rationalization and participation: implementation of new technologies and problems of the work councils in the FRG', *Economic and Industrial Democracy*, 11: 111–27.

Altmann, N., Deiss, M., Doehl, V. and Sauer, D. (1986) 'Ein "Neuer Rationalisierungstyp"? – Neue Anforderungen an die Industriesoziologie', *Soziale Welt*, 37: 2/3: 191–206.

Altmann, N., Köhler, C. and Meil, P. (1992) 'No end in sight: current debates on the future of industrial work', in N. Altmann et al. (eds), *Technology and Work in German Industry*, London: Routledge.

Amadieu, J.-F. (1990) 'France', in W. Sengenberger, G. Loveman and M.J. Piore, *The Re-emergence of Small Enterprises: Industrial Restructuring in Industrialised Countries*, Geneva: International Institute for Labour Studies.

Amadieu, J.-F. (1992) 'Labour–management co-operation and work organization change: deficits in the French industrial relations system', in OECD, *New Directions in Work Organisation*, Paris: OECD.

Amin, A. (1992) 'Big firms versus the regions in the Single European Market', paper presented at the Annual Conference of the BSA, April 1992, University of Kent.

Amin, A. and Robins, K. (1990) 'The re-emergence of regional economies? The mythical geography of flexible accumulation', *Environment and Planning: Society and Space*, 8: 7–34.

Amin, A. and Dietrich, M. (1991) 'From hierarchy to hierarchy: the dynamics of contemporary corporate restructuring in Europe', in *Towards a New Europe*, Aldershot: Edward Elgar.

Amin, A. and Dietrich, M. (eds.) (1991) *Towards a New Europe: Structural Change in the European Economy*, Aldershot: Edward Elgar.

Anglo-German Foundation (1988) *New Technology-based Firms in Britain and Germany*, London: Anglo-German Foundation.

Anglo-German Foundation, with RSA (1993) *Debunking the Myths about the German Company*, ed. G. Binney, London: AGF.

Ashford, D. (1990) 'Decentralising France: how the Socialists discovered pluralism', *West European Politics* 13 (4): 46–65.

Atkinson, J. and Meager N. (1986) *Changing Working Patterns*, Report by the Institute of Manpower Studies, London: IMS.

Auerbach, P. (1989) 'Multinationals and the British economy', in F. Green, *The Restructuring of the UK Economy*, Brighton, Sussex: Harvester.

Bade, F.-J. (1987) 'Die Wachstumspolitische Bedeutung Kleiner und Mittlerer Unternehmen', in M. Fritsch and C.J. Hull (eds), *Arbeitsplatzentwicklung und Regionalentwicklung*, Berlin: Sigma.

Badham, R. and Matthews J. (1989) 'The new production systems debate', *Labour and Industry*, 2 (2): 194–246.

Baglioni, G. (1990) 'Introduction', in G. Baglioni and C. Crouch (eds), *European Industrial Relations*, London: Sage.

Bannock, G. (1973) *The Juggernauts: The Age of the Big Corporation*, London: Pelican Books.

Bannock, G. (1976) *The Smaller Business in Britain and Germany*, London: Wilton House Publications.

Bannock, G. (1981) *The Economics of Small Firms*, Oxford: Basil Blackwell.

Bannock, G. (1994) 'Innovation in small business banking', *Signal*, Spring/ Summer, Newsletter of the Anglo-German Foundation, London: Anglo-German Foundation.

Bannock, G. and Albach, H. (1991) *Small Business Policy in Europe*, Report for the Anglo-German Foundation, London: AGF.

Batstone, E. and Gourlay, S. (1986) *Unions, Unemployment and Innovation*, Oxford: Basil Blackwell.

Bauer, M. (1988) 'The politics of state-directed privatisation: the case of France 1986–88', *West European Politics*, 11 (4): 49–60.

Bayliss, B.T. and Butt, A.A. (1980) *Capital Markets and Industrial Investment in Germany and France*, London: Saxon House.

Bechtle, G. and Düll, K. (1992) 'The future of the mass production worker', in N. Altmann, C. Köhler and P. Meil (eds), *Technology and Work in German Industry*, London: Routledge.

Bechtle, G. and Lutz, B. (1989) 'Die Unbestimmtheit post-tayloristischer Rationalisierungsstrategie und die ungewisse Zukunft industrieller Arbeit – Überlegungen zur Begründung eines Forschungsprogramms', in K. Düll and B. Lutz (eds), *Technikentwicklung und Arbeitsteilung im Internationalen Vergleich*, Frankfurt and New York: Campus.

Beisheim, M., von Eckardstein, G. and Müller M. (1991) 'Partizipative Organisationsformen und industrielle Beziehungen', in W. Müller-Jentsch (ed.) *Konfliktpartnerschaft*, Munich: Rainer Hampp Verlag.

Berger, J. (1990) 'Market and state in advanced capitalist societies', in A. Martinelli and N.J. Smelser (eds), *Economy and Society: Overviews in Economic Sociology*, London: Sage.

Berger, J., Domeyer, V. and Funder, M. (eds) (1990) *Kleinbetriebe im wirtschaftlichen Wandel*, Frankfurt: Campus.

Berghahn, V.R. and Karsten D. (1987) *Industrial Relations in West Germany*, Oxford: Berg.

Best, M.H. (1990) *The New Competition: Institutions of Industrial Restructuring*, Cambridge: Polity Press.

Best, M. and Humphries J. (1987) 'The city and industrial decline', B. Elbaum and W. Lazonick (eds.), *The Decline of the British Economy*, Oxford: Clarendon Press.

Bialas, C. and Ettl, W. (1993) 'Wirtschaftliche Lage, soziale Differenzierung und Probleme der Interessenorganisation in den neuen Bundesländern', *Soziale Welt*, 44 (1): 52–74.

Bögenhold, D. (1985) *Die Selbständigen*, Frankfurt: Campus.

Böhm, J. (1992) *Der Einfluss der Banken auf Grossunternehmen*, Hamburg: Steuer-und Wirtschaftsverlag.

Bolton Report (1971) *Report of the Committee of Inquiry on Small Firms*, London: Her Majesty's Stationery Office.

Bonneau, M. et al. (1989) 'Gestion de l'emploi et de la formation chez les sous-traitant: résultats provisoires', research report, Paris: Centre de Recherche sur l'Emploi et les Qualifications.

Bosch, G. (1988) 'Der bundesdeutsche Arbeitsmarkt im internationalen Vergleich', *WSI-Mitteilungen*, 3: 176–85.

Boucek, T. (1993) 'Developments in post-war French political economy: the continuing decline of *dirigisme*?', in J. Sheldrake and P. Webb (eds), *State and Market: Aspects of Modern European Development;* Aldershot: Dartmouth.

Bournois, F. (1991) 'Pratiques de gestion des ressources humaines en Europe: données comparées', *Revue française de gestion*, May: 46–50.

Boyer, R. (1988) *The Search for Labour Market Flexibility*, Oxford: Clarendon Press.

Boyer, R. (1991a) 'New directions in management practices and work organization', Discussion Paper no. 9130, Paris: CEPREMAP.

Boyer, R. (1991b) 'The eighties: the search for alternatives to Fordism', in B. Jessop et al. (eds), *The Politics of Flexibility*, Aldershot: Edward Elgar.

Boyer, R. (1992a) 'How to promote cooperation within conflicting societies?', paper presented at the conference on 'Convergence and Divergence in Economic Growth and Technical Change', MERIT, University of Limburg, Maastricht.

Boyer, R. (1992b) 'Neue Richtungen von Managementpraktiken und Arbeitsorganisation. Allgemeine Prinzipien und nationale Entwicklungspfade', in A. Demirovic et al. (eds), *Staat und Hegemonie*, Münster: Westfälisches Dampfboot.

Boyer, R. (1993) 'The convergence hypothesis revisited: globalization but still the century of nations?', paper prepared for the Conference 'Domestic Institutions, Trade and the Pressures for National Convergence', Bellagio, Italy, Feb.

Bridgford, J. (1990) 'French trade unions: crisis in the 1980s', *Industrial Relations Journal*, 2: 126–35.

Brown, R. (1990) 'A flexible future in Europe? Changing patterns of employment in the United Kingdom', *British Journal of Sociology*, 41 (3): 304–28.

Brown, W. and Wadhwani S. (1990) 'The economic effects of industrial relations legislation since 1979', *National Institute Economic Review*, Feb.: 57–70.

Büchtemann, C. and Schupp, J. (1992) 'Repercussions of reunification: patterns and trends in the socio-economic transformation of East Germany', *Industrial Relations Journal*, 23 (2): 90–106.

Bühner, R. (1990) *Unternehmenszusammenschlüsse*, Stuttgart: Poeschel.

Cable, J.R. (1985) 'Capital market information and industrial performance: the role of West German banks', *Economic Journal*, 95 (337): 118–32.

Cable, J. and Dirrheimer, M.J. (1983) 'Hierarchies and markets: an empirical test of the multidivisional hypothesis in West Germany', *International Journal of Industrial Organization*, 1: 43–62.

Campbell, A. and Warner, M. (1991) 'Training strategies and microelectronics in the engineering industries of the UK and Germany', in P. Ryan (ed.), *International Comparisons of Vocational Education and Training for Intermediate Skills*, London: Falmer Press.

Casey, B. (1991) 'Recent developments in the German apprenticeship system', *British Journal of Industrial Relations*, 29 (2): 205–22.

Cavestro, W. (1989) 'Automation, new technology and work content', in S. Wood (ed.), *The Transformation of Work*, London: Unwin Hyman.

Cawson, A. (1994) 'Sectoral governance in consumer electronics in Britain and France', in J.R. Hollingsworth, P. Schmitter and W. Streeck (eds), *Governing Capitalist Economies*, New York and London: Oxford University Press.

Cerny, P.G. (1989) 'From *dirigisme* to deregulation? The case of financial markets', in P. Godt (ed.), *Policy-making in France*, London: Frances Pinter.

Chandler, A.D. (1990) *Scale and Scope: The Dynamics of Industrial Capitalism*, Cambridge, Mass.: Harvard University Press.

Chandler, A.P. and Daems H. (1980) 'Introduction', in A.P. Chandler and H. Daems (eds), *Managerial Hierarchies*, Cambridge, Mass., and London: Harvard University Press.

Chandler, A.P. and Daems, H. (eds), (1980) *Managerial Hierarchies*, Cambridge, Mass., and London: Harvard University Press.

Child, J. (1987) 'Information technology, organization, and the response to strategic challenges', *California Management Review*, 30 (1): 35–50.

Child, J. and Kieser, A. (1979) 'Organization and managerial roles in British and West German companies: an examination of the culture-free thesis', in C.J. Lammers and D.J. Hickson (eds), *Organizations Alike and Unlike*, London: Routledge & Kegan Paul.

Claessens, D., Klönne A. and Tschoeppe, A. (1989) *Sozialkunde der Bundesrepublik Deutschland*, Reinbeck: Rowohlt Verlag.

Clarke, S. (1988) 'Overaccumulation, class struggle and the regulation approach', *Capital and Class*, 36: 59–92.

Coakley, J. and Harris, L. (1992) 'Financial globalisation and deregulation', in J. Michie (ed.), *The Economic Legacy 1979–92*, London: Academic Press.

Confederation of British Industry (CBI) (1991) *Competing with the World's Best*, report of the CBI Manufacturing Advisory Group, London: CBI.

Coriat, B. (1992) 'Incentives, bargaining and trust: alternative scenarios for the future of work', paper presented at the conference on 'Convergence and Divergence in Economic Growth and Technical Change', MERIT, University of Limburg, Maastricht.

Cressey, P. and Di Martino, V. (1991) *Agreement and Innovation: The International Dimension of Technological Change*, Hemel Hempstead, Herts.: Prentice-Hall.

Crewe, L. (1991) 'New technologies, employment shifts and gender divisions within the textile industry', *New Technology, Work and Employment*, 6 (1): 43–53.

Cross, M. (1988) 'Changes in working practices in UK manufacturing, 1981–88', *Industrial Relations Review and Report*, 415, May: 2–10.

Crouch, C. (1993) *Industrial Relations and European State Traditions*, Oxford: Clarendon Press.

Curran, J. (1993) 'The flexibility fetish', *Capital and Class*, 50: 99–126.

Daniel, W. (1987) *Workplace Industrial Relations and Technical Change*, London: Frances Pinter.

Daniel, W.W. and Millward, N. (1983) *Workplace Industrial Relations in Britain*, London: Heinemann.

Dascher, O. (1974) 'Probleme der Konzernverwaltung', in H. Mommsen, D. Petzina, B. Weisbrod (eds), *Industrielles System und Politische Entwicklung in der Weimarer Republik*, Düsseldorf: Droste Verlag.

Deakin, S. (1992) 'Labour law and industrial relations', in J. Michie (ed.), *The Economic Legacy, 1979–1992*, London: Academic Press.

Deeg, R. (1994) 'Reviving the German state? Institutional transfer and social learning examined in the case of Saxony', paper presented at the Ninth International Conference of Europeanists, Chicago, 31 March – 1 April.

Deiss, M. (1992) 'Towards a polarization of skill structures', in N. Altmann, C. Köhler and P. Meil (eds), *Technology and Work in German Industry*, London: Routledge.

Delbridge, R., Turnbull, P. and Wilkinson, B. (1992) 'Pushing back the frontiers: management control and work intensification under JIT/TQM factory regimes', *New Technology Work and Employment*, 7 (2): 97–106.

Delorme, R. (1992) 'Staat und ökonomische Entwicklung', in A. Demirovic, H.-P. Krebs and T. Sablowski (eds), *Hegemonie und Staat*, Münster: Westfälisches Dampfboot.

Demirovic, A., Krebs, H.-P. and Sablowski, T. (eds), (1992) *Hegemonie und Staat*, Münster: Westfälisches Dampfboot.

de Smidt, J. and Wever, E. (1990) 'Firms, strategy and changing environments', in M. de Smidt and E. Wever (eds), *The Corporate Firm in a Changing World Economy*, London: Routledge.

Deutsche Bundesbank (1984) 'The share market in the Federal Republic of Germany and its development potential', *Monthly Report of the Deutsche Bundesbank*, 36 (4): 11–19.

De Vroey, M. (1984) 'A regulation approach interpretation of contemporary crisis', *Capital and Class*, 23: 45–66.

Dicken, P. (1992) *Global Shift: The Internationalization of Economic Activity*, 2nd edn, London: Paul Chapman.

Dierkes, M. and Zimmermann, K. (1989) *Wirtschaftsstandort Bundesrepublik*, Frankfurt: Campus.

DiMaggio, P.J. and Powell, W.W. (1991) 'Introduction', in W.W. Powell and P.J. DiMaggio (eds), *The New Institutionalism in Organizational Analysis*, Chicago and London: University of Chicago Press.

DIW (1994) *DIW Economic Bulletin*, 31 Jan.

Doran, A. (1984) *Craft Enterprises in Britain and Germany*, Study by Economists' Advisory Group, London: Anglo-German Foundation.

Dore, R. (1986) *Flexible Rigidities*, London: Athlone Press.

Dubois, P. (1993) 'The design of computerised production management systems: a question of time?', in M. Heidenreich (ed.), *Computers and Culture in Organizations*, Berlin: Sigma, Rainer Bohn Verlag.

Dubois, P. and Linhart, D. (1994) 'Industrial networks and corporate cultures: the French case', in C. Mako and P. Novoszáth (eds), *Convergence versus Divergence: The Case of the Corporate Culture*, Budapest: Institute for Social Conflict Research, Hungarian Academy of Sciences and Communication and Consultation Co. Ltd.

Dunford, M. (1991) 'Industrial trajectories and social relations in areas of new industrial growth', in G. Benko and M. Dunford (eds), *Industrial Change and Regional Development*, London: Belhaven.

Dunne, P. and Hughes, A. (1990) 'Small businesses: an analysis of recent trends in their relative importance and growth performance in the UK with some European comparisons', Small Business Research Centre, Working Paper no. 1, Cambridge: SBRC.

Dyas, G.P. and Thanheiser, H.T. (1976) *The Emerging European Enterprise*, London: Macmillan.

Ebster-Grosz, D. (1994) 'Successful cross-cultural configurations in Anglo-German business collaboration', paper presented at the AIB Conference, Manchester, March.

Edwards, J. and Fischer, K. (1991) 'Banks, finance and investment in West Germany since 1970', Centre for Economic Policy Research Discussion Paper 497, London: CEPR.

Edwards, P.K. (1987) *Managing the Factory*, Oxford: Basil Blackwell.

Edwards, P., Hall, M., Hyman, R., Marginson, P., Sisson, K., Waddington, J. and Winchester, D. (1992) 'Great Britain: still muddling through', in A. Ferner and R. Hyman (eds), *Industrial Relations in the New Europe*, Oxford: Basil Blackwell.

Eglau, H.-O. (1989) *Wie Gott in Frankfurt. Die Deutsche Bank und die deutsche Industrie*, Düsseldorf: ECON Verlag.

Elger, T. (1991) 'Task flexibility and the intensification of labour in UK manufacturing in the 1980s', in A. Pollert (ed.), *Farewell to Flexibility?*, Oxford: Basil Blackwell.

Elston, J.A. and Albach, H. (1994) 'Bank affiliation and firm capital investment in Germany', Wissenschaftszentrum Berlin Discussion Paper FS IV 94–10, Berlin: WZB.

Eltis, W. (1992) 'The contribution of Japanese industrial success to Britain and Europe', paper presented to the Institut de l'Entreprise, Paris, 3 June.

Esping-Anderson, G. (1993) *Changing Classes*, London: Sage.

Esser, J. (1988) 'Symbolic privatisation: the politics of privatisation in West Germany' *West European Politics*, 11 (4): 61–73.

Esser, J. (1990) 'Bank power in West Germany revised', *West European Politics*, 13 (4): 17–32.

Eyraud, F. and Tschobanian, R. (1985) 'The Auroux reforms and company level industrial relations in France', *British Journal of Industrial Relations*, 23 (2): 241–58.

Eyraud, F., d'Iribarne, A. and Maurice, M. (1988) 'Des entreprises face aux technologies flexibles: une analyse de la dynamique du changement', *Sociologie du travail*, 1 (30): 55–77.

Feldenkirchen, W. (1992) 'Concentration in German industry, 1870–1939', in B. Supple (ed.), *The Rise of Big Business*, Aldershot: Edward Elgar.

Fichter, M. (1993) 'A house divided: a view of German unification as it has affected organised labour', *German Politics*, 2 (1): 21–39.

Fischer, J. and Minssen, H. (1987) 'Weder Reprofessionalisierung noch vollendeter Taylorismus. Neue Leistungspolitik in der Bekleidungsindustrie', *Soziale Welt*, 38 (2): 197–210.

Fox, A. (1985) *History and Heritage: The Social Origins of the British Industrial Relations System*, London: George Allen & Unwin.

Franks, J. and Mayer, C. (1990) 'Capital markets and corporate control: a study of France, Germany and the UK', *Economic Policy*, 10, 191–231.

Franks, J. and Mayer, C. (1992) 'Corporate control: a synthesis of the international evidence', unpublished working paper, London Business School.

Gallie, D. (1989) 'Trade union allegiance and decline in British urban labour markets', Economic and Social Research Council: Social Change and Economic Life Initiative Working Paper 9, Oxford: Nuffield College.

Gallie, D. (1991) 'Patterns of skill change: upskilling, deskilling or the polarization of skills?', *Work, Employment and Society*, 5 (3): 319–52.

Geary, D. (1991) 'The industrial bourgeoisie and labour relations in Germany, 1871–1933', in D. Blackbourn and R. Evans (eds), *The German Bourgeoisie*, London: Routledge.

Ghertman, M. (1986) 'New multinationals in Europe', in K. Macharzina and W.H. Staehle (eds), *European Approaches to International Management*, London: de Gruyter.

Gibbs, D. (1989) 'Government policy and industrial change: an overview', in D. Gibbs (ed.), *Government Policy and Industrial Change*, London: Routledge.

Glyn, A. (1992) 'The "productivity miracle", profits, and investments', in J. Michie (ed.), *The Economic Legacy, 1979–1992*, London: Academic Press.

Goetschy, J. and Rozenblatt, P. (1992) 'France: the industrial relations system at a turning point?', in A. Ferner and R. Hyman (eds), *Industrial Relations in the New Europe*, Oxford: Basil Blackwell.

Goold, M. and Campbell, A. (1987) *Strategies and Styles: The Role of the Centre in Managing Diversified Corporations*, Oxford: Basil Blackwell.

Gordon, C. (1990) 'The business culture in the United Kingdom', in C. Randlesome (ed.), *Business Cultures in Europe*, Oxford: Heinemann.

Goss, D. (1990) *Small Business and Society*, London: Routledge.

Gourvish, T.R. (1992) 'British business and the transition to a corporate economy: entrepreneurship and management structures', in B. Supple (ed.), *The Rise of Big Business*, Aldershot: Edward Elgar.

Grabher, G. (1988) *Unternehmensnetzwerke und Innovation*, Research Unit Labour Market and Employment, Wissenschaftszentrum Berlin.

Grahl, J. and Teague, P. (1991) 'A new deal for Europe', in A. Amin and M. Dietrich (eds), *Towards a New Europe: Structural Change in the European Economy,* Aldershot: Edward Elgar.

Grant, W. and Paterson, W. (1994) 'The chemical industry: a study in internationalization', in J.R. Hollingsworth, P. Schmitter and W. Streeck (eds), *Governing Capitalist Economics*, New York and London: Oxford University Press.

Gray, S. and McDermott, C. (1990) *Mega-Merger-Mayhem*, London: Mandarin.

Greenhalgh, C. and Gregory, M. (1994) 'Why manufacturing still matters', *Employment Policy Institute Economic Report*, 8 (5), Aug.

Hakim, C. (1988) 'Self-employment; a review of recent trends and current issues', *Work, Employment and Society*, 2 (4): 421–50.

Hall, P. (1984) 'Patterns of economic policy: an organizational approach', in S. Bornstein, D. Held and J. Krieger (eds), *The State in Capitalist Europe*, London: Unwin Hyman.

Hall, P. (1986) *Governing the Economy*, London: Oxford University Press.

Hall, P. (1990) 'The state and the market', in P. Hall, J. Hayward and H. Machin (eds), *Developments in French Politics*, London: Macmillan.

Hall, P. (1993) 'Policy paradigms, social learning and the state: the case of economic policy-making in Britain', *Comparative Politics*, 25 (3): 275–96.

Hamilton, F.E.I. (1987) 'Multinational enterprises', in W.F. Lever (ed.), *Industrial Change in the United Kingdom*, London: Longman Scientific.

Hannah, L. (1976a) *The Rise of the Corporate Economy*, London: Methuen.

Hannah, L. (ed.) (1976b) *Management Strategy and Business Development*, London: Macmillan.

Hannah, L. (1980) 'Visible and invisible hands in Great Britain', in A.D. Chandler and H. Daems (eds), *Managerial Hierarchies*, Cambridge, Mass.: Harvard University Press.

Hanqué, B. and Soskice, D. (1994) 'The French political economy', paper presented to a seminar at the Wissenschaftszentrum Berlin, November.

Harvey, D. (1989) *The Condition of Postmodernity*, Oxford: Basil Blackwell.

HBS, IGM, IAT, FhG (1992) *Lean Production/schlanke Produktion. Neues Produktionskonzept humanerer Arbeit?*, Düsseldorf: Hans-Böckler Stiftung.

Heald, D. (1988) 'The United Kingdom: privatisation and its political context', *West European Politics*, 11 (4): 31–48.

Heidenreich, M. (1993) 'The expansion of the educational system and the introduction of production control systems: a crossnational perspective', in M. Heidenreich (ed.), *Computers and Culture in Organizations*, Berlin: Sigma, Rainer Bohn Verlag.

Henderson, J. (1989) *The Globalization of High Technology Production*, London: Routledge.

Hendry, C. (1990) 'New technology, new careers: the impact of flexible specialization on skills and jobs', *New Technology, Work and Employment*, 5 (1): 31–43.

Hildebrandt, E. and Seltz, R. (1989) *Wandel betrieblicher Sozialverfassung durch systemische Kontrolle? Die Einführung computergestützter Produktionsplanungs- und Steuerungssysteme im bundesdeutschen Maschinenbau*, Berlin: Rainer Bohn Verlag.

Hirsch-Kreinsen, H. (1989) 'Entwicklung einer Basistechnik – NC Steuerungen von Werkzeugmaschinen in den USA und der Bundesrepublik', in K. Duell and B. Lutz (eds), *Technikentwicklung im internationalen Vergleich*, Frankfurt and New York: Campus.

Hirsch-Kreinsen, H. and Wolf, H. (1987) 'Neue Produktionstechniken und Arbeitsorganisation. Interessen und Strategien betrieblicher Akteure', *Soziale Welt*, 38 (2): 181–9.

Hirst, P. (1989) *After Thatcher*, London: Collins.

Hirst, P. and Thompson G. (1992) 'The problem of "globalization": international economic relations, national economic management and the formation of trading blocks', *Economy and Society*, 21 (4): 357–96.

Hirst, P. and Zeitlin J. (1989) *Reversing Industrial Decline?*, Leamington Spa: Berg.

Hirst, P. and Zeitlin, J. (1990) 'Flexible specialization vs. post-Fordism: theory, evidence and policy implications', Birkbeck Public Policy Centre Working Paper, London: Birkbeck College.

Hirst, P. and Zeitlin J. (1992) 'Flexible specialization versus post-Fordism', *Economy and Society*, 20 (11): 1–56.

Hoang-Ngoc, L. and Lallement, M. (1992) 'The decentralization of industrial relations in France: trends towards microcorporatism?', paper presented at the International Working Party on Labour Market Segmentation, Cambridge, July.

Hollingsworth, J.R. (1993) 'A comparative study of social systems of production', paper prepared for Workshop on Social Systems of Production, Madison, Wisconsin, Feb.

Hollingsworth, J.R., Schmitter, P. and Streeck, W. (eds) (1994) *Governing Capitalist Economies*, New York and London: Oxford University Press.

Hood, N. (1986) 'Role and structure of British multinationals', in K. Macharzina and W.H. Staehle (eds), *European Approaches to International Management*, London: de Gruyter.

Horovitz, J. (1980) *Top Management Control in Europe*, New York: St Martin's Press.

Hoss, P. and Wirth, B. (1992) 'Relations of trust in East German industry?', paper presented at the Conference on Convergence and Divergence in Economic Growth and Technical Change, MERIT, University of Limburg, Maastricht, Dec.

Hughes, A. (1990) 'Industrial concentration and the small business sector in the UK: the 1980s in historical perspective', Small Business Research Centre Working Paper no. 6, Cambridge: SBRC.

Hughes, A. (1992) 'Competition policy and the competitive process: Europe in the 1990s, *Metroeconomica*, 43 (1–2): 1–50.

Hyman, R. (1988) 'Flexible specialization: miracle or myth?, in R. Hyman and W. Streeck (eds), *New Technology and Industrial Relations*, Oxford: Basil Blackwell.

Hyman, R. (1991) 'Plus ça change?: the theory of production and the production of theory', in A. Pollert (ed.), *Farewell to Flexibility?*, Oxford: Basil Blackwell.

Hyman, R. and Ferner, A. (1992) 'Introduction: industrial relations in the New Europe', in R. Hyman and A. Ferner (eds), *Industrial Relations in the New Europe*, Oxford: Basil Blackwell.

Imrie, R. and Morris, J. (1992) 'A review of recent changes in buyer–supplier relations', *Omega*, 20 (5–6): 641–52.

Ingham, G. (1984) *Capitalism Divided? The City and Industry in British Social Development*, London: Macmillan.

Institute of Manpower Studies (IMS) (1986) *Changing Working Patterns*, A report for the NEDO, London: IMS.

Jacobi, O. (1991) 'Debureaucratization and flexibility', in B. Jessop et al. (eds), *The Politics of Flexibility*, Aldershot: Edward Elgar.

Jacobi, O. and Müller-Jentsch, W. (1990) 'West Germany: continuity and structural change', in G. Baglioni and C. Crouch (eds), *European Industrial Relations*, London: Sage.

Jacobi, O., Keller, B. and Müller-Jentsch, W. (1992) 'Germany: codetermining the future', in A. Ferner and R. Hyman (eds), *Industrial Relations in the New Europe*, Oxford: Basil Blackwell.

Jepperson, R.L. (1991) 'Institutions, institutional effects, and institutionalism', in W.W. Powell and P.J. DiMaggio (eds), *The New Institutionalism in Organizational Analysis*, Chicago and London: University of Chicago Press.

Jessop, B. (1989) 'Conservative regimes and the transition to post-Fordism: the cases of Great Britain and West Germany', in M. Gottdiener (ed.), *Capitalist Development and Crisis Theory: Accumulation, Regulation, and Spatial Restructuring*, London: Macmillan.

Jessop, B. (1990) 'Regulation theories in retrospect and prospect', *Economy and Society*, 19 (2): 153–216.

Jessop, B. (1991) 'The welfare state in the transition from Fordism to post-Fordism', in B. Jessop et al. (eds), *The Politics of Flexibility*, Aldershot: Edward Elgar.

Jessop, B. (1992) 'Regulation und Politik', in A. Demirovic et al. (eds), *Hegemonie und Staat*, Münster: Westfälisches Dampfboot.

Johnson, St. (1991) 'The small firm and the UK labour market in the 1980s', in A. Pollert (ed.), *Farewell to Flexibility*, Oxford: Basil Blackwell.

Jones, B. (1988) 'Work and flexible automation in Britain: a review of developments and possibilities', *Work, Employment and Society*, 2 (4): 451–86.

Jürgens, U. (1991) 'Industrielle Restrukturierung und Wandel des betrieblichen Arbeitseinsatzes: Methodisches Design und ausgewählte Ergebnisse eines internationalen zwischenbetrieblichen Vergleichs westlicher Automobilkonzerne', in M. Heidenreich and G. Schmidt (eds), *International Vergleichende Organisationsforschung*, Opladen: Westdeutscher Verlag.

Julius, D. and Thomsen, S.E. (1988) *The Explosion of FDI among the G-5*, Discussion Paper No. 8, London: Royal Institute of International Affairs.

Julius, D.A. and Thomsen, S.E. (1989) *Inward Investment and Foreign-owned Firms in the G-5*, London: Royal Institute for International Affairs.

Kaedtler, J. and Kottwitz, G. (1994) 'Industrielle Beziehungen in Ostdeutschland: Durch Kooperation zum Gegensatz von Kapital und Arbeit?', *Industrielle Beziehungen*, 1 (1): 13–38.

Keller, B. (1990) 'The future of labour relations in the Federal Republic of Germany', *Labour and Society* 15 (4): 379–99.

Keller, B. and Henneberger, F. (1991) 'Privatwirtschaft und öffentlicher Dienst: Parallelen und Differenzen in den Arbeitspolitiken', in W. Müller-Jentsch (ed.), *Konfliktpartnerschaft*, München and Mering: Rainer Hampp Verlag.

Kern, H. (1994) 'Intelligente Regulierung. Gewerkschaftliche Beiträge in Ost und West zur Erneurerung des deutschen Produktionsmodells', *Soziale Welt*, 45, (1): 33–59.

Kern, H. and Sabel, C. (1994) 'Verblasste Tugenden. Zur Krise des deutschen Produktionsmodells', *Soziale Welt*, 9: 605–24.

Kern, H. and Schumann, M. (1984) *Das Ende der Arbeitsteilung? Rationalisierung in der Industriellen Produktion*, Munich: C.H. Beck.

Kindleberger, C. (1964) *Economic Growth in France and Britain, 1851–1950*, Cambridge (Mass.): Harvard University Press.

Knight, J. (1992) *Institutions and Social Conflict*, Cambridge: Cambridge University Press.

Kocka, J. (1970) 'Vorindustrielle Faktoren in der deutschen Industrialisierung', in M. Stürmer (ed.), *Das kaiserliche Deutschland. Politik und Gesellschaft 1870–1918*, Düsseldorf: Droste Verlag.

Kocka, J. (1975a) *Unternehmer in der deutschen Industrialisierung*, Göttingen: Vandenhoek & Ruprecht.

Kocka, J. (1975b) 'Expansion – Integration – Diversifikation. Wachstums-strategien industrieller Großunternehmen in Deutschland vor 1914', in H. Winkel (ed.), *Vom Kleingewerbe zum Großbetrieb*, Berlin: Duncker & Humboldt.

Kocka, J. and Siegrist, H. (1979) 'Die hundert größten deutschen Industrie-unternehmen im späten 19. und frühen 20. Jahrhundert', in N. Horn and J. Kocka (eds), *Law and the Formation of the Big Enterprise in the 19th and Early 20th Century*, Göttingen: Vandenhoek & Ruprecht.

Köhler, C. and Schmierl, K. (1992) 'Technological innovation – organiza-tional conservatism', in N. Altmann *et al.* (eds), *Technology and Work in German Industry*, London: Routledge.

Kotthoff, H. and Reindl, J. (1990) *Die soziale Welt kleiner Betriebe*, Göttingen: Otto Schwartz.

Krätke, S. (1991) 'Cities in transformation: the case of West Germany', in G. Benko and M. Dunford (eds), *Industrial Change and Regional Develop-ment*, London: Belhaven.

Landes, D. (1969) *The Unbound Prometheus: Technological Change and Industrial Development*, Cambridge: Cambridge University Press.

Lane, C. (1989) *Management and Labour in Europe: The Industrial Enter-prise in Germany, Britain and France*, Aldershot: Edward Elgar.

Lane, C. (1990) 'Vocational training, employment relations and new produc-tion concepts in Germany: some lessons for Britain', *Industrial Relations Journal*, 21 (4): 247–59.

Lane, C. (1991) 'Industrial reorganization in Europe: patterns of convergence and divergence in Germany, France and Britain', *Work, Employment and Society*, 5 (4): 515–39.

Lane, C. (1992) 'European business systems: Britain and Germany com-pared', in R. Whitley (ed.), *Firms and Markets in Europe: The Role of Social Institutions in Structuring Market Economies*, London: Sage.

Lane, C. (1993) 'Gender and the labour market in Europe: Britain, Germany, and France compared', *Sociological Review*, 41 (2): 274–301.

Lane, C. (1994) 'Industrial order and transformation of industrial relations:

Britain, Germany and France', in R. Hyman and A. Ferner (eds), *New Frontiers in European Industrial Relations*, Oxford: Basil Blackwell.

Lash, S. and Urry, J. (1987) *The End of Organized Capitalism*, Cambridge: Polity Press.

Leborgne, D. and Lipietz, A. (1988) 'New technologies, new modes of regulation: some spatial implications', *Space and Society*, 6 (3).

Levine, A.L. (1967) *Industrial Retardation in Britain, 1880–1914*, London: Weidenfeld & Nicolson.

Lévy-Leboyer, M. (1980) 'The large corporation in modern France', in A.D. Chandler and H. Daems (eds), *Managerial Hierarchies*, Cambridge, Mass.: Harvard University Press.

Linhart D., Duell, K. and Bechtle, G. (1989) 'Neue Technologien und industrielle Beziehungen im Betrieb – Erfahrungen aus der Bundesrepublik Deutschland und Frankreich', in K. Duell and B. Lutz (eds), *Technikentwicklung und Arbeitsteilung im internationalen Vergleich*, Frankfurt and New York: Campus.

Lipietz, A. (1986) 'New tendencies in the international division of labour: regimes of accumulation and modes of regulation', in A. Scott and M. Storper (eds), *Production, Work, Territory*, Boston, Mass.: Allen & Unwin.

Lipietz, A. (1992a) 'Vom Althusserismus zur "Theorie der Regulation"', in A. Demirovic et al. (eds), *Hegemonie und Staat*, Münster: Westfälisches Dampfboot.

Lipietz, A. (1992b) 'Allgemeine und konjunkturelle Merkmale der ökonomischen Staatsintervention', in A. Demirovic et al. (eds), *Hegemonie und Staat*, Münster: Westfälisches Dampfboot.

Littler, C. (1982) *The Development of the Labour Process in Capitalist Societies*, London: Heinemann.

Locke, R.R. (1984) *The End of the Practical Man: Entrepreneurship and Higher Education in Germany, France and Great Britain 1880–1940*, Greenwich, Conn.: JAI Press.

Löhn, J. (1989) 'Der Standort Bundesrepublik: Die technologische Basis und Zukunft', in M. Dierkes and K. Zimmermann (eds), *Wirtschaftsstandort Bundesrepublik*, Frankfurt: Campus.

Lutz, B. (1992) 'The contradictions of post-Tayloristic rationalization and the uncertain future of industrial work', in N. Altmann, C. Köhler and P. Meil (eds), *Technology and Work in German Industry*, London: Routledge.

Lutz, B. and Veltz, P. (1989) 'Maschinenbauer versus Informatiker – Gesellschaftliche Entwicklung in Deutschland und Frankreich', in K. Duell and B. Lutz (eds), *Technikentwicklung und Arbeitsteilung im internationalen Vergleich*, Frankfurt and New York: Campus.

Macharzina, K. (1986) 'Features of European multinationals', in K. Macharzina and W.H. Staehle (eds), *European Approaches to International Management*, London: De Gruyter.

Mahnkopf, B. (1991) 'Vorwärts in die Vergangenheit? Pessimistiche Spekulationen über die Zukunft der Gewerkschaften in der neuen Bundesrepublik', in A. Westphal, H. Herr, M. Heine and U. Busch (eds), *Wirtschaftspolitische Konsequenzen der deutschen Vereinigung*, Frankfurt: Campus.

Mahnkopf, B. (1992) 'The "skill-oriented" strategies of German trade unions: their impact on efficiency and equality objectives', *British Journal of Industrial Relations*, 30, March: 61–81.

Mahon, R. (1987) 'From Fordism to?: new technology, labour markets and unions', *Economic and Industrial Democracy*, 8: 5–60.

Mahoney, M., Wagner, K. and Paulssen, M. (1994) Changing Fortunes: an industry study of British and German productivity growth over three decades', WZB Discussion Paper FSI 94–304, Berlin: Wissenschaftszentrum Berlin.

Manske, F. (1991) *Kontrolle, Rationalisierung und Arbeit*, Berlin: Sigma, Rainer Bohn Verlag.

Marchington, M. and Parker, P. (1990) *Changing Patterns of Employee Relations*, London: Harvester Wheatsheaf.

Marginson, P., Edwards, P.K., Martin, R., Purcell, J. and Sisson, K. (1988) *Beyond the Workplace*, Oxford: Basil Blackwell.

Marsden, D. and Ryan, P. (1991) 'Initial training, labour market structure and public policy: intermediate skills in British and German Industry', in P. Ryan (ed.), *International Comparisons of Vocational Education and Training for Intermediate Skills*, London: Falmer Press.

Marsden, D. and Thompson, M. (1990) 'Flexibility agreements in Britain', *Work, Employment and Society*, 4: 83–104.

Martin, R. (1988) 'Technological change and manual work', in D. Gallie (ed.), *Employment in Britain*, Oxford: Basil Blackwell.

Martin, R. and Tyler, P. (1992) 'The regional legacy', in J. Michie (ed.), *The Economic Legacy 1979–1992*, London: Academic Press.

Martinelli, F. and Schoenberger, F. (1991) 'Oligopoly is alive and well: notes for a broader discussion of flexible accumulation', in G. Benko and M. Dunford (eds), *Industrial Change and Regional Development: The Transformation of New Industrial Spaces*, London: Belhaven Press.

Mason, C.M. (1987) 'The small firms sector', in W.F. Lever, *Industrial Change in the United Kingdom*, London: Longman Scientific.

Mason, G., van Ark, B. and Wagner, K. (1993) 'Productivity, product quality and workforce skills: food processing in four European countries', WZB Discussion Paper FSI 93–309, Berlin: Wissenschaftszentrum Berlin.

Maurice, M., Sorge, A. and Warner, M. (1980) 'Societal differences in organising manufacturing units', *Organization Studies*, 1: 63–91.

Mayer, M. and Whittington, R. (1994) 'Managing the large diversified firm in contemporary Europe', paper presented at the workshop on Social Constitution of Economic Actors, Humboldt University, Berlin, 22–24 April.

McGee, J. and Segal-Horn, S. (1992) 'Will there be a European food processing industry?', in S. Young and J. Hamill (eds), *Europe and the Multinationals*, Aldershot: Edward Elgar.

Millward, N. and Stevens, M. (1986) *British Workplace Industrial Relations, 1980–1984*, Aldershot: Gower.

Millward, N., Stevens, D., Smart, D. and Hawes, W.R. (1992) *Workplace Industrial Relations in Transition: The DE/ESRC/PSI/ACAS Surveys*, Aldershot: Dartmouth.

Mooser, J. (1984) *Arbeiterleben in Deutschland 1900–1970*, Frankfurt: Suhrkamp.

Morris, J. and Imrie, R. (1991) *Transformations in the Buyer–Supplier Relationship*, London: Macmillan.

Müller-Jentsch, W., Rehermann, K. and Sperling, H.-J. (1992) 'Socio-technical rationalization and negotiated work organisation: recent trends in Germany', in OECD (ed.), *New Directions in Work Organization: The Industrial Relations Response*, Paris: OECD.

Neumann, W. and Unterwedde, H. (1986) *Industriepolitik. Ein deutsch-französischer Vergleich*, Opladen: Leske & Budrich.

New, C.C. and Myers, A. (1986) *Managing Manufacturing Operations in the UK 1975–85*, London: Institute of Manpower Studies.

Nielsen, K. (1991) 'Towards a flexible future: theories and politics', in B. Jessop, K. Nielsen, H. Kastendiek and O.K. Pedersen (eds), *The Politics of Flexibility*, Aldershot: Edward Elgar.

Nolan, P. (1989) 'Walking on water? Performance and industrial relations under Thatcher', *Industrial Relations Journal*, 20 (2): 81–92.

Northcott, J., Rogers, P., Knetsch, W. and de Lestapis, B. (1985) *Microelectronics in Industry. An International Comparison: Britain, Germany, France*, London: Policy Studies Institute.

Oakey, R., Rothwell, R. and Cooper, S. (1988) *The Management of Innovation in High-Technology Small Firms*, London: Frances Pinter.

O'Brien, P. and Keyder, C. (1978) *Economic Growth in Britain and France, 1780-1914*, London: George Allen & Unwin.

OECD (1989) *Employment Outlook*, Paris: OECD.

OECD (1991) *Employment Outlook*, Paris: OECD.

OECD (1992) 'Recent developments in self-employment', in *Employment Outlook*, Paris: OECD, pp. 155–93.

Ohmae, K. (1990) *The Borderless World: Power and Strategy in the Interlinked Economy*, London: Collins.

Olle, W. (1985) ' "Job export" und 'Job creation" – Zur Beschäftigungsentwicklung in multinationalen Konzernen', in P. Mettler (ed.), *Multinationale Konzerne in der Bundesrepublik Deutschland*, Frankfurt: Haag & Herchen.

Orru, M., Woolsey Bighart, N. and Hamilton, G.G. (1991) 'Organizational isomorphism in East Asia', in W.W. Powell and P.J. DiMaggio, *The New Institutionalism in Organizational Analysis*, Chicago and London: University of Chicago Press.

Pavitt, K. (1970) 'Performance in industrially advanced countries', in M. Goldsmith (ed.), *Technological Innovation and the Economy*, London: John Wiley.

Penn, R. (1990) 'Skilled maintenance work at BT', *New Technology, Work and Employment*, 5 (2): 135–44.

Penn, R. (1992) 'Contemporary relationships between firms in a classical industrial locality', *Work, Employment and Society*, 6 (2): 209–28.

Piore, M. and Sabel, Ch. (1984) *The Second Industrial Divide: Possibilities for Prosperity*, New York: Basic Books.

Pohl, H. (1992) 'On the history of organisation and management in large German enterprises since the nineteenth century', in B. Supple (ed.), *The Rise of Big Business*, Aldershot: Edward Elgar.

Pollard, S. (1965) *The Genesis of Modern Management*, London: Edward Arnold.

Pollert, A. (1988) 'The "flexible firm": fixation or fact?'. *Work, Employment and Society*, 2 (3): 281–316.

Pollert, A. (ed.) (1991) *Farewell to Flexibility?*, Oxford: Basil Blackwell.

Porter, M. (1990) *The Competitive Advantage of Nations*, London: Macmillan.

Powell, W.W. and DiMaggio, P.J. (eds) (1991) *The New Institutionalism in Organizational Analysis*, Chicago and London: University of Chicago Press.

Prais, S.J. (1976) *The Evolution of Giant Firms in Britain*, Cambridge: Cambridge University Press.

Pries, L., Schmidt, R. and Trinczek, R. (1990) *Entwicklungspfade von Industriearbeit*, Opladen: Westdeutscher Verlag.

Prowse, S. (1994) *Corporate Governance in an International Perspective: A Survey of Corporate Control Mechanisms among Large Firms in the United States, the United Kingdom, Japan and Germany*, Basle: Bank for International Settlements.

Puhle, H.-J. (1970) 'Parlament, Parteien und Interessenverbände 1890–1914', in M. Stürmer (ed.), *Das kaiserliche Deutschland*, Düsseldorf: Droste Verlag.

Quack, S. and Hildebrandt, S. (1994) 'Hausbank or fournisseur? Bank services for small and medium-sized enterprises in Germany and France', paper presented at the ESF EMOT Workshop on 'Financial Services', at the Centre de Recherche sur d'Espargne, Paris, 30 September – 1 October.

Rainnie, A. (1991) 'Just-in-time, subcontracting and the small firm', *Work, Employment and Society*, 5 (3): 353–76.

Rainnie, A. (1993) 'The reorganisation of large firm subcontracting: myth and reality', *Capital and Class*, 49: 53–75.

Ramsey, H. (1991) 'Reinventing the wheel? A review of the development and performance of employee involvement', *Human Resource Management Journal*, 1 (4): 1–22.

Rose, M. (1993) 'Trade unions: ruin, retreat or rally?', *Work, Employment and Society*, 7 (2): 291–312.

Rosenhaft, E. and Lee, W.R. (1990) 'State and society in modern Germany – Beamstenstaat, Klassenstaat, Wohlfahrtsstaat', in W.R. Lee and E. Rosenhaft (eds), *The State and Social Change in Germany, 1880–1980*, New York, Oxford and Munich: Berg.

Rothwell, S. (1987) 'Selection and training for advanced manufacturing technology' in T.D. Wall, C.W. Clegg and N.J. Kemp, *The Human Side of Advanced Manufacturing Technology*, Chichester, Sussex: John Wiley.

Rowthorn, B. (1992) 'Government spending and taxation in the Thatcher era', in J. Michie (ed.), *The Economic Legacy 1979–1992*, London: Academic Press.

Rubery, J. (1989) 'Precarious forms of work in the United Kingdom', in G. Rogers and J. Rogers (eds), *Precarious Jobs in Labour Market Regulation*, Brussels: International Institute for Labour Studies.

Rubery, J., Tarling, R. and Wilkinson, F. (1987) 'Flexibility, marketing and the organisation of production', *Labour and Society*, 12 (1): 131–51.

Sabel, C.F. (1989) 'The reemergence of regional economies', Research Unit Labour Market and Employment. Wissenschaftszentrum Berlin, Discussion Paper FSI 89–3.

Sabel, C.F. (1990) 'Skills without a place: the reorganization of the corporation and the experience of work', paper presented at the 1990 BSA Conference in Guildford.

Sally, R. (1994) 'Multinational enterprises, political economy and institutional theory: domestic embeddedness in the context of internationalization', *Review of International Political Economy*, 1 (1): 161–92.

Sauer, D., Deiss, M., Doehl, V., Bieber, D. and Altmann, N. (1992) 'Systemic rationalization and inter-company divisions of labour', in N. Altmann, C. Köhler and P. Meil, *Technology and Work in German Industry*, London: Routledge.

Saxenian, A.L. (1989) 'The Cheshire cat's grin: innovation, regional development and the Cambridge case', *Economy and Society*, 18 (4).

Sayer, A. (1989) 'Postfordism in question', *International Journal of Urban and Regional Research*, 13 (4): 666–95.

Schmidt, M.G. (1992) 'Political consequences of German unification', *West European Politics*, 15 (4): 1–75.

Schmidt, R. and Trinczek, R. (1991) 'Duales System: Tarifliche und betriebliche Interessenvertretung', in W. Müller-Jentsch (ed.), *Konfliktpartnerschaft*, Munich and Mering: Rainer Hamp Verlag.

Schmierl, K. and Schutz-Wild, R. (1994) 'Phoenix aus der Asche? Die Investitionsgüterindustrie in den neuen Bundesländern', *Blick durch die Wirtschaft*, 18 May.

Schoenberger, E. (1989) 'Multinational corporations and the new international division of labour: a critical appraisal', in S. Wood (ed.) *The Transformation of Work*, London: Unwin Hyman.

Schultz-Wild, R. (1992) 'Diffusion of CIM-technologies: dynamic dissemination and alternative paths of innovation', in N. Altmann, C. Köhler and P. Meil (eds), *Technology and Work in German Industry*, London: Routledge.

Schumann, M., Baethge-Kinsky, V., Neumann U. and Springer, R. (1990) *Breite Diffusion der Neuen Produktionskonzepte – zögerlicher Wandel der Arbeitsstrukturen*, Zwischenbericht, Göttingen: Soziologisches Forschungsinstitut.

Schumann, M., Baethge-Kinsky, V., Kuhlmann, K. and Neumann, U. (1994) 'Der Wandel der Produktionsarbeit im Zugriff neuer Produktionskonzepte', *Soziale Welt*, 9: 11–43.

Scott, J. (1985) *Corporations, Classes and Capitalism*, 2nd edn, London: Hutchinson.

Scott, M.G. and Roberts I. (1988) 'Employment relationships and the labour process in the small firm', Department of Business and Management, University of Stirling, paper given at the Aston/UMIST 6th Annual Labour Process Conference, Birmingham.

Scott, W.R. (1991) 'Unpacking institutional arguments', in W.W. Powell and P.J. DiMaggio (eds), *The New Institutionalism in Organizational Analysis*, Chicago and London: University of Chicago Press.

Scott, A. and Storper, M. (1987) 'High technology industry and regional development: a theoretical critique and reconstruction', *International Social Science Journal*, 112.

Segrestin, D. (1990) 'Recent changes in France', in G. Baglioni and C. Crouch (eds), *European Industrial Relations*, London: Sage.

Semlinger, K. (1989) 'Fremdleistungsbezug als Flexibilitätsreservoir. Unternehmenspolitische und arbeitspolitische Risiken in der Zuliefererindustrie', *WSI Mitteilungen*, 9: 517–25.

Sengenberger, W. and Loveman, G. (1988) *Smaller Units of Employment*, a Synthesis Report on Industrial Reorganisation in Industrialised Countries, Geneva: International Labour Office.

Sengenberger, W. and Pyke, F. (1990) 'Small firm industrial districts and local economic regeneration: research and policy issues', Paper no. 1 of the International Conference on Industrial Districts and Local Economic Regeneration, Geneva: International Institute for Labour Studies.

Sengenberger, W., Loveman, G. and Piore, M. (1990) 'Introduction: economic and social reorganisation in the small and medium-sized enterprise sector', in W. Sengenberger et al. (eds), *The Re-emergence of Small Enterprises*, Geneva: International Institute for Labour Studies.

Senker, P. and Simmonds, P. (1991) 'Changing technology and design work in the British engineering industry, 1981–88', *New Technology, Work and Employment*, 6 (2): 91–9.

Service des Statistiques Industrielles (1988) *L'Industrie française dans les régions*, Paris: La Documentation Française.

Shutt, J. and Whittington, R. (1984) 'Large firm strategies and the rise of small units', School of Geography, Manchester, Working Paper Series no. 15.

Shutt, J. and Whittington, R. (1987) 'Fragmentation strategies and the rise of small units', *Regional Studies*, 19.

Siegrist, H. (1980) 'Deutsche Großunternehmen vom späten 19. Jahrhundert bis zur Weimarer Republik', *Geschichte und Gesellschaft*, 6 (1): 60–102.

Silvia, S. (1994) 'German unification and emerging divisions within German employers' associations: cause or catalyst?', paper presented at the Ninth International Conference of Europeanists, Chicago, 31 March – 2 April.

Skidelsky, R. (1993) 'Save small firms and they will save us', *Independent*, 1 July 1993.

Small Business Research Centre (1992) *The State of British Enterprise: Growth, Innovation and Competitive Advantage of Small and Medium-sized Firms*, Cambridge: SBRC, University of Cambridge.

Smyser, W.R. (1992) *The Economy of United Germany*, London: Hurst.

Sorge, A. and Streeck, W. (1987) 'Industrial relations and technical change: the case for an extended perspective', in St. Tolliday and J. Zeitlin (eds), *Between Fordism and Flexibility*, Cambridge: Polity Press.

Sorge, A., Warner, M., Hartman, G. and Nicholas, I. (1983) *Microelectronics and Manpower in Britain and Germany*, Aldershot: Gower.

Steedman, H. (1990) 'Improvements in workforce qualifications: Britain and France 1979–88', *National Institute Economic Review*, August: 50–61.

Stelzer-O'Neill, B. (1994) 'Unternehmensfinanzierung in Grossbritannien', *Blick durch die Wirtschaft*, 10 August.

Stewart, R., Barsoux, J.-L., Kieser, A., Ganther, H.-D. and Walgenbach, P. (1994) *Managing in Britain and Germany*, report for the Anglo-German Foundation, London: AGF.

Stille, F. (1990) 'Industrial policy in West Germany: the 1980s', in K. Cowling and H. Tomann (eds), *Industrial Policy after 1992*, London: Anglo-German Foundation.

Stoffaes, C. (1989) 'Industrial policy and the state: from industry to enterprise', in P. Godt (ed.), *Policy Making in France*, London: Frances Pinter.

Stopford, J.M. and Turner, L. (1985) *Britain and the Multinationals*, Chichester, Sussex: John Wiley.

Storey, D.J. (1982) *Entrepreneurship and the New Firm*, London: Croom Helm.

Storey, J. and Sisson, K. (1990) 'Limits to transformation: human resource management in the British context', *Industrial Relations Journal*, 21 (1): 60–5.

Streeck, W. (1989) 'Successful adjustment to turbulent markets: the automobile industry', in J.P. Katzenstein (ed.), *Industry and Politics in West Germany*, Ithaca, N.Y.: Cornell University Press.

Streeck, W. (1992) *Social Institutions and Economic Performance*, London: Sage.

Supple, B. (1983) 'States and industrialization: Britain and Germany in the nineteenth century', in D. Held et al. (eds), *States and Societies*, Oxford: Martin Robertson.

Syzman, J. (1983) *Governments, Markets and Growth*, Oxford: Martin Robertson.

Telesis (1986) *Competing for Prosperity. Business Strategies and Industrial Policies in Modern France*, research report by B. Déchéry for the Policy Studies Institute, London.

Thelen, K.A. (1991) *Union of Parts: Labour Politics in Postwar Germany*, Ithaca, N.Y. and London: Cornell University Press.

Tichy, G. (1990) 'Bestandsbedingungen und probleme kleiner Unternehmungen', in J. Berger, V. Domeyer and M. Funder (eds), *Kleinbetriebe im wirtschaftlichen Wandel*, Frankfurt: Campus.

Turner, L. (1991) *Democracy at Work: Changing World Markets and the Future of Labour Unions*, Ithaca, N.Y.: Cornell University Press.

Turner, L. and Auer, P. (1994) 'A diversity of new work organisation. Human-centred, lean, and in-between', *Industrielle Beziehungen*, 1 (1): 39–61.

Tylecote, A. (1982) 'German ascent and British decline, 1870–1980: the role of upper-class structure and values', in E. Friedman (ed.), *Ascent and Decline in the World System*, London: Sage.

Tylecote, A. (1991) 'Performance pressures, short-termism and innovation', in J. Cheese (ed.), *Attitudes to Innovation in Germany and Britain: A Comparison*, London: Centre for Science and Technology.

United Nations (1988) *Transnational Corporations in World Development*, New York: UN Centre on Transnational Corporations.

van Tulder, R. and Junne, G. (1988) *European Multinationals in Core Technologies*, Chichester, Sussex: John Wiley.

van Waarden, F. (1993) 'Über die Beständigkeit nationaler Politikstile und Politiknetzwerke. Eine Studie über die Genese ihrer institutionellen Verankerung', in R. Czada and M. Schmidt (eds), *Verhandlungsdemokratie, Interessenvermittlung, Regierbarkeit*, Opladen: Westdeutscher Verlag.

Vickery, L. (1986) 'France', in P. Burns and J. Dewhurst (eds), *Small Business in Europe*, London: Macmillan.

Vitols, S. (1994) 'German banks and the modernization of the small firm sector: long-term finance in a comparative perspective', paper presented at the 9th International Conference of Europeanists, Chicago, March–April.

Vonortas, N.S. (1990) 'Emerging patterns of multinational enterprise operations in developed market economies: evidence and policy', *Review of Political Economy* 2 (5): 188–220.

Vosskamp, U. and Wittke, V. (1992) 'Junge Facharbeiter in der Produktion – eine Herausforderung für betriebliche Arbeitspolitik', *SOFI-Mitteilungen*, June: 28–34.

Walsh, J. (1991a) 'Restructuring, productivity and workplace relations: evidence from the textile industry', *New Technology, Work and Employment*, 6 (2): 124–37.

Walsh, V. (1991b) 'Inter-firm technological alliances: a transient phenomenon or new structures in capitalist economies?', in A. Amin and M. Dietrich (eds), *Towards a New Europe*, Aldershot: Edward Elgar.

Wassermann, W. (1990) 'Die Interessenvertretung der Arbeitnehmer in Klein- und Mittelbetrieben', in J. Berger et al. (eds), *Kleinbetriebe im wirtschaftlichen Wandel*, Frankfurt: Campus.

Wasserman, W. (1992) *Arbeiten im Kleinbetrieb*, Cologne: Bundverlag.

Weimer, S. (1990) 'Arbeitsbedingungen in Kleinbetrieben', in J. Berger, V. Domeyer and M. Funder (eds), *Kleinbetriebe im wirtschaftlichen Wandel*, Frankfurt and New York: Campus.

Weimer, S. (1992) 'The development and structure of small-scale firms', in N. Altmann, C. Köhler and P. Meil (eds), *Technology and Work in German Industry*, London: Routledge.

Weir, M. and Skocpol, Th. (1985) 'State structures and the possibilities for "Keynesian" responses to the great depression in Sweden, Britain and the United States', in P. Evans, D. Rueschemeyer and Th. Skocpol (eds), *Bringing the State Back In*, Cambridge: Cambridge University Press.

Whitley, R. (1992) 'Societies, firms and markets: the social structuring of business systems', in R. Whitley (ed.), *European Business Systems*, London: Sage.

Whitley, R. (1994) 'Dominant forms of economic organization in market economies', *Organization Studies*, 15 (2): 153–82.

Whittaker, D.H. (1990) *Managing Innovation*, Cambridge: Cambridge University Press.

Willemsen, A. (1989) 'Der Standort Bundesrepublik: Die Sicht der Wirtschaft', in M. Dierkes and K. Zimmermann (eds), *Wirtschaftsstandort Bundesrepublik*, Frankfurt: Campus.

Williams, K., Williams J. and Haslam, J. (1983) *Why Are the British Bad at Manufacturing?*, London: Routledge & Kegan Paul.

Williams, K., Cutler T., Williams, J. and Haslam C. (1987) 'The end of mass production?', *Economy and Society*, 16 (3): 405–39.

Williams, K., Williams, J. and Haslam, C. (1990) 'The hollowing out of British manufacturing and its implications for policy', *Economy and Society*, 19: 456–90.

Willman, P. and Winch, G. (1985) *Innovation and Management Control*, Cambridge: Cambridge University Press.

Wilson, F.L. (1991) 'Democracy in the workplace: the French experience', *Politics and Society*, 19 (4): 439–62.

Wittke, V. (1989) 'Systemische Rationalisierung – Zur Analyse aktueller Umbruchprozesse in der industriellen Produktion', *SOFI-Mitteilungen*, 17.

Wohlmuth, K. (1985) 'Multinationale Konzerne und Wirtschaftspolitik in der Bundesrepublik Deutschland', in P. Mettler (ed.), *Multinationale Konzerne in der Bundesrepublik Deutschland*, Frankfurt: Haag & Herchen.

Wright, M., Chiplin, B. and Coyne, J. (1989) 'The market for corporate control: the divestment option', in J. Fairburn and J. Kay (eds), *Mergers and Merger Policy*, London: Oxford University Press.

Young, S. and Hamill, J. (eds.) (1992) *Europe and the Multinationals*, Aldershot, Hants.: Edward Elgar.

Zeitlin, J. (1994) 'Why are there no industrial districts in the United Kingdom?', in A. Bagnasco and C. Sabel (eds), *Ce que petit fair: Les petites et moyennes enterprises en Europe*, English version, London: Frances Pinter.

Index